Microprocessor
Systems

WILEY SERIES IN COMPUTING

Consulting Editor
Professor D. W. Barron
Computer Studies Group, Southampton University,
Southampton, England

BEZIER · Numerical Control – Mathematics and Applications
DAVIES and BARBER · Communication Networks for Computers
BROWN · Macro Processors and Techniques for Portable Software
PAGAN · A Practical Guide to Algol 68
BIRD · Programs and Machines
OLLE · The Codasyl Approach to Data Base Management
DAVIES, BARBER, PRICE, and SOLOMONIDES · Computer Networks and
   their Protocols
KRONSJO · Algorithms: Their Complexity and Efficiency
RUS · Data Structures and Operating Systems
BROWN · Writing Interactive Compilers and Interpreters
HUTT · The Design of a Relational Data Base Management System
O'DONOVAN · GPSS – Simulation Made Simple
LONGBOTTOM · Computer System Reliability
AUMIAUX · The Use of Microprocessors
ATKINSON · Pascal Programming
KUPKA and WILSING · Conversational Languages
SCHMIDT · GPSS – Fortran
PUZMAN/PORIZEK · Communication Control in Computer Networks
SPANIOL · Computer Arithmetic
BARRON · Pascal – The Language and its Implementation
HUNTER · The Design and Construction of Compilers
MAYOH · Problem Solving with ADA
AUMIAUX · Microprocessor Systems

Microprocessor Systems

M. Aumiaux

Département de Formation Permanente Ecole Superieure d'Electronique de l'Ouest-Angers

Translation by
Arleta Starza
and David Brailsford

1807 1982

JOHN WILEY & SONS

Chichester · New York · Brisbane · Toronto · Singapore

First published 1980 © Masson, Editeur, Paris under the title
Les Systèmes à Microprocesseur by Michel Aumiaux

Library of Congress Cataloging in Publication Data:

Aumiaux, Michel.
  Microprocessor systems.

  (Wiley series in computing)
  Translation of: Les systèmes à microprocesseur.
  Includes index.
  1. Microprocessors.   I. Title.   II. Series.
  QA76.5.A789613   001.64'04   81-16251

  ISBN 0 471 10129 X   AACR2

British Library Cataloguing in Publication Data:

Aumiaux, M.
  Microprocessor systems. – (Wiley series in computing)
  1. Microcomputers
  2. Microprocessors
  I. Title
  001.64'04   QA76.5

  ISBN 0 471 10129 X

Typeset by Pintail Studios Ltd, Ringwood
Printed by The Pitman Press, Bath.

Preface

In a previous book *The Use of Microprocessors* we studied the fundamental microcomputer LSI circuits, i.e. memories, programmable interfaces, and the microprocessor itself. But a knowledge of microcomputers, no matter how good, is not sufficient when one is faced with designing or implementing a microprocessor system. In addition, one has to be well acquainted with all aspects of the hardware and software environment of microcomputers.

Study of the hardware environment permits the microprocessor to be interfaced to any industrial component or part, including specialized controllers such as those for interrupts, direct memory access, VDUs, floppy disks, etc. Study of the software environment allows the application in question to be programmed in assembly language and implemented with the aid of a development system.

In the present book we have tried to give as complete and detailed a study as possible of the microcomputer environment within a microprocessor system. Such an objective can only be attained by constant attention to detail and clear exposition. Attention to detail is important, because we know how misleading incomplete information can be for a user who wishes to implement a microprocessor system; and for this reason we have illustrated the contents of this book at every possible opportunity with examples relating to the INTEL 8080A or 8085A microprocessors and the MOTOROLA 6800 or 6802 microprocessors. A clear exposition is equally important because the programming of specialized controllers and the use of a development system are complex operations, which have resulted in complex technical documentation, not designed for teaching purposes.

Microprocessor Systems is the first book, to my knowledge, to treat in detail the three fundamental topics: interfacing, programming in assembler, and the use of a development system. In addition, we believe that it will be useful for present and future designers of microprocessor systems, as well as for large numbers of people who have an interest in microprocessors.

Michel Aumiaux
1 August 1979

Contents

Chapter I

Application and management of microprocessor-based systems

The construction of a logic system, automated system, or process controller requires, at the outset, a choice of the fundamental technique to be used, i.e.

(1) Hard-wired logic;
(2) Microprocessor programmed logic; or
(3) Minicomputer programmed logic.

Hard-wired logic can, among other things, assist a programmed logic system if the latter is incapable of executing all required system functions. In making our choice, the potential for using a microprocessor, in the form of a microcomputer, will be evaluated.

If such a use is made, a sequence of different stages will be required in analysing and implementing an industrial application. These stages are shown in Figure 1. We shall study these stages in outline and try to distinguish, so far as is possible, the major or minor choice criteria that will apply throughout our study of industrial applications.

I. THE EVALUATION OF SYSTEM REQUIREMENTS AND CONSTRAINTS

The first task in designing any logic system, or automated system, is always the evaluation of system requirements and constraints; in other words, a definition of the design criteria. To do this, however, one must first define the problem in detail together with the anticipated results.

1

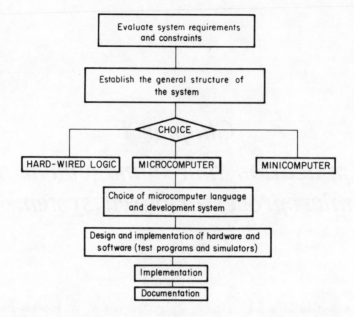

Figure 1. Analysis and implementation of an industrial system

I.1. Problem-definition and anticipated results

I.1.1. System requirements

(a) Hardware requirements

(1) I/O and command circuits. We must define the number of inputs, the number of outputs, and also the I/O and command circuits.
(2) The amount of data to be placed in memory. Is there data to be stored? If so, how much? How will this data be used? The answers to these questions will enable one to decide whether or not a particular memory has adequate capacity, and thus to choose the appropriate type of memory.

(b) Software requirements

(1) The number of operations to be performed. It is important to know the number of operations to be performed by the system because this strongly influences the choice of solution: hard-wired logic, microprocessor, or minicomputer.
(2) The nature of these operations. Simple logic functions are more easily carried out by hard-wired logic than by a microprocessor or minicomputer. By contrast,

microprocessors perform addition and subtraction in binary, or in BCD, without difficulty and with no need for supplementary circuits. When provided with a program, microprocessors can also perform multiplication and division, though with a non-negligible execution time.

So far as minicomputers are concerned, they contain hard-wired circuits for addition, subtraction, multiplication, and division and so are able to execute rapidly any form of arithmetic operation.

I.1.2. System constraints

(1) Speed. Processing speed determines the execution time of the principal functions to be implemented: logic operations, arithmetic operations, reading of data, sending of command signals, sequencing, etc.

Basically, the technology used determines the speed. The greatest speed is actually obtained by hard-wired logic using ECL technology. Next in order come bit-slice microprocessors, followed by minicomputers, 16-bit microprocessors and then 8-bit microprocessors: the 16-bit microprocessors, which handle words 16 bits long, are naturally faster in program execution than 8-bit microprocessors.

At present, the leading manufacturers of integrated circuits are engaged in a fierce battle to get their own technology (e.g. SOS, HMOS and VMOS) accepted as the standard.

(2) Space requirements. From this point of view, a single-board microcomputer, when practicable, is the most favoured, followed by a microcomputer and then a minicomputer, with hard-wired logic being the least suitable so far as space considerations are concerned.

(3) Power consumption. The two main factors determining power consumption are the technology used and the degree of integration. So far as the technology is concerned, CMOS is the least demanding in terms of power consumption. LSI circuits are therefore more favoured from the viewpoint of power consumption than are the SSI or MSI circuits traditionally used in hard-wired logic.

(4) Cost. This is made up of three separate costs: hardware, software (taking into account the programming and implementation of the application in question), and the eventual investment cost of a microprocessor system. This cost criterion is much more complex than the others.

II. DEFINITION OF GENERAL SYSTEM STRUCTURE

This phase consists of breaking down the industrial application into modules, each of which carries out a particular well-defined major function: the modules are then connected together so as to implement the industrial application. It is desirable to distinguish clearly the input/output modules from the processing modules. The inputs and outputs of each module will then be well defined.

III. CHOICE OF SYSTEM

III.1. Hard-wired logic

Hard-wired logic is of interest in two major cases:

(1) The construction of small logic systems, or automatic circuits, involving not more than twenty to forty standard integrated circuits and not requiring frequent modification. The 'hard-wired logic' solution is, in effect, the one which involves the least development cost, particularly if the analysis is carried out with the aid of a method such as the *phase method*, proposed and developed by the author in Vol. II of his book *Logique binaire et ordinateurs* (*Binary Logic and Computers*). Development requires no special investment beyond standard laboratory equipment such as voltmeters, universal controllers, oscilloscopes, etc.

(2) The construction of logic systems involving more than twenty to forty standard integrated circuits and requiring an operating speed superior to that offered by a micro or minicomputer, but not requiring the storage of substantial amounts of data.

The majority of 8-bit microprocessors involve MOS N-channel technology. The execution time of an instruction is of the order of microseconds, which is slow compared with bipolar technology such as ECL. It is true that bit-slice microprocessors enable instructions to be executed in about 50 nanosec, but their implementation is much more complicated than that of a system constructed using a standard microprocessor architecture, such as the 8080A, the 6800, the Signetics 2650, etc. Also, such implementation is not possible in all organizations and, even for those organizations having the required expertise, it would entail very substantial development costs, at least at present. Moreover, the operating speed of bit-slice microprocessors would not be sufficient for certain applications.

III.2. Microcomputers

Let us recall that a microprocessor cannot be used by itself but must be linked to a RAM memory, a ROM memory, and one or more I/O circuits. These circuits, assembled on one or more boards, form a microcomputer.

The microcomputer format has the advantage of flexibility, low space requirements, and the availability of devices which greatly facilitate implementation. These devices range from simple kit monitors to powerful development systems with floppy disks, printer, and console, which allow programming in assembler or high-level languages.

Whenever an industrial application requires arithmetic calculations without any great emphasis on speed one must consider the microprocessor possibility. The same argument applies to applications requiring the storage of large amounts of data, or involving a large variety of industrial I/O devices (bearing in mind the great flexibility of microprocessors in linking to any kind of I/O device). In particular, for non-standard I/O devices, the microcomputer is the most sensible solution if its speed is compatible with the requirements of the application. The development cost of software for an industrial microprocessor system is substantial. It would therefore have to be written off against a medium- or large-scale production run.

When using a microcomputer, users generally have available the three types of memory required for maximum flexibility:

(1) EPROM memory for applications subject to frequent modification, or for small-scale applications;
(2) ROM memory for medium- or large-scale applications not requiring program modifications; and
(3) RAM memory for the storage of data, variables, and the results of calculations.

The range of possible microcomputer applications can be made as wide as possible by using EPROM/ROM sockets, which can equally well accept an EPROM or a ROM, and also by using interfaces where the individual I/O bits can be programmed for input or output, either in groups of n, or individually. This is not the case for microcomputers which are connected to fixed, non-programmable, interface boards. Also, a microcomputer I/O card can control twelve inputs and twelve outputs. However, if the application required sixteen inputs and four outputs, then two I/O cards would be necessary even though only twenty input/outputs would be used out of the forty-eight available.

III.3. Minicomputers

A minicomputer has a much more powerful instruction set than a microcomputer. Its operating speed and memory capacity are also much higher. All minicomputers offer the possibility of hard-wired multiplication and division, with much more rapid execution than for software multiplication and division. In this way, the arithmetic unit of a minicomputer is capable of effecting a multiplication or division by simply decoding the corresponding instruction.

A minicomputer can be connected to a large number of standard peripheral devices, but it is not well suited to non-standard I/O circuits. In particular, each of its inputs and outputs is designated by the designer as an input or as an output, in contrast to what happens with a programmable parallel interface. Flexibility is not the strong point of minicomputers but, on the other hand, their software is very powerful, and this reduces the time and development costs of an application. However, a minicomputer does cost more than a microcomputer and it is primarily of interest for one-off or short production-run industrial systems.

We have gathered these different ideas together in the flowchart of Figure 2, giving in diagrammatic form the solution which seems best at first sight. We emphasize the qualification 'at first sight', since in our flowchart the decision at each decision-lozenge is necessarily yes or no. We cannot avoid interpreting this as 'definitely yes', or 'definitely no', and yet the answers, as we well know, are not

6

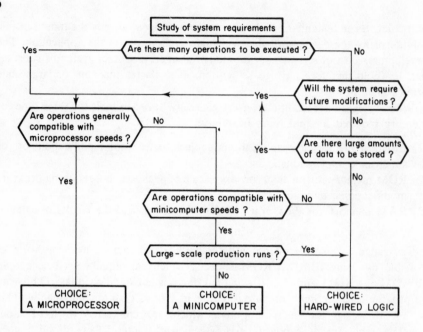

Figure 2. Flowchart of system choice

always so cut-and-dried. Thus there remains the possibility of a mistake every time the answer to a question is not a firm yes or no, but rather a 'maybe yes, maybe no' answer.

To summarize: this flowchart merely attempts to facilitate a choice by indicating that solution which, at the very least, it would be unwise to reject without careful consideration.

One of the flowchart tests is 'Are operations generally compatible with microprocessor speeds?' Now it would be a pity to reject the microprocessor solution solely because it could not execute one or two operations sufficiently rapidly. It might be desirable to retain the microcomputer and augment it with a few hard-wired logic circuits. If, for example, the problem is that of insufficient speed in executing multiplication, it is certainly a good idea to connect an arithmetic multiplication circuit to the microprocessor to effect hardware multiplication. In the same way, for long production runs of systems executing calculations which are too fast for a microprocessor, it is probably worth considering a hard-wired logic solution by adding an arithmetic circuit such as the ADVANCED MICRO DEVICES (AMD) AM 5911.

IV. CHOICE OF MICROCOMPUTER, LANGUAGE, AND DEVELOPMENT SYSTEM

If the choice comes down in favour of a microcomputer, and we shall only concern ourselves with this eventuality, we must consider the following points:

(1) The choice of format;

(2) The choice of language and development system; and

(3) The choice of supplier.

We shall investigate these points and the choice criteria for each.

IV.1. Choice of microcomputer format

Once a decision has been made in favour of a microcomputer, five possibilities, each with its attendant advantages and disadvantages, are open to us. We shall examine each one in turn and then look at the choice criteria.

IV.1.1. Examination of each possibility

(a) Purchase of a microcomputer as a 'packaged system'

Format. The microcomputer comes cased, as would a measuring instrument or a minicomputer, with the case also containing a power supply. The different manual functions are grouped at the front of the case. On the back panel are input/output connectors, as well as connectors for the data and address buses to facilitate extension of the system (for the advantages and disadvantages of this system see Table I).

Table I. Advantages and disadvantages of a packaged system

Puchase of a microcomputer as a 'packaged system'	
Advantages	*Disadvantages*
(1) Most compact packaging, not requiring any hardware knowledge	(1) A microcomputer in this form is very expensive
(2) Fastest system implementation, provided such a 'complete system' is available, helped by the manufacturer's pre-prepared application, development and test programs	(2) Does not provide the opportunity for familiarity with and mastery of microcomputer system hardware
(3) Most reliable implementation for a first-time industrial application, especially when the organization does not have staff trained in digital logic	(3) Dependence on one manufacturer since second sources for complete systems do not generally exist
(4) Most flexible implementation method because of the options frequently offered with such a complete system and also benefiting from the manufacturer's successive improvements to the system	
(5) Input/output interfaces are usually available (including analog interfaces) and are orientated towards industrial applications: opto-electronic isolators, highly noise-immune logic, relays, thyristors, etc.	

(b) Purchase of a microcomputer as a 'multi-card system'

Format. The manufacturer specifies a range of cards, that is, a set of compatible and complementary cards of identical dimensions which are assembled using a 'card-cage' capable of taking several cards at a time (typically between six and ten). (These are often small cards in the European (Eurocard) format of 100 mm x 160 mm.) The bottom of the cage has a printed circuit onto which connectors are soldered for receiving and transmitting all the signals from the data, address, and command buses (for the advantages and disadvantages of this system, see Table II).

Table II. Advantages and disadvantages of a multi-card system

Purchase of a microcomputer as a multi-card system	
Advantages	*Disadvantages*
(1) Flexible solution which effects a pleasing compromise between the purchase of a complete system and the construction of a microprocessor from components	(1) It is not cased and requires a separate power supply
(2) Enables one to benefit from the manufacturer's technological improvements to the range of boards	(2) Four or five boards are usually needed to assemble this type of microcomputer; this leads to a relatively powerful system which is, consequently, too cumbersome for small industrial applications
(3) Offers a relatively wide range of boards; in particular industrial I/O boards (including analog boards, which will be cheaper to buy than to make when they are needed for small- or medium-scale production runs)	

(c) Purchase of a microcomputer as a 'single-board system'

Format. The manufacturer produces a single board onto which are connected the processor, RAM, ROM, parallel programmable interfaces, and a serial programmable interface which enables the board to be connected to an input/output device, such as a teletype or a visual display screen. This format has been adopted by today's largest manufacturer of microprocessors (INTEL).

Boards such as the SBC (single board computer) 80/20 (INTEL) are well known and are usually either

(a) in the American format of 6 inches x 12 inches (122 mm x 310 mm); or
(b) in the DIN European format (160 mm x 233.4 mm).

In order to extend the facilities of the system, the bus signals are brought out to the lower part of the board and are designed to slot into a connector (for the advantages and disadvantages of this system see Table III).

Table III. Advantages and disadvantages of a single-board system

Purchase of a microcomputer as a 'single-board system'	
Advantages	Disadvantages
(1) The cheapest possible purchase price for a microcomputer (2) Enables one to benefit from manufacturer's improvements as technical progress is made	(1) Less flexibility for system extension than with a multi-board system (2) The limited power of a single-board microcomputer

(d) Construction of a microprocessor from components

Format. The user designs and constructs his microcomputer starting from purchased LSI circuits. He could, of course, choose one of the three types of packaging we have just seen or, as is sometimes advantageous, he could adopt a completely different type of layout; this latter option is often necessary when a microcomputer is to be built into a small space; for example, in telemetry applications, cine-cameras and television sets (for the advantages and disadvantages of this system see Table IV).

Table IV. Advantages and disadvantages of constructing a microcomputer

Construction of a microcomputer from components	
Advantages	Disadvantages
(1) Global cost per unit is very low over large production runs (more than 500 units) (2) Allows for flexible installation possibilities (integration of the system in a case of specific dimensions)	(1) Requires personnel trained in digital logic and often in industrial electronics (2) Requires complex and cumbersome equipment: A complete development system Logic analyser Oscilloscope Test equipment Logic probe
(3) Provides scope for acquiring experience and mastery of hardware-related problems in microcomputer systems. But is such an investment in 'know-how' advisable or necessary for the given organization?	(3) Highest development cost solution
	(4) Long implementation delay compared with other solutions

(e) Purchase of a microcomputer in a 'microsystem' form

Format. LSI technology now permits the fabrication of a microcomputer on a single chip. This gives a microcomputer of limited power which is, none the less, capable of supporting small microprocessor-based systems (which we shall henceforth call microsystems).

Let us point out that the facilities of such microsystems can be extended by attaching standard LSI components: ROM or EPROM, RAM, parallel interfaces, etc. However, this takes us back to the previous solution and involves knowing how to construct a microcomputer from components.

A microsystem without additional components can, obviously, only be used for small industrial applications. It is particularly suitable for small peripheral controllers or specialized terminals, but can also be used in appliances for the general public (for the advantages and disadvantages of this system see Table V).

Table V. Advantages and disadvantages of purchasing a microsystem

Purchase of a microcomputer in the form of a microsystem

Advantages	Disadvantages
(1) Greatly reduced bulkiness which allows for microsystem installation in any type of apparatus	(1) A microcomputer of very limited power
(2) Cost is extremely small relative to functions performed	
(3) Development time is reduced to software development only (if power supply is purchased)	
(4) This approach, when possible, applies equally well to small- and medium-volume production runs (microsystems with EPROM) as to large-scale production (microsystem with ROM)	

IV.1.2. Choice criteria for a microcomputer

(a) Number of units to be manufactured.   The design of an industrial application and the construction of N units entails a global cost C_N which is the sum of three partial costs:

$$C_N = N \times C_M + C_D + C_I$$

where C_M is the unit cost of hardware components required (i.e. to produce one instance of the industrial application); C_D is the cost of hardware and software development; that is, the labour cost resulting from the design and implementation of hardware and software for the industrial application; and C_I is the cost of investing in test-equipment; development system, test simulators, logic analyser, probes, etc. If this investment is used for other industrial applications, C_I will be an appropriate fraction of the global investment.

The global cost per unit is thus:

$$C = C_M + \frac{C_D}{N} + \frac{C_I}{N}$$

The number of units, N, is therefore an important factor in unit-cost, C. For large-volume runs ($N > 500$), C differs only slightly from C_M. The search for a minimal unit cost involves reducing C_M, which means choosing a microcomputer in its least expensive form: this suggests either constructing it from components, or purchasing a microsystem (for very small industrial applications). For medium-volume runs ($100 < N < 500$, say), the development and investment costs can lead to a unit cost significantly greater than C_M. In principle, the best solution is the purchase of a microcomputer in a single-board or multi-board form. For small-volume runs ($N < 100$), the term $(C_D + C_I)/N$ is greater than C_M, which results in one of three solutions: a single-boardsystem, a multi-board system, or a complete system (the latter being particularly suitable when N is less than 10). *Note.* Remember that microsystems may be suitable for certain very simple applications (irrespective of whether they involve large, medium or small runs).

(b) Delays. The shortest implementation delays are obtained using complete systems or microsystems (when practicable). Single-board and multi-board systems lead to longer delays, but these are still considerably shorter than those resulting from constructing a microcomputer from components.

(c) Competence of personnel. The construction of a microcomputer should be attempted only by personnel who are qualified and experienced in digital logic. The less experience a company has with digital logic, the more it should be in favour of purchasing a ready-made or packaged microcomputer.

IV.2. Choice of language and development system

IV.2.1. Analysis of possible languages

(a) Hexadecimal. The operation code of each instruction is an 8-bit binary word. This word is represented by two hexadecimal characters. The exercises which we gave in *The Use of Microprocessors* were all translated into hexadecimal. This is the best language for familiarizing oneself with microprocessors and their programming. It can, however, only be used for the smallest of programs since it soon becomes tedious. It is suitable, therefore, as an introduction to microprocessors but not as a language for industrial application programming.

(b) Assembler language (or low-level language). In this language, the operation code is expressed by a mnemonic for the instruction; ADD for addition, for example. An address is represented by a LABEL, which is a string of one to six alphanumeric characters, the first being a letter of the alphabet. Some possible labels are CAN, START, END, N12, etc. Of course, each label designates only one address.

An assembler language has a particular syntax which must, obviously, be scrupulously adhered to. Programs written in assembler language are subsequently translated into binary by a service program, called an assembler.

Assembler programming leads to programs which, having been translated into binary (to produce *object programs*), require less memory space and have a shorter execution time than programs written in a high-level language, such as BASIC or FORTRAN. Assembler language, however, has the drawback of being specific to a single microprocessor (or a family of microprocessors). A program written for the INTEL 8080A would have to be rewritten if subsequently used on a MOTOROLA 6800. Moreover, a user knowing only the 6800 would not be able to maintain an application whose programs had been written for the 8080A.

(c) High-level language. In order to overcome the above-mentioned difficulties of assembler language, computer scientists have created *high-level languages* whose primary characteristic should be their universality. We say 'should be' because, unfortunately, these same computer scientists have skilfully developed numerous variants of the same language thus diminishing the universality of these high-level languages and the advantages conferred thereby. Fortunately, there exists another characteristic of these languages, namely the speed of program-development which they allow. Each high-level language instruction corresponds, on average, to a group of four or six assembler instructions. This results in considerable time-saving and, consequently, a reduction in software development cost.

On the other hand, the universality of high-level languages leads to suboptimal industrial application programs in the following senses:

(1) The object program memory requirement is 1.5 to 3 times greater than for a program written in assembler language and translated into binary: inevitably the hardware cost, which includes the cost of memory, is increased.
(2) The execution time is 1.5 to 3 times longer than for a source-program written in assembler language.

Note. The user program, written either in assembler or in high-level language, is known as a *source program*. When translated into binary it is called an *object program.*

Many microprocessor manufacturers now make available compilers for high-level languages, the language BASIC being particularly popular. These compilers are often stored on floppy disks, or, more usefully, are permanently 'burnt in' to EPROM memory. This latter method greatly speeds up access times to the translator programs, and makes program-development in a high-level language an attractive possibility.

IV.2.2. Language choice criteria

Table VI. Language choice criteria

Criterion	Language giving best performance for a given criterion
Implementation delay	A high-level language
Program execution time	Assembler language
Memory occupation (by object program)	Assembler language
Control of input/output devices	Assembler language

IV.2.3. Choice of development system

The language chosen will determine the characteristics expected from the development system. There are three possible solutions for industrial application development:

(1) Monitor in ROM or EPROM. Some microcomputer boards contain a small service program which allows an input/output device (e.g. a teletype or a VDU) to be connected to the microcomputer. This program, known as the MONITOR, is usually included in ROM. This solution is useful for developing small programs.

(2) Assembler board and RAM board. A 16k-byte RAM BOARD can be attached to ready-made microcomputers, in particular to 'multiboard systems'. A RAM board is required in order that the assembler program can reside in RAM memory during the translation process. Together, these two boards allow for assembler language programming, provided that an input/output device is connected to the microcomputer board. The advantages of this solution may lead manufacturers to market development minisystems whose function will be reduced to assembler programming. Their cost will be much lower than that of a complete development system.

(3) Complete development system. Apart from an assembler, such a system contains other service programs; for example, compilers which translate programs written in high-level languages into machine language. A development system permits the execution of a program in its industrial application and at its usual speed, while also allowing program development. The microcomputer used for this is not that of the industrial application but that of the development system. This process is known as *emulation*, and it is carried out using a program called an emulator. Such service programs are stored in mass memory, which is almost always a floppy disk (also called a diskette). This development system consists of an input/output device (TTY or CRT) as well as a printer for program listings. A development system is expensive, but is indispensable for large-scale industrial applications.

(4) Time-sharing. It is also possible to develop a program under time-sharing,

starting from an input/output device situated in a factory (or elsewhere) and connected to a large computer. The initial investment is minimal, but the development cost is high when one takes into account the two costs of time sharing:

(a) A fixed cost for attaching the terminal; and
(b) A variable cost determined by the connect-time while the terminal is in use. (Moreover, this costed time is difficult to control.)

This method, unlike a complete development system, does not, of course, permit real-time emulation of an industrial application.

Note. When an application is to be reproduced in medium- or large-scale runs, the question of purchasing a development system (and perhaps also a logic analyser) will have to be considered. Such a system enables one to store in real-time the states of the microprocessor pins during N operation cycles and to display subsequently, whenever one wishes, the state of each of these pins during the N cycles. Logic-analysers are either specific for one microprocessor or adaptable to several types of microprocessor.

IV.3.   Choice of supplier

IV.3.1.   First step

When the choice of microcomputer format has been made the first step in choosing a supplier is easily made by eliminating those whose products do not satisfy either the desired format or the technical characteristics required by the industrial application. In fact, this first step is taken practically at the same time as the choice of microcomputer package.

IV.3.2.   Criteria for the choice of supplier

(a) Availability.   This is one of the most important criteria. The user should positively avoid choosing new products whose marketing has been announced but not, in fact, begun. It sometimes happens that availability of a product is announced for a certain date but, due to unforeseen difficulties, is subsequently delayed by several months. Sometimes, following such delays, the marketing of a given product is cancelled (as happened in 1978 with a 64K-bit memory, when the supplier finally withdrew the product).

(b) Financial stability of the supplier.   This is also an important point to consider. A firm which has sound financial backing is a guarantee that a given product will continue to be sold. From this point of view, one should consider the following: 'Does the sale of microprocessors lead to the sale of the company's more profitable products?'

In effect, the fierce competition facing microprocessor manufacturers does not allow them to make substantial profits nor, in all probability, will it allow them to do so in the future. Moreover, it is vital for the manufacturers that micro-processors should lead to sales of more expensive and profitable equipment such as RAM, PROM, and EPROM memories.

(c) Supplier's range of products. It is important to find a supplier offering the greatest number of auxiliary microprocessor products (such as programmable interfaces, memories, peripheral controllers, buffers, etc.) as well as products in the software domain (such as assemblers, cross-assemblers, interpreters, com-pilers, etc.). The supplier should also have development systems available.

(d) Supplier's technical back-up. Once again, this is a very important criterion. The supplier should have one or more application engineers (who exist in reality and not just on paper!), competent and ready to offer help if one should face problems. Here, the supplier's sales force and the distributor's technical assistance should be taken into consideration.

(e) The existence of second sources. A second source is an enterprise other than the microprocessor manufacturer which produces and sells the same products as the manufacturer. Such a second source is genuine if subject to a licensing agree-ment. If this is not the case, the product has been copied but not officially recog-nized, and the second source is not genuine.

The existence of such second sources, be they licensed or otherwise, is an additional assurance of product availability and marketing continuity. It is, likewise, a guarantee of competition and, consequently, of reasonable prices as a result of non-excessive profit margins.

V. DESIGN AND IMPLEMENTATION OF HARDWARE AND SOFTWARE

V.1. Hardware/software split

The designer may have to use logic circuits to implement certain functions which would otherwise be impossible for the microprocessor to carry out; for example, an arithmetic circuit if fast calculations have to be made. If there are frequent or relatively long timing operations, a programmable timer is recommended. Such a timer is indispensable when executing operations at very precise time intervals; every ten seconds, for example.

There are cases where a specific logic circuit cannot be dispensed with, but more usually the industrial system microprocessor designer is faced with a choice between hardware or software implementation because, in fact, certain functions can be carried out either by several integrated circuits or by a program. As examples we can cite a keyboard decoder and the serialization of a byte with the addition of START and STOP bits.

We know that for long production-runs the hardware cost must be minimized: therefore, so far as is compatible with the industrial system's characteristics, the maximum possible number of functions should be carried out by means of software.

V.2. Study of industrial application hardware

This part of the process, which is relatively unimportant in designing a microprocessor project, consists of choosing relevant LSI components and possibly certain other auxiliary circuits such as decoders, bus buffers, multiplexers, etc. Of course, one must also decide on memory sizes and the number and types of parallel interfaces (a task which, as we have seen, does not exist if we purchase a microcomputer). In any case, there remains the analysis and implementation of the actual industrial application, assuming this has not been done already, as well as the circuits that may be required for attaching the industrial system (optoelectronic isolators and interfaces for voltage and power-level compatibility).

VI. IMPLEMENTATION

This is carried out with development tools which we shall study in Chapter IV.

VII. DOCUMENTATION

It is very important to produce a complete set of documents. In particular, the functions of the different programs and subroutines should be well defined, and annotated flowcharts, with notes on registers destroyed and input/output data, should be included.

VIII. THE MICROPROCESSOR IN ITS PRINCIPAL INDUSTRIAL APPLICATIONS

In this section we outline the main areas of microprocessor application as well as listing the standard functions carried out by microprocessors in each of these areas.

VIII.1. The microprocessor in data processing

In this area, microprocessors are used in card-punches on peripheral data-processing centres and in what we might call 'devolved data processing' to distinguish it from distributed data processing, in which the whole 'intelligence' of the data system is centralized and carried out by a single computer. There are two types of information to be transmitted:

(1) Information requiring rapid transmission: for example, between an aeroplane and the control tower;
(2) Information not requiring rapid transmission, which can be transmitted by slower procedures: for example, statistical data.

Since the information source does not have an 'intelligence' capable of determining the urgency of the information to be transmitted, data transmission should
be fast. This results in an increased system cost, since cost increases with
transmission speed. Moreover, if the computer is to monitor and process all the
information, its size would have to be greatly increased.

In order to remedy this, a minimum amount of 'intelligence' will have to be
decentralized to the information source. This would analyse the incoming information and transmit to the computer only what it requires, with an appropriate
transmission speed, a technique we shall call 'devolved data processing'. This
minimum of 'intelligence' is precisely what a microcomputer can provide, it being
then used as an intelligent terminal. The benefit is twofold: first, the cost is low;
second, implementation is no longer necessarily confined to a computer scientist
but can be carried out by any microprocessor specialist, be he electronic engineer,
technician, or computer scientist. We should also point out that the microprocessor is capable of detecting errors in the data it receives.

VIII.2. The microprocessor in process control

Process control systems are generally complex and designed for the automatic
monitoring and control of industrial processes such as refining or laminating (or,
more generally, of production processes for materials requiring a number of
manufacturing stages and being, perhaps, unpleasant for human operatives
because of extreme environmental conditions or contact with dangerous
products). Such process control requires the acquisition of analog or digital data,
coming from different parts of the plant, followed by the analysis of this data and
the control of such parameters as motor speed and activation commands for
shutters, motors, furnace control circuits, *etc*. In this area, the microprocessor has
many applications.

VIII.2.1. Driving a data-acquisition system

Large amounts of analog and digital data are transmitted by cable to a data-
gathering system, consisting of a multiplexer, an amplifier, a sample-and-hold
circuit, and an analog-to-digital converter. Because of lack of space, we shall not
describe here the functioning of a data-acquisition system. Interested readers can
refer to our work *Pratique de l'electronique*, Vol. 2, Editions Masson (*The
Practice of Electronics*, Vol. 2, Masson), in which we have set aside a chapter for
detailed study of such a system.

The control of the different parts of the system is called 'driving the system':
this function is easily carried out by microprocessors.

VIII.2.2. Localized control

Localized control is to process control as devolved data processing is to ordinary
data processing. We have seen that the latter can be organized as 'centralized data

processing' or 'devolved data processing'. In the same way, industrial process control can be structured along the lines of 'centralized control' or 'localized control'.

In the first instance, all the data, which in this case we shall refer to as input variables, are transmitted by cable to the central computer. (This is equivalent to the central computer in a data processing system.) At present such cables may be several hundred metres long. For instance, a petrol refinery may require a thousand input variables, each system variable being being at an average distance of 500 m from the central microcomputer, preceded by its data-acquisition system. This results in a high installation cost, taking into account the cost of cable.

In the case of localized control, several microcomputers are placed relatively close to the input variables. Each microprocessor, preceded by its data-acquisition system, controls and commands a group of several dozen input variables. It receives orders from the central minicomputer and it periodically transmits the states of logic variables, or numerical values of the previously processed and converted analog quantities. This second solution presents several advantages:

(1) Reduced installation cost. Localized control considerably reduces the cost of transmission cable. In our example, centralized control requires the transmission of a thousand variables along 500 m of cable. Under localized control, these 500-m links reduce to just a few dozen wires for each output of the microcomputer. When the variables are close to the microcomputer, adapter circuits are no longer required. Experience shows that the installation cost of localized control for one variable is half that for centralized control, despite the additional cost of the microcomputers.

(2) Simple and easily handled software so far as the central minicomputer is concerned. In the case of centralized control the minicomputer must monitor all the programs. This calls for a high processing speed and substantial software, which is difficult to implement. On the other hand, process control with a localized control structure allows the microcomputer to execute conventional subroutines, such as data examination, calibration of data sensors (temperature-correction, standardization), thermocouple linearization, calibration of measuring apparatus, etc. This greatly reduces the number and length of minicomputer programs since the minicomputer receives only pre-processed data, which is already in a convenient form, and, of course, results in simpler and more easily managed software, which is a non-negligible advantage.

(3) Increased reliability. Localized control leads to several small sub-appliances instead of one large appliance, as in centralized control. The increased reliability is due, in part, to the fact that a microprocessor has only a limited number of simple tasks to carry out and, in part, to the microcomputer's great reliability as a result of its construction from a very limited number of integrated circuits. In fact, reliability increases as the number of components decreases. Moreover, localized control reduces the number of tasks to be

carried out by the central minicomputer and simplifies many of the remaining tasks. All this reduces the risk of breakdowns and results in global reliability for the process control.

(4) Simplified maintenance. Maintenance is obviously facilitated by the organization of process control into small sub-appliances, as in the case under localized control; moreover, each microcomputer can carry out test functions and inform the minicomputer of certain system failures.

VIII.2.3. Digital control

Digital control has never worked well with minicomputers because their cost forces one to assign the regulation of n control loops to the minicomputer and to double-up each minicomputer in case of a possible system failure. This leads to complex interconnections, often lacking in safety.

The microcomputer is an ideal solution for a digital control function. Its low cost and its reliability allow for the installation of a microcomputer for each control loop. Since the system is capable of dealing with a failure by switching to manual control there is no need to double the number of microcomputers. Maintenance is, of course, made considerably easier.

VIII.3. The microprocessor in measuring instruments

In this area the microprocessor supports the working of the front panel by testing the push-buttons and the illumination of the displays. It easily executes mathematical calculations and, for a small additional cost, provides the measuring-instrument manufacturer with many extras, such as, for example, statistical calculations. The microprocessor also guarantees the sequencing of logical operations, thereby replacing hard-wired logic.

VIII.4. Public domain

Here the applications are many and varied and microprocessors are particularly well suited. They are used, for example, in cars, television sets, weighing machines, domestic electric appliances, and cash registers.

Chapter II
Input/output techniques

Three techniques exist for carrying out data transfers between the microprocessor system and the outside world:

(1) Programmed input/output;
(2) Interrupt driven input/output; and
(3) Direct memory access input/output.

We shall study each one of these three techniques in detail. It does, however, seem advisable to begin by recalling certain basic notions which we developed in *The Use of Microprocessors*, if only to define our terminology. With this in mind, we shall briefly look at the addressing of input/output devices and at the signals of a standard processor. By processor, we mean the circuit or circuits required for the processor architecture; for example, the 8080A microprocessor circuit, its 8224 clock circuit, and also the 8228 circuit, all of which taken together are known as the INTEL 8080A microprocessor.

II.1. ADDRESSING INPUT/OUTPUT DEVICES

There are two ways of implementing input/output.

II.1.1. I/O using memory instructions (memory-mapped I/O)

In this method, the I/O device is read from or written to as if it were a memory location. For this, the microprocessor must have at least:

(1) A memory-read instruction;
(2) A memory-write instruction;
(3) A read-control signal; and
(4) A write-control signal.

20

The selection of an I/O device then requires three address bits as follows:

(1) Two bits to select either RAM, ROM, or I/O devices. Usually the A_{14} and A_{15} address bits are used for this selection. For example, if we choose the combination $A_{14} = 0$ and $A_{15} = 0$ for the RAM, and the combination $A_{14} = 1$ and $A_{15} = 1$ for the ROM, the I/O devices will then use up the two remaining bit-configurations.
(2) One linear selection bit (a specific bit for I/O) to select one of n I/O devices. This bit must be other than A_0 or A_1, which are allocated to the selection of one of the input device registers. Figure 3 gives an example of addressing within memory-mapped I/O.

In this figure, RAM is addressed if, and only if,

$$\overline{CS1} \cdot \overline{CS2} = 1, \text{ where } A_{15} = 0 \text{ and } A_{14} = 0$$

A convenient way of arranging chip selection as well as memory location and register addressing, for a 1K byte RAM and a 2K ROM, is as follows:

	A15	A14	A13	A12	A11	A10	A9	A8	A7	A6	A5	A4	A3	A2	A1	A0
RAM	0	0				x	x	x	x	x	x	x	x	x	x	x
ROM	1	1			x	x	x	x	x	x	x	x	x	x	x	x
Interface No. 1	1	0									0	0	1	x	x	
Interface No. 2	1	0									0	1	0	x	x	
Interface No. 3	1	0									1	0	0	x	x	

In Figure 3 we show only those address bits required for chip selection in the general sense; that is, either the ROM, or the RAM, or one of the three interfaces.

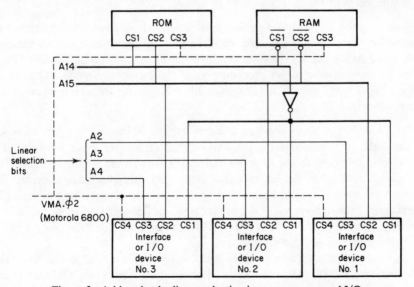

Figure 3. Addressing by linear selection in memory-mapped I/O

The broken line indicates the additional connection to be added when using the MOTOROLA 6800 microprocessor.

The ROM chip is addressed by the logic function $A14 \cdot A15$. If this ROM only possessed a single CHIP SELECT (CS) input, the function $A14 \cdot A15$ would again be the correct logic for CS.

We would have: CS ROM $= A14 \cdot A15$. *We shall henceforth indicate this addressing function by 'CS ADDRESS'.* Thus, for Figure 3, we have:

'ROM CS ADDRESS' $= A15 \cdot A14$
'RAM CS ADDRESS' $= \overline{A15} \cdot \overline{A14}$
'INTERFACE No. 1 CS ADDRESS' $= A15 \cdot \overline{A14} \cdot A2$
'INTERFACE No. 2 CS ADDRESS' $= A15 \cdot \overline{A14} \cdot A3$
'INTERFACE No. 3 CS ADDRESS' $= A15 \cdot \overline{A14} \cdot A4$

II.1.2. I/O using I/O instructions

In this method the microprocessor treats the memories and the input/output devices in different ways. It needs at least:

a memory-read instruction;
a memory-write instruction;
a memory-read control signal;
a memory-write control signal;
a peripheral-(I/O device) read instruction;
a peripheral-write instruction;
a peripheral-read control signal; and
a peripheral-write control signal.

The selection of memories or I/O devices is made implicitly by the choice of instruction. One bit (for example, the A15 bit) suffices to differentiate between RAM and ROM. As for the selection of one of the n input/output devices, this is done by the linear selection procedure as in the memory-mapped I/O method. Figure 4 gives an example of addressing in an I/O structure where separate I/O instructions are used.

Note 1. In the memory-mapped I/O method the addressing requires an AND circuit if the input/output device has only one 'CS chip select' input. However, it is possible in this case to use decoded addressing rather than linear selection. The decoder is enabled by the bit, or bits, which select the input/output devices. We give an example of this in Figure 5, in which we have denoted the selecting of input/output devices by $A_{15} = 1$ and $A_{14} = 0$. The decoder is enabled by this bit-configuration. In Figure 5 the RAM is at hexadecimal address 0000 and the ROM is at hexadecimal address C000.

This method of addressing works well, and we believe that it has now been adopted for MOTOROLA 6800 applications (see Figure 6). Of course, the decoder could be some circuit other than the 8205; the only precaution to take would be to check whether or not it is an inverter. With this method of addressing,

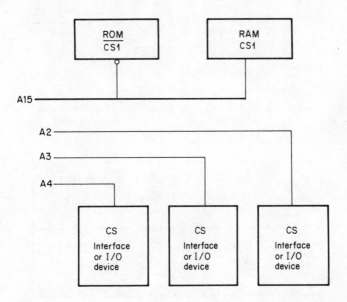

Figure 4. Addressing in an I/O structure which uses I/O instructions

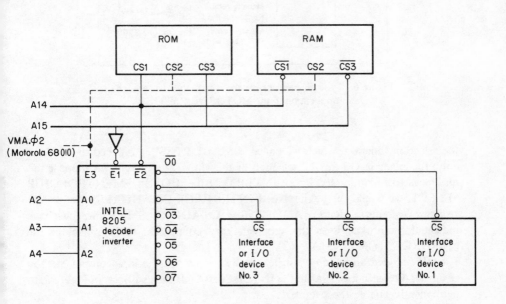

Figure 5. Decoded addressing in memory-mapped I/O

INTEL 8080A	Memory read	$\overline{\text{MEMR}}$	Inverted signal
	Memory write	$\overline{\text{MEMW}}$	
	Peripheral read	$\overline{\text{I/OR}}$	
	Peripheral write	$\overline{\text{I/OW}}$	
MOTOROLA 6800	Read	R/W	Direct signal
	Write	$\overline{\text{R/W}}$	
ZILOG Z80	Read	$\overline{\text{RD}}$	Inverted signal
	Write	$\overline{\text{WR}}$	
INTEL 8085	Read	$\overline{\text{RD}}$	Inverted signal
	Write	$\overline{\text{WR}}$	

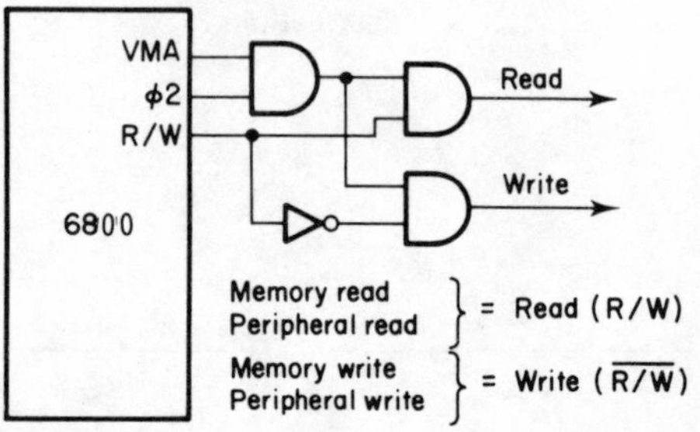

Figure 6. Typical microprocessor read and write signals; application to the MOTOROLA 6800

the selection function, which we called 'CS ADDRESS', is reduced to one term only: for example $\overline{\text{OO}}$ for the selection of the No. 1 interface. If we suppose the interfaces to be addressed by an INVERTED (i.e. COMPLEMENTED) CHIP SELECT, we would then write 'No. 1 INTERFACE $\overline{\text{CS}}$ ADDRESS' = $\overline{\text{OO}}$. We recognize, of course, that $\overline{\text{CS}}$ ADDRESS = $\overline{\text{CS ADDRESS}}$. In Figure 5 we have indicated by broken lines the supplementary connection to be made for the MOTOROLA 6800 (VMA · ϕ2).

Such decoded addressing can be equally used when the input/output method requires I/O instructions (as in the INTEL 8080A). It then suffices, in Figure 5, to permanently enable the decoder:

$$\overline{\text{E1}} = \overline{\text{E2}} = 0 \quad \text{E3} = 1$$

Note 2. All microprocessors possess, in direct or inverted form, the read or write signals which we have listed. In this book we shall use the notations PERI READ and PERI WRITE for I/O devices; for the MOTOROLA 6800 these signals will be R/W and $\overline{R/W}$, respectively.

II.2. Programmed input/outputs

Several circuits allow for such transfers, with or without a status test. We shall study those which are normally used, including (a) programmable interfaces, (b) tri-state buffers, and (c) tri-state latches.

II.2.1. Data transfer by programmable interface

We know that a microprocessor has two kinds of LSI programmable interface: one for parallel data transfer (the 8255 for the INTEL 8080A, the PIA for the MOTOROLA 6800) and another one for serial transmission (the 8251 for the 8080A and the ACIA for the 6800). By sending one or two bytes to the command register of the interface it is possible to program the I/O transfer to communicate with the outside world. We saw this type of data transfer many times in our earlier book.

II.2.2. Data transfer by a tri-state buffer

It is not always necessary to use a parallel programmable interface for data transfer. For example, Figure 7 shows two thumb-wheel switches connected to a tri-state buffer. Any circuit having the ability to place its outputs at high impedance can be directly connected to the data bus by an 8-bit tri-state buffer.

The buffer should deposit 8 output bits on the data bus whenever the microprocessor carries out a read instruction from the input port which is now the

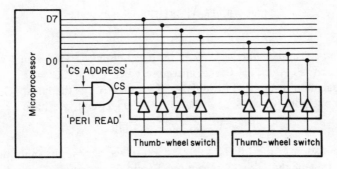

Figure 7. Connection of two thumb-wheel switches to the data bus

26

buffer; in other words, whenever the port is addressed ('CS ADDRESS' = 1) and when, in addition, the 'PERI READ' signal is activated.

The logic function for the 'chip select' (CS) input of the tri-state buffer then is:

$$CS = \text{'CS ADDRESS'} \cdot \text{'PERI READ'}$$

Note. In the I/O method using I/O instructions 'CS ADDRESS' is not a unique select; that is, it is not only used to select an input/output device: it is also an address bit used with the RAM and ROM. So, to ensure that an input/output device is not also addressed by a memory instruction, we must activate 'PERI READ' for a read from I/O port, or 'PERI WRITE' for a write to the I/O port.

Conversely, in the memory-mapped I/O method, 'CS ADDRESS' is a unique address which is specific to the corresponding input/output device. In this case, if the I/O port can only be read, the signal 'PERI READ' is not required. This will be the case for applications using the MOTOROLA 6800 microprocessor.

Figure 8 shows a possible tri-state buffer.

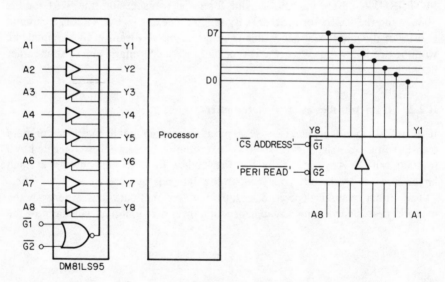

Figure 8. The DM81LS95 tri-state buffer

The National Semi-Conductor (NS) DM81LS95 circuit. This is an 8-bit buffer, enabled when $\overline{G1} + \overline{G2} = 0$ and, therefore when $\overline{G1} = \overline{G2} = 0$.

(1) Application to the INTEL 8080A. If we take A3 as the linear selection bit for that input port which is now the DM81LS95 circuit, we have:

$$\overline{G1} = A3 \quad \overline{G2} = \overline{I/OR}$$

(2) Application to the MOTOROLA 6800. If we choose the input port using the O3 output of the address scheme in Figure 5, we have:

$$\overline{G1} = \overline{G2} = \overline{O3}$$

II.2.3. Tri-state latch data transfer (for input and output)

The DM81LS95 buffer mentioned above transmits to its outputs, when required, the data presented on its inputs; but this data has to be present at the time of the read, since it is not memorized. If this memorizing function is necessary, then, instead of a tri-state buffer, a tri-state latch must be used. For a write operation, a buffer alone is not sufficient since the data does not stay stable on the data bus. It must be memorized by a latch.

A tri-state latch contains, for each bit, a flip-flop and a tri-state buffer. To memorize information it generally has a signal controlling data-memorization. The output buffers, of course, have a tri-state command; most frequently, it involves combining one or more 'chip select' inputs into an addressing function for the tri-state latch.

As an example, we shall give an application of the INTEL tri-state latch (the 8212 circuit). the MODE (MD) input should be set to 1 for the 'output' mode, in which case the output buffers are always enabled; this ensures stable data at the 8212 output, which needs to be so for seven-segment displays.

Setting the MODE input to 0 ensures input of data as received and, in this case, the tri-state command for the latch output is formed by two chip-select inputs designated $\overline{DS1}$ and DS2. the data-latching command is designated by STB (STROBE).

We choose, as an application example, the 8212 used as an output port for controlling two seven-segment displays with their decoders (Figure 9). We shall use, so far as the 8080A allows us, the I/O method using I/O instructions, and we choose A3 as the linear selection bit. This A3 bit should be active at level 0. In this

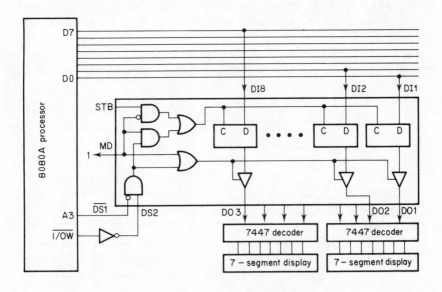

Figure 9. The 8212 used as an output port

28

way, the output port address supplied by the 8212 is 11110111, or F7. The instruction OUT F7 will thus transfer the contents of the accumulator to the seven-segment display, exactly as we were able to do with the parallel interface. The output buffers are permanently enabled by level 1 of the MODE input. The latch is loaded by the simultaneous presence of the address F7 and of I/OW.

The block-diagram of Figure 9 applies just as easily to the MOTOROLA 6800. Let us take 'CS ADDRESS' = O3, in accordance with the addressing in Figure 5; we then have

$$\overline{DS1} = \text{'}\overline{CS} \text{ ADDRESS'} = \overline{O3}. \ DS2 = \text{'PERI WRITE'} = 1$$

II.2.4. Polling method

Certain I/O devices can themselves request a transfer; for example, a keyboard when one of its keys has been pressed. Such devices, which are particularly well adapted to interrupt mode, can nevertheless be driven in program mode as well.

We know, in fact, that any I/O device which is not permanently available delivers, via a STATUS BIT, information such as 'busy', 'ready', or 'register empty'. In order to monitor several I/O devices, each of which has a status bit, it suffices to examine regularly the state of each of the I/O devices by reading and testing their status bits. This technique is known as 'POLLING'. In order to facilitate this, it is convenient to group together the status bits and to use them to create one or more input ports, implemented via tri-state buffers as described above. Figure 10 shows an input port which groups together eight status bits: the implementation uses a NATIONAL SEMI-CONDUCTOR DM81LS85 buffer. A read instruction transfers the eight status bits to the accumulator, where each bit is tested. If it has the logic value '1', the program branches to the subroutine corresponding to the I/O device. The order of testing of the status bits determines the ordering of priorities.

Figure 11 shows an example of a polling subroutine in which top priority has been given to the No. 5 I/O device. This polling subroutine assumes that the

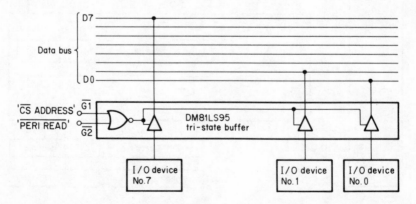

Figure 10. An input port which groups together 8 status bits

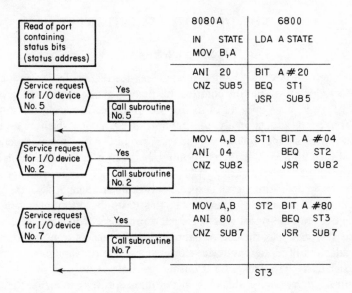

Figure 11. Polling subroutine

SUB5, SUB2, etc. interrupt subroutines do not overwrite the contents of register A in the 6800, or the contents of registers A and B in the 8080A. For this, we need to save the register contents on the stack at the beginning of these sub-routines and to restore them at the end, just before the return instruction (RET for the 8080A, RTS for the 6800). The interrupt subroutine ends with the instruction RT for the 8080A and RTI for the 6800. Let us recall that this latter RTI instruc-tion automatically restores the context; that is, the contents of the accumulators, the flags, and the program counter.

If the service requests of the input/output device are not automatically handled this will have to be done by a program. To do this, we must first assign a select address for the peripheral chip; in other words, a 'CS ADDRESS', which resets all the other service request flip-flops to zero. As soon as the STATUS port has been read, this resetting can be carried out by a write instruction to the address defined by 'CS ADDRESS'. The CLEAR inputs of these flip-flops are linked together for this purpose in the following way:

$$\text{CLEAR inputs} = \overline{\text{'CS ADDRESS'}} \cdot \overline{\text{'PERI WRITE'}}$$

Since there is no reading of data at the STATUS port address, the 'PERI WRITE' signal is unnecessary in the memory-mapped I/O method (as in the MOTOROLA 6800). In this case, we will simply have

$$\text{CLEAR inputs} = \overline{\text{'CS ADDRESS'}}$$

The polling program should be executed regularly, which takes up much of the microprocessor's time. When this is unacceptable, interrupt mode should be used.

II.3. INPUT/OUTPUT VIA INTERRUPTS

II.3.1. Interrupts

For those interrupt devices which generate a service request by themselves, such as a keyboard or push-button control, the polling method does not give good results. In fact, it takes up a lot of microprocessor time in testing the status bits and, moreover, it adapts badly to real-time systems in which microprocessor intervention should follow the service request with minimal delay. An interrupt-driven approach is therefore advisable, if not indispensable, in such a case. With fast peripherals, such as a floppy disc or a VDU, the interrupt method is also recommended. Although it is specifically adapted to input devices, it can be used equally well with output devices. In this case, the interrupt will not be a service request, but the signal sent to the microprocessor would either be 'transfer completed' (for example, the end of a direct memory-access transfer), or a signal of the availability of an output device (for example, the transmitter of a programmable serial interface might send 'transmit register empty').

By contrast with polling, which is a synchronous process, interrupt functioning is asynchronous. Moreover, on receipt of an interrupt request the microprocessor will co-ordinate operations by finishing the instruction in execution. But, in order to be able to detect a possible request, it tests the 'interrupt request' input at the start of each instruction (or at the end, depending on the microprocessor). These requests can be sent out by a programmable parallel interface, a programmable serial interface, or by any other external device. In particular, a tri-state latch suits this process admirably. Figure 12 gives an example of this. The circuit used is the INTEL 8212, which appears to be a component with flexibility, economy, and wide applicability. It is, in fact, designed to generate an interrupt on its $\overline{\text{INT}}$ output. In this diagram, an 8-bit input device, possessing a latching command, is connected to the data bus by the tri-state latch. This input device could be an ASCII keyboard set up for 7 or 8 parallel bits. Alternatively, it could simply comprise two thumb-wheel switches equipped with a push-button for inserting a value into memory; for example, a minimum or maximum threshold in the case of data-acquisition systems. The latching command (usually designated by STROBE) will

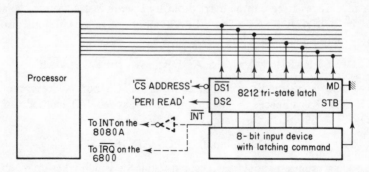

Figure 12. Interrupt generated by a tri-state latch

bring about the transfer of 8 bits from the input device into the tri-state latch, will latch them, and will then activate the 8212 $\overline{\text{INT}}$ output. For the 8080A, this output will be linked to the INT input via an inverter, and for the 6800 it will be linked directly to $\overline{\text{IRQ}}$. The MODE (MD) input will have to be set to zero (input mode) and the output buffers will then be enabled by $\overline{\text{DS1}} \cdot \text{DS2}$. This enabling should only take place when, on the one hand, the 8212 is addressed and, on the other hand, a read command is sent by the microprocessor. These enabling conditions are satisfied by the following relationships:

$$\overline{\text{DS1}} = \text{'}\overline{\text{CS}}\text{ ADDRESS'}$$

$$\text{DS2} = \text{'PERI READ'}$$

The I/O port comprising the tri-state latch can now only be read; also, the signal 'PERI READ' is not required in memory-mapped I/O mode (as in the MOTOROLA 6800).

II.3.2. Principles of interrupt handling

II.3.2.1. The initiation of an interrupt request. Within an industrial application interrupt requests can be initiated by input/output devices using either a programmable parallel interface, a programmable serial interface, or by user-supplied external logic; however, such requests can only be generated from devices specifically designed to function in interrupt mode. The reason for an interrupt request is usually a request for service (most frequently an I/O transfer), or to signal the end of service after some operation has been requested and performed.

Let us recall that any interrupt request generated by an input/output device usually involves two actions:

(1) Setting to '1' a status bit assigned to this input/output device, thereby indicating the interrupt request; and
(2) Activating an 'interrupt request' signal.

The interrupt request should, of course, be relayed to the microprocessor, which has, for this purpose, one or more 'interrupt request' inputs. If it has several such inputs, these are prioritized; that is, in the event of simultaneous interrupt requests, one of them will have priority and, furthermore, a priority ordering exists for each of the inputs. These are generally known as *prioritized interrupt levels*; the ZILOG Z 80, which has three such interrupts, provides an example. When the number of circuits permitted to carry out interrupts is greater than the number of 'interrupt request' inputs on the microprocessor (remembering that this number is usually one), there are two possible solutions:

(1) The 'interrupt request' outputs are merged and linked to the single 'interrupt request' input of the microprocessor. If the latter possesses several interrupt levels, the requests must be sent out by the user at the various levels, corresponding to the user-desired priority ordering;

(2) The 'interrupt request' outputs are addressed to an 'interrupt controller', which prioritizes the requests and relays them to the microprocessor.

II.3.2.2. The process of branching to the subroutine to be executed. Whenever the 'interrupt request' input of the microprocessor (or one of these inputs if there are several) is activated, the microprocessor:

(1) Activates the 'interrupt acknowledge' signal if interrupts have been enabled by the program;
(2) Completes the execution of the current instruction;
(3) Inhibits any new interrupt request;
(4) Saves, on the stack, the return address of the program, or subroutine, which was interrupted by the arrival of the interrupt;
(5) Saves the 'machine state'; that is, the accumulator(s), the registers, the program counter, the stack pointer, and the flags. This operation does not exist in every microprocessor: the 8080A does not do it, for example, whereas the 6800 does;
(6) Executes a specific process, built into the microprocessor, with the object of branching to the interrupt subroutine to be executed. This specific process will be studied, later on, for the 8080A and the 6800.

An interrupt controller is a circuit which usually has eight levels of prioritized interrupts and which is designed so that several controllers can be connected in parallel (cascaded) if the eight levels prove insufficient. When one or more 'interrupt request' inputs of the controller become active, the controller supplies, on its output pins, either the address of the interrupt subroutine corresponding to the highest priority input/output device, or a code corresponding to the highest priority interrupt level. This code, represented in three or four bits, is called a vector. When concatenated with the other address bits, it produces, directly or indirectly, depending on the microprocessor, the address of the prioritized interrupt subroutine; that is, the subroutine appropriate to the input/output device which has requested an interrupt with the given priority. This technique is called *vectored addressing*. We shall see this in action when we study the MOTOROLA 6828 controller.

II.3.3. Interrupt handling on the INTEL 8080A

II.3.3.1. Branching to the subroutine to be executed. When this microprocessor receives an interrupt request it tests the INTE flip-flop, which, depending on whether its value is 0 or 1, inhibits or acknowledges interrupts. If INTE = 1, it activates the 'interrupt acknowledge' signal ($\overline{\text{INTA}}$), resets INTE to 0, finishes the instruction in execution and stops program execution while it enters an interrupt handling sequence. In order to do this:

(1) It saves a return address to the interrupted program (i.e. the contents of the program counter);
(2) It subsequently initiates a 'FETCH' cycle, without, however, putting an

address on the address bus. The purpose of this cycle is to fetch the operation code for the next instruction to be executed. External logic will previously have deposited this operation code on the data bus as a result of the $\overline{\text{INTA}}$ signal. This op-code must necessarily be a subroutine call; the instruction is, therefore, either a RST or a CALL;

(3) In the event of a call instruction, the microprocessor initiates two more FETCH cycles and activates $\overline{\text{INTA}}$ twice to fetch the two bytes of the address part of the CALL instruction;

(4) The execution of the instruction causes the microprocessor to branch to the address of the subroutine to be executed.

II.3.3.2. Handling of interrupts without an interrupt controller. External logic places a RESTART instruction on the data bus via a tri-state buffer. To do this, the tri-state buffer is enabled by the $\overline{\text{INTA}}$ signal. When the microprocessor executes the FETCH cycle the RESTART instruction is sent, which is then decoded in the microprocessor instruction register. This RESTART instruction, which is a subroutine call reduced to a single byte, is executed by the microprocessor, and causes a branch to an address indicated within the instruction. It only remains for the programmer to place an interrupt subroutine or a polling subroutine at this address. Eight RST instructions exist: RST0, RST1, RST2, RST3, RST4, RST5, RST6, RST7. These eight instructions are subroutine calls to the respective decimal addresses, 0, 8, 16, 24, 32, 40, 48, and 56; or to the equivalent hexadecimal addresses, 00, 08, 10, 18, 20, 28, 30, and 38. The decimal address is obtained by multiplying the RST level by 8. Thus, the corresponding decimal address for RST5 is $8 \times 5 = 40$. The number 8 arises from the fact that 8 bytes are reserved for each RST level in low-order ROM or EPROM memory addresses. If the interrupt program appropriate to the RST parameter consists of eight bytes at most, it can be located in these reserved memory addresses. Otherwise, it suffices to place in the first three reserved addresses a jump instruction, which jumps to the actual address of the subroutine to be executed. Thus if we wish to put at address 0520 the subroutine corresponding to an interrupt request at level 0, we should plant the instruction JUMP 0520 at hexadecimal addresses 00. 01 and 02 (Figure 13).

Figure 14 gives an example of planting an RST instruction using a tri-state buffer. To the inputs A1 to A8 of the DM81LS95 we have given values corresponding to the instruction RST0 (i.e. C7 in hexadecimal). The block-diagram of Figure 14 applies when only one input/output device is allowed to generate interrupt requests, or when prioritization is carried out by polling.

II.3.3.3. Interrupt handling with the 8259 interrupt controller. The INTEL interrupt controller is the 8259 circuit, which has replaced the 8214.

This circuit accepts up to eight prioritized interrupt requests on its inputs IR0 to IR7, where the highest priority must be connected to IR0. As soon as an interrupt request appears on one of the inputs IR0 to IR7, the interrupt controller memorizes it and sends an interrupt request to the microprocessor. The latter

34

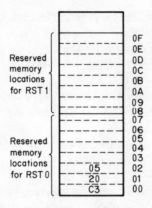

Figure 13. ROM contents for RST0

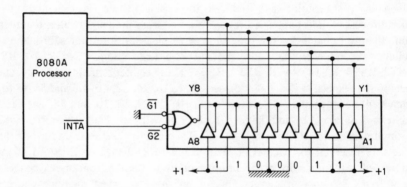

Figure 14. External logic for a RESTART interrupt

Table VII. RST instructions

RSTN	Operation code	Branching address	
		Decimal	Hex
RST0	C7	0	00
RST1	CF	8	08
RST2	D7	16	10
RST3	DF	24	18
RST4	E7	32	20
RST5	EF	40	28
RST6	F7	48	30
RST7	FF	56	38

completes the instruction currently in execution and generates a negative pulse on $\overline{\text{INTA}}$. The 8259 receives this signal and subsequently places the hexadecimal code, CD, of a CALL instruction onto the data bus. The FETCH cycle, initiated by the microprocessor at the same time as it activates $\overline{\text{INTA}}$, fetches the CD into the operation code position of the instruction register. This code is interpreted as a CALL, which causes the microprocessor to generate a second, and then a third, negative pulse on $\overline{\text{INTA}}$, each pulse being associated with a new FETCH cycle.

The 8259 has been designed to place on the data bus the least significant byte, followed by the most significant byte, of the address-part of the CALL instruction; this occurs at the arrival of the second and third negative pulses, respectively, on the $\overline{\text{INTA}}$ input (which is linked to the $\overline{\text{INTA}}$ output of the microprocessor). This address is that of a 4- or 8-byte memory region (depending on what has been programmed into the 8259). As this region is far too small to contain the entire interrupt subroutine appropriate to this interrupt request, it contains, instead, the three bytes of an unconditional jump to the subroutine.

In this way, the 8259 controller provides the microprocessor with a CALL instruction having an address-part specific to the interrupt level to be handled and also specific to the IR input. The address relative to IR0 is sent out by the microprocessor to the 8259 when the latter is being programmed with the initialization words, ICW1 and ICW2.

(a) 8259 Registers. From the user's point of view, the 8259 can be considered as containing the following registers:

(1) A *request register*, which receives the eight 'interrupt request' inputs IR0 to IR7. This is called an INTERRUPT REQUEST REGISTER by INTEL and designated IRR;
(2) A *mask register*, which, when programmed, is able to inhibit or enable each interrupt level individually. This is called an INTERRUPT MASK REGISTER by INTEL and designated IMR;
(3) A *service register*, which memorizes either a single request being serviced (i.e., in execution) or more than one request if the request in execution gets interrupted by a request of higher priority. This is called an IN-SERVICE REGISTER by INTEL and designated ISR;
(4) Three *initialization registers*, which are loaded in advance by the microprocessor with the necessary data for successful operation of the interrupt controller as follows;
    (a) Whether one, or more, controllers are in use;
    (b) Information regarding chaining in the case of several controllers;
    (c) Address of the interrupt subroutine corresponding to interrupt level zero. This address constitutes the second and third byte of the CALL instruction, which must be sent to the microprocessor by the controller.

The contents of these registers are called INITIALIZATION COMMAND WORDS and are designated by ICW1, ICW2, and ICW3;

(1) Three *command registers*, which permit the user to choose one of a number of modes of operation allowed by the 8259. Their contents are called OPERATION COMMAND WORDS and are designated by OCW1, OCW2, and OCW3;

(2) Two *status registers* read by the microprocessor.

(b) 8259 Signals. The pins of this circuit are:

(1) The eight prioritized interrupt levels IR0 to IR7, the highest priority level being IR0;

(2) The eight bi-directional bits of the data bus. In the microprocessor to controller direction, they allow the microprocessor to write into the command register. In the reverse direction, they allow the microprocessor to read the status register and allow the controller to send the three bytes of the CALL instruction (which is a subroutine call with a 16-bit address) to the microprocessor;

(3) The signal $\overline{RD}$ is the read signal. It is connected to $\overline{I/OR}$ on the processor;

(4) The signal $\overline{WR}$ is the write signal. It is connected to $\overline{I/OW}$ on the processor;

(5) The signal INT is the interrupt request sent to the microprocessor;

(6) The signal $\overline{INTA}$ receives the 'interrupt acknowledged' signal generated by the microprocessor on its $\overline{INTA}$ (same name) pin in response to INT;

(7) The signal $\overline{CS}$ for enabling the 8259;

(8) The address bit A0. Together with $\overline{RD}$ and $\overline{WR}$, it allows the selection of one of the 8259 registers;

(9) The signal $\overline{SP}$ and the lines CAS0, CAS1, and CAS2, which are only used when several 8259 controllers are cascaded.

(c) 8259 initialization words. Together, ICW1 and ICW2 deliver to the 8259 the start address of the 4- or 8-byte memory region assigned to each interrupt level. This memory region contains a jump instruction to the address of the corresponding subroutine. Thus if the subroutine corresponding to interrupt level IR0 starts at hexadecimal address 1530, the instruction JMP 1530 is planted, starting at the first address of the memory region assigned to IR0. Yet again, though, we must know this first IR0 address: for this purpose, we have the initialization words ICW1 and ICW2. Knowing the first address of the memory region assigned to IR0, as well as the number of bytes assigned to each region (8 or 4 depending on whether the 2^2 bit of ICW1 is 0 or 1), the 8259 then calculates the first address of each of the memory regions assigned to the interrupt levels. It only remains for the user to place in these locations (which he has now chosen using ICW1 and ICW2) the appropriate instructions to jump to the interrupt subroutines. Figure 15 illustrates this using the example of IR0 and IR1. If the memory region is programmed to be of size 4 bytes, the first address of the IR0 memory region is determined as indicated in Figure 15. Figure 16 helps to determine the layout of ICW1 and ICW2. The 8259 recognizes ICW1 and ICW2 by the following characteristics:

for ICW1 A0 = 0 2^0 bit of ICW = 0 2^4 bit of ICW = 1

for ICW2 A0 = 0

As soon as the 8259 receives the initialization words, it is ready to function in its simplest mode, characterized as follows:

(1) All the interrupt levels IR0 to IR7 are enabled (mask register set to zero);
(2) Fixed prioritization of these levels: IR0 has the highest priority (fixed priority mode).

At the same time, the 8259 could be programmed for other prioritized modes by means of the command words OCW1 and OCW2.

OCW2 contains the A8 to A15 bits of the first address of the IR0 memory region. We are missing the A0 to A4 bits of this address. These five bits will be

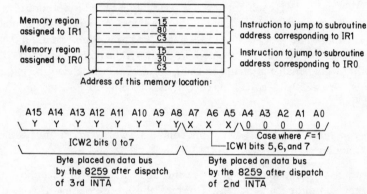

Figure 15. Use of a memory region for branching to interrupt subroutine corresponding to IR0

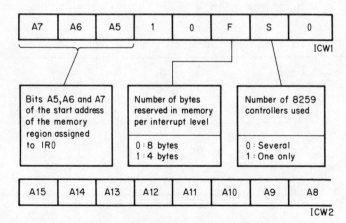

Figure 16. The ICW1 and ICW2 initialization words

supplied by the controller, when operating at the required interrupt level (see Table VIII).

Study of Table VIII shows that it is sufficient: (1) to encode the level number in bits A2, A3, and A4, if $F = 1$, and to set A0 and A1 to zero; (2) to encode the level number in bits A3, A4, and A5, if $F = 0$, and to set A0, A1, and A2 to zero.

It should be noted that the address bit A5 can only be programmed by the user when the chosen format is $F = 1$. If $F = 0$, we must have A5 = 0.

If the microprocessor system contains several 8259 controllers ($S = 0$ for ICW1), a third initialization word is needed: ICW3. But, by way of simplification, let us suppose, for the moment, that the system contains only one 8259 controller. Our controller, having received ICW1 and ICW2, is now ready to receive interrupts, level 0 having the highest priority.

(d) 8259 command word OCW1 (mask word). Having sent the initialization words ICW1 and ICW2, each 'interrupt request' input of the 8259 controller can be individually masked; that is, inhibited by the 'mask register' programmed by OCW1. The mask does not act on the IR (interrupt request) input, but on the ISR bit corresponding to the 'service register'. In this way, the command word OCW1 = 11111000 would enable interrupt levels 0, 1, and 2. On receiving the initialization words, the 8259 interprets every command with A0 = 1 as an OCW1 (Figure 17).

(e) 8259 command word OCW2. This command word almost always carries out two functions:

(1) A compulsory function; to signal to the 8259 the end of execution of an interrupt subroutine and to reset to zero the corresponding IRS but. All interrupt subroutines should end, therefore, by sending OCW2 followed by a RET instruction;
(2) An optional function; to set the priority ordering so as to differ from that of the fixed priority mode. For this, the 8259 allows different priority modes to be set.

Table VIII. Least significant bits of the call instruction address

	Case F = 1 4 bytes per level					Case F = 0 8 bytes per level					
	A4	A3	A2	A1	A0	A5	A4	A3	A2	A1	A0
IR0	0	0	0	0	0	0	0	0	0	0	0
IR1	0	0	1	0	0	0	0	1	0	0	0
IR2	0	1	0	0	0	0	1	0	0	0	0
IR3	0	1	1	0	0	0	1	1	0	0	0
IR4	1	0	0	0	0	1	0	0	0	0	0
IR5	1	0	1	0	0	1	0	1	0	0	0
IR6	1	1	0	0	0	1	1	0	0	0	0
IR7	1	1	1	0	0	1	1	1	0	0	0

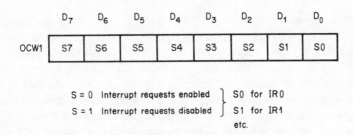

Figure 17. OCW1 command word

The 8259 recognizes OCW2 by the following characteristics:

$$A0 = 0 \quad 2^3 \text{ bit of OCW} = 0 \quad 2^4 \text{ bit of OCW} = 0$$

(i) Fixed priority mode (fully nested mode). This is the classic method by which highest priority is given to level 0 and lowest priority to level 7. We recall that the controller automatically places itself in this mode after receiving ICW1 and ICW2. An interrupt in course of execution can itself be interrupted if an interrupt of a higher priority arrives. In this case, the bits corresponding to these two levels are set to '1' in the ISR service register, indicating that neither of the interrupt subroutines is finished. Each of the interrupt subroutines should signal to the controller that it is finished by resetting its ISR bit. To do this, the user-program sends OCW2 to the 8259 at the end of the interrupt subroutine, which resets the highest priority ISR bit, i.e. the one which corresponds to the interrupt level which has just been serviced. In this mode, OCW2 has the value 00100000, or 20 hexadecimal and this value has to be sent to the 8259 command register. In order that this sending is not disturbed by a pending interrupt, the handling of any further interrupts must be inhibited, which gives the following general form to the subroutine:

```
SUB         EI
            *
            *
            *
            DI
            MVI A, 20
            OUT CR (8259 command register)
            EI
            RET
```

The RET instruction causes the microprocessor to branch back to the interrupted subroutine, if there was one. If there are no other interrupt requests pending, the microprocessor returns, by means of the stack, to the place in the main program where it was interrupted. We recall that each branch to a subroutine causes the return address to the interrupted program to be saved in the stack.

(ii) Rotating priority mode. This mode is used when peripheral interrupt requests have equal priorities. In this situation we need to reset to zero the IRS bit for the interrupt in execution, and to be able, eventually, to assign the lowest priority to any one of these interrupt levels. This last operation (which can be carried out either during the interrupt subroutine, or at the end of it), usually entails a priority rotation. Let us explain this rotation by means of an example.

Suppose that a level 2 interrupt is being serviced. Its bit was set to '1' at the time of the interrupt request. The priority order is then as shown in Figure 18.

The different possibilities which we have just alluded to give several variants, which we shall now study.

(1) Automatic rotation at the end of an interrupt (AUTO ROTATE AT EOI).
   (a) The end of interrupt subroutine execution is signalled to the 8259 controller by sending from the subroutine the programmed command word OCW2 = 10100000;
   (b) This latter command word causes the resetting to zero of the corresponding ISR interrupt bits;
   (c) The command word gives lowest priority to the interrupt which has just finished and causes a rotation of priorities. Since the peripherals are in theory of equal priority, no new interrupt request can arrive during the execution of an interrupt subroutine. Thus we need only enable interrupt-mode operation (which is automatically disabled by the microprocessor as soon as it receives an interrupt request) at the end of an interrupt subroutine. The last four instructions are then:

```
MVI A OCW2  (with OCW2 = A0)
OUT CR      (CR = Command register of controller)
EI          interrupt enable
RET         subroutine return
```

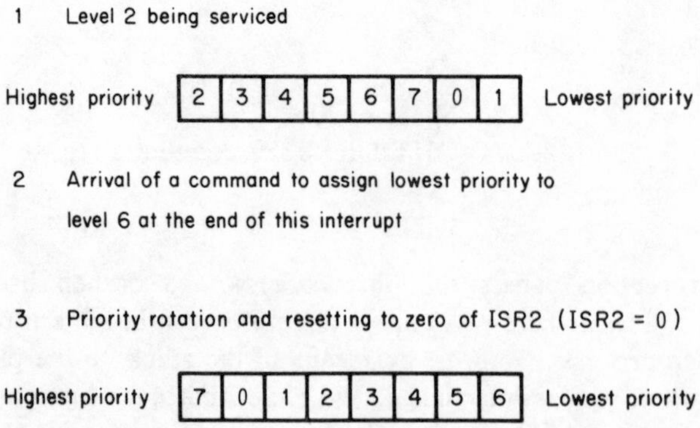

1   Level 2 being serviced

Highest priority | 2 | 3 | 4 | 5 | 6 | 7 | 0 | 1 | Lowest priority

2   Arrival of a command to assign lowest priority to
    level 6 at the end of this interrupt

3   Priority rotation and resetting to zero of ISR2 (ISR2 = 0)

Highest priority | 7 | 0 | 1 | 2 | 3 | 4 | 5 | 6 | Lowest priority

Figure 18. Example of rotating priorities

(2) Specific rotation at the end of an interrupt (SPECIFIC ROTATE AT EOI).

(a) The end of execution of an interrupt subroutine is signalled to the 8259 controller by sending the command word $OCW2 = 11100L_2L_1L_0$.

(b) This latter word (which is programmed into the subroutine) causes the ISR bit specified by the binary code in bits $L_2L_1L_0$ to be reset to zero. The code should be that of the interrupt level corresponding to the subroutine; for example, 4 for the subroutine corresponding to IR4.

(c) the command word gives lowest priority to the interrupt whose level is specified by $L_2L_1L_0$ and initiates a priority rotation.

(3) Specific rotation during an interrupt (SET PRIORITY).

(a) The command word placed in the interrupt subroutine does not influence the ISR bits nor does it signify the end of the interrupt subroutine. This OCW2 command word is $11000L_2L_1L_0$.

(b) The command word does, however, fix a new lowest priority. This is defined by the level encoded in the three $L_2L_1L_0$ bits and is followed by a priority rotation. Note that, exceptionally, this command does not signal the end of a subroutine.

(4) Change of priority at the end of an interrupt (SPECIFIC EOI).

(a) The end of execution of the interrupt subroutine is signalled to the 8259 controller by sending from the subroutine the programmed command word $OCW2 = 01100L_2L_1L_0$.

(b) The command word resets to zero the ISR bit corresponding to the interrupt.

(c) The command word gives the lowest priority to the interrupt whose level is specified by $L_2L_1L_0$, but there is no rotation of priorities.

From these considerations we deduce that all interrupt subroutines should signal end of execution to the controller by sending a command word, which resets to zero the ISR bit corresponding to this subroutine (this bit was previously set to '1' by the interrupt request from the corresponding peripheral). The priorities are now modified so as to assign the lowest priority to the peripheral which has just been serviced; this is done automatically (automatic rotation at the end of an interrupt), or by encoding in three bits the level assigned to the peripheral which should now take the lowest priority.

There is one and only one command which allows priority to be set in the middle of a subroutine and not necessarily at the end; this is the SET PRIORITY command.

Table IX outlines the OCW2 command words for the 'rotating priority' mode. These words can be derived from Figure 19.

Note 1. All interrupt subroutines should finish with an OCW2 command word in order to reset to zero the ISR bit corresponding to this subroutine. In the *fixed priority* mode the code for this ISR bit is automatically looked up and obtained by the 8259. But in the *rotating priority* mode it would not be possible for the 8259 to find it; this is why the code, in this mode, is indicated at the end of each subroutine by the $L_2L_1L_0$ bits.

Table IX. OCW2 commands in the rotating priority mode

	Command word								ISR reset to zero	Priority rotation	Lowest priority assigned
	D_7	D_6	D_5	D_4	D_3	D_2	D_1	D_0			
Auto rotate at EOI	1	0	1	0	0	0	0	0	Yes	Yes	To level which has just been serviced
Specific rotate at EOI	1	1	1	0	0	L_2	L_1	L_0	Yes	Yes	To level specified by $L_2L_1L_0$
Set priority	1	1	0	0	0	L_2	L_1	L_0	No	Yes	To level specified by $L_2L_1L_0$
Specific EOI	0	1	1	0	0	L_2	L_1	L_0	Yes	No	To level specified by $L_2L_1L_0$

Sub-modes of the rotating priority mode

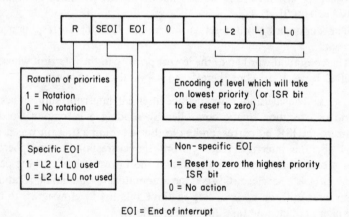

EOI = End of interrupt

Figure 19. Format of OCW2 command word

Note 2. Knowing how to determine and use ICW1, ICW2, OCW1 and OCW2 is sufficient to enable one to manage up to 8 'interrupt request' inputs. The 8259 is then relatively easy to use, and performs well. To illustrate this simplicity, we shall program a specific example for the 8259. For this, we must know how to address each of the 8259 registers. This addressing is not very elegant but it is simple. One single address bit, A0, is used jointly for ordering the arrival of commands and for determining the 2^0 and 2^4 bits of the initialization or command word.

If the following sequence is followed in the main program

sending of ICW1 initialization word
sending of ICW2 initialization word
sending of OCW1 command word,

the addressing reduces to

$A0 = 0$ for ICW1 and OCW2
$A0 = 1$ for ICW2 and OCW1

Let us put the A7 bit of the address onto the 8259 $\overline{CS}$ input (linear selection). The two register addresses of the 8259 are then:

01111110, or 7E hexadecimal, for ICW1 and OCW2;
01111111, or 7F hexadecimal, for ICW2 and OCW1.

We shall now program the 8259 in fixed priority mode and enable only the interrupt levels 0, 1, and 2; also, let us choose the addresses 2000, 2100, and 2200 as the first addresses of subroutines corresponding to IR0, IR1, and IR2; finally, we take 1260 as first address of the memory region assigned to IR0.

The instructions JMP 2000, JMP 2100, and JMP 2200 should be placed starting at the respective addresses 1260, 1264, and 1268.

If we then take $F = 1$ and $S = 1$, in the command word and the first address of the memory region assigned to IR0 to be 1260 we obtain the following 8259 program:

```
MVI ⎫  A, 76H   (the letter H signifies hexadecimal)
OUT |  7EH      ICW1 = 76
MVI |  A, 12H   ICW2 = 12
OUT ⎬  7FH      OCW1 = F8
MVI |  A, F8H
OUT |  7FH
EI  ⎭
```

Each of the subroutines corresponding to IR0, IR1 and IR2 ends with:

```
DI
MVI    A, 20H
OUT    7EH
EI
RET
```

(f)   The 8259 OCW3 command word (Table X)

(1) OCW3 polling command word. The 8259 controller accepts the programmed polling mode and then behaves as a form of priority encoder. This mode is useful

Table X. Command word OCW3

Objective	Nature of command	Command word								
		D_7	D_6	D_5	D_4	D_3	D_2	D_1	D_0	in hex
Polling	Polling command word	X	0	0	0	1	1	0	0	0C
Read of a status word	Command word preceding the read of 'mask register' IMR	OCW3 not required								
	Command word preceding the read of 'request register' IRR	X	0	0	0	1	0	1	0	0A
	Command word preceding the read of 'service register' ISR	X	0	0	0	1	0	1	1	0B
Special mask	Command word for setting the special mask SMM to 1	X	1	1	0	1	0	0	0	68
	Command word for resetting special mask SMM to 0	X	1	0	0	1	0	0	0	48

X represents either 0 or 1. For the hex value we have taken $X = 0$.

when several interrupt subroutines are identical, or, perhaps, when the 8259 is situated on a board which does not receive $\overline{\text{INTA}}$. This mode is obtained very simply by inhibiting the interrupts with a DI instruction and then sending an OCW3 command word of the form $X0001100$. The letter X signifies that the bit could be either 0 or 1. On receiving the next $\overline{\text{RD}}$ signal, the 8259 places on the data bus an 8-bit polling word. Only 4 of these 8 bits are of interest to us. The 2^7 bit (called I) serves as the bit which indicates, when its value is '1', that a service request is either in course of execution, or has just been made. In such cases, the highest priority level is encoded on bits W_0, W_1, and W_2 (see Figure 20). The programmer should then follow the command word with a read instruction and it then only remains to decode the highest priority level and to branch to the corresponding subroutine. When using this mode, we shall then find the following instructions in the main program and not in the interrupt subroutine, as was the case for OCW2:

```
DI          disable interrupts
MVI         A, OCW3
OUT         CR (command register)
IN          ADDR
```

This IN instruction, which follows the sending of OCW3, will deposit the polling word on the data bus and then into the accumulator. The polling sub-

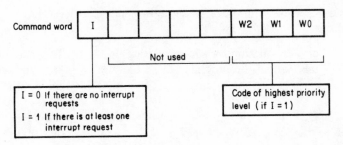

Figure 20. Polling word

routine will consist of testing I and then, if $I = 1$, of decoding $W_2W_1W_0$, and of branching to the correct interrupt subroutine.

(2) OCW3 command word for reading out the status word. The programmer can always find out where he is, within the rather complex functioning of the 8259 controller, by reading the status word. But, since there are several registers which can be read, a single OCW3 command word permits one to choose the information one wishes to have. The sending of this command word is, of course, followed by a read of a status word. The three registers which can be read are:

(a) The 'mask register' IMR, giving each of the inhibited interrupt levels. This does not require an OCW3 command word to be sent in advance;

(b) The 'request register' IRR, showing each of the activate interrupt levels of the 8259. In order to read the contents of this register, one must, previously, have sent the command word $OCW3 = X0001010$;

(c) The 'service register', ISR, in which each interrupt level in service has its bit set to 1. An interrupt level is in service if it is in course of execution, or if its execution has been started but interrupted by a higher priority level. In order to read the contents of this register, one must send the command word $OCW3 = X0001011$ in advance. Recall that the letter X signifies that the corresponding bit could take on either the value 0 or 1.

(3) OCW3 command word for special masking. During the execution of a subroutine, any other interrupt request can only be considered if the interrupt subroutine has allowed new interrupts via the EI (Enable Interrupt) instruction. However, only interrupts corresponding to higher priority levels can take place. The object of this special masking is to allow any new interrupt request, *whatever its priority*; this occurs while the special mask, called SMM by INTEL, is held at level '1'. The same OCW3 command word can reset it at '0', in which case the operation reverts to normal. This special operation, carried out inside the interrupt subroutine, requires a prior masking of the level corresponding to this subroutine, and this is done by an OCW1 command word. The OCW3 command word is:

(a) $OCW3 = X1101000$ for setting the mask to '1'.
(b) $OCW3 = X1001000$ for setting the mask to '0'.

Let us explain this with an example corresponding to level 4:

SUB4	no new interrupt is allowed during	This part of the
•	this part of the program.	program does not
•		contain the EI
•		instruction.
MVI A,	OCW1 Mask for IR4	OCW1 =
OUT CR	(the 8259 command reg.)	00010000 = 10
MVI A,	OCW3	
OUT CR	(the 8259 command reg.) setting SMM	OCW3 =
EI	interrupt enable special mask to 1	01101000 =
•	During this part of the program any	
•	new interrupt, whatever its priority,	
•	could intervene.	
DI	inhibition of interrupts to send an	
	OCW3 command word.	
MVI A,	OCW3 resetting SMM	OCW3 =
OUT CR	(the 8259 command reg.) special mask to 0	01001000 = 48
MVI A,	OCW1 Removal of	OCW1 =
OUT CR	(command reg.) IR4 mask	00000000 = 00
•		
•	normal operation	
•		
EOI	(some appropriate EOI action via OCW2)	
RET		

(g) Example of several 8259 controllers in series. Several INTEL 8259 controllers can be used to extend the number of interrupt levels to 64. Past 64, one must use the polling mode implemented by the 8259. The connection of several 8259 controllers is very simple. One of the controllers becomes the master controller, the others being slave controllers. Each INT output of a slave is connected to an IR input of the master according to the priorities assigned to that slave controller. The IR0 input will only be used if there are eight slave controllers (Figure 21).

Naturally, the INT input of the master is connected to the INT input of the microprocessor. The $\overline{SP}$ input is set to 1 for the master and grounded for all the slaves. These wired connections between the INT outputs of the slaves and the IR inputs of the master will be communicated to the controllers by an initialization word called ICW3. For the ICW3 of the master, it suffices to set to 1 the bit corresponding to an IR input receiving the INT output of a slave. Thus, for Figure 22 we have:

ICW3 of master: 01001000 (IR3 and IR6)

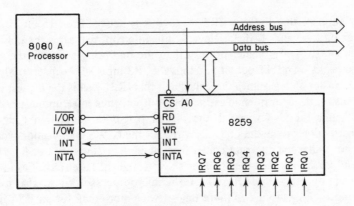

Figure 21. Interfacing an 8259 circuit

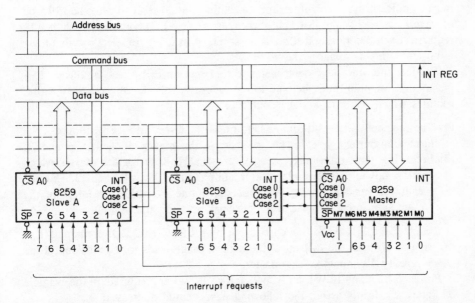

Figure 22. Microprocessor system with twenty-two interrupt levels provided by three 8259s

For the ICW3 of each slave we must encode, on the three least significant bits of ICW3, the level of the IR input to which the INT output of the slave is connected. So for the same Figure 22 we have:

ICW3 of slave A: 00000011 (INT linked to IR3)
ICW3 of slave B: 00000110 (INT linked to IR6)

The inputs CAS0, CAS1, and CAS2 of the master are linked to the corresponding pins of the slaves, these pins functioning as inputs.

48

Let us suppose that the level IR5 of slave A is active. The IR5 bit of slave A then takes on the value 1. If, for slave A, this interrupt request is the only one at that moment, or if it is higher priority than the one being serviced, the slave A 8259 enables its own INT output and thus the IR3 input of the master. The ISR3 bit of the master also assumes the value 1. If this IR3 level is the highest priority for the master, it, in turn, enables the INT output, thus interrupting the 8080A. When it sends the $\overline{\text{INTA}}$ signal, the master places the operation code of the CALL instruction on the data bus. By virtue of the ICW3 initialization words the master knows that the interrupt comes from slave A. Using the three lines CAS0, CAS1, and CAS2 it sends the code for slave A and the latter identifies itself. On receiving the operation code for CALL the microprocessor knows that it should activate the $\overline{\text{INTA}}$ output two more times (twice more than for an RST instruction). Slave A, having identified itself, then sends first the least significant byte of the address corresponding to the interrupt subroutine to be executed, and then the most significant byte. This interrupt subroutine should reset to zero the ISR5 bit of slave A, as well as the ISR3 bit of the master. Two EOI commands will then be required. Each 8259 has a distinct address bit for its $\overline{\text{CS}}$ (chip select), so that there is no ambiguity as regards the addresses.

The fact that one slave controller interrupt sets an ISR bit of the master to 1 means that attention must be paid to the following rules for those interrupt subroutines which relate to a slave controller:

(1) The first task of the subroutine is to mask the lesser priority IR inputs of the master: in our example, for IR5 of slave A, this means inputs 4, 5, 6, and 7.
(2) Following that, one must reset to zero that ISR bit of the master which corresponds to the slave interrupt; in our example, this will be ISR3. This will permit the master, during interrupt subroutine execution, to interrupt the present subroutine because of a higher priority interrupt sent out by slave A.

Resetting the ISR bit to 0 is carried out by a SPECIFIC EOI command. It is this request to reset the ISR bit of the master which leads to the masking of the lesser priority IR inputs of the master.

For each 8259, an ICW1, an ICW2, and an ICW3 are required. In the example of Figure 22, let us assign the following hexadecimal addresses:

2000H for level 0 of the master controller
2020H for level 0 of slave controller A
2040H for level 0 of slave controller B.

The letter H after the address signifies hexadecimal notation. The initialization words are then:

master controller	ICW1 = 00010100 = 14H
	ICW2 = 00100000 = 20H
	ICW3 = 01001000 = 48H
slave A controller	ICW1 = 00110100 = 34H
	ICW2 = 00100000 = 20H

$$\text{ICW3} = 00000011 = 03\text{H}$$

slave B $\text{ICW1} = 01010100 = 54\text{H}$

controller $\text{ICW2} = 00100000 = 20\text{H}$

$$\text{ICW3} = 00000100 = 06\text{H}$$

(h) Addressing the 8259 registers. This mode of addressing is very specific since there is only one A0 selection bit for nine possible registers. Three registers, however, are read-only, IRR, ISR, and IMR, while the remaining six are write-only; these are the three initialization registers corresponding to ICW1, ICW2, and ICW3, and the three command registers corresponding to OCW1, OCW2, and OCW3. But this, of course, is not sufficient. In addition, two other selection criteria intervene (see Table XI):

Table XI. Addressing the 8259 controller registers

Instruction	A0	Register address	Remarks
Read	0	IRR or ISR	Selection carried out by the value of the
	1	IMR	previously sent command word
Write	0	ICW1, OCW2, OCW3	Selection carried out by the value of D_4 and D_3: D_4 D_3 1 X ICW1 0 0 OCW2 0 1 OCW3
	1	ICW2, ICW3, OCW1	Selection carried out by the order in which they arrive at the controller

(1) The value of the command word bits D4 and D3;
(2) The order of arrival of initialization or command words: the first word written will always be ICW1 and the second will always be ICW2.

The 8259, then, only possesses two addresses or, if one prefers, two ports: one for A0 = 0, the other for A0 = 1. We will call them, arbitrarily,

PT59A for A0 = 0 and PT59B for A0 = 1

II.3.4. Interrupt handling on the MOTOROLA 6800

II.3.4.1. Branching to the subroutine to be executed. When the micro-processor receives an interrupt request it finishes the instruction in execution, tests the interrupt mask, and, if the latter is at 0 (interrupts enabled), it stops the program in execution and enters an interrupt processing sequence. For this:

(1) It saves the return address to the interrupted program as well as saving the machine context; that is, the contents of accumulators A and B, the program counter, and the values of flags;

(2) It sets the interrupt mask to 1 in order to inhibit any further interrupts;
(3) It loads the program-counter with the contents of memory-locations FFF8 (most significant byte) and FFF9 (least significant byte) for the case of an interrupt request on the $\overline{IRQ}$ input. If this request occurs on the $\overline{NMI}$ input, it loads the program-counter with the contents of memory locations FFFC (most significant byte) and FFFD (least significant byte).
(4) The microprocessor then branches to the address indicated by the contents of the program-counter, at which address it should find the interrupt subroutine address.

II.3.4.2. Interrupt handling without an interrupt controller. It suffices to place the address of the subroutine to be executed at interrupt addresses, FFF8–FFF9 for IRQ, and FFFC–FFFD for NMI.

This type of interrupt handling applies when there is only one input/output device capable of generating interrupt requests (assuming $\overline{NMI}$ be reserved for the detection of power-failure), or when the interrupts are handled by polling. In the first case, the address of the subroutine to be executed is that of a single interrupt subroutine. In the second case, it is the address of a polling subroutine.

The choice by MOTOROLA of interrupt addresses FFF8 and FFF9 means placing the ROM at high addresses, and enabling this ROM for the bit-configuration A15 = 1 and A14 = 1. Let us take, as an example, a 2K byte ROM.

The addressing can be represented as follows:

A15 A14 A13 A12 A11 A10 A9 A8 A7 A6 A5 A4 A3 A2 A1 A0

ROM   1   1   ●   ●   ●   X   X   X   X   X   X   X   X   X   X   X

The symbol X represents either 0 or 1 in the address placed on the address bus. The three dots on the address bits A11, A12, and A13 signify that these three bits are not being used and they can take the value 0 or 1 in the address sent out by the microprocessor. Let us first give these dots the value 0, then the value 1, in the following address:

11●●●11111111000

We then obtain the addresses

1111111111111000, or FFF8, which is the 8th address of a ROM starting from a highest address of FFFF.

1100011111111000, or C7F8, which is the 8th address of a ROM starting from a highest address of C7FF.

Therefore, even if the microprocessor places on its address bus the address FFF8 in order to read its contents it will, in fact, read the contents of the memory location C7F8. It follows that, whatever the size of the ROM, the address FFF8 always corresponds to the 8th address of this memory, starting from its highest address. The result is similar for the FFF9 address. The only rule for the user to observe will be to place the address of the subroutine to be executed at the two highest ROM addresses which have F8 and F9, respectively, as their least significant byte of the address.

II.3.4.3. Interrupt handling using the 6828 interrupt controller.

(1) The 6828 registers. From the point of view of the user, the 6828 controller comprises two registers:

(a) A *request register*, which receives the eight 'interrupt request' inputs $\overline{IN0}$ to $\overline{IN7}$ (this is called REQUEST REGISTER by MOTOROLA): $\overline{IN7}$ has the highest priority.
(b) A *mask register*, which inhibits attention to interrupt requests for levels lower than the level set by the contents of this four-bit mask register.

(2) Programming the 6828. This interrupt controller allows only one mode of operation; that is, the one where priorities are predetermined and fixed, the highest having a level of 7. Also, it has neither a command register nor a status register. The only programming to be performed is that of the mask register consisting of four bits. A write instruction to address $11111111111XXXX0$ loads the mask register with the contents XXXX, the value of which ranges from 0000 (no interrupt level is masked) to 1000 (every interrupt level is masked). We recall that the mask register inhibits all interrupt requests of a level lower than the mask contents. The programming of this register is not carried out via the data bus and hence the bus contents are immaterial in the present situation.

(3) Functioning of the 6828. The interrupt controller should be inserted between address bits A1 A2 A3 A4 of the address bus and the corresponding bits of the ROM memory. We know that following an interrupt request the microprocessor reads the contents of memory location FFF8 followed by FFF9. For the first read, it deposits the value FFF8 on the address bus and reads the contents of the data bus. The insertion of an interrupt controller leads to this latter being addressed by FFF8. Following this addressing, the controller replaces the four ROM address bits A1 A2 A3 A4, with the value of a vector corresponding to the prioritized interrupt request. The memory position read therefore has the address:

$$11111111111Z4Z3Z2Z10 \text{ (i.e. } A0 = 0)$$

We now place, in the two memory locations with addresses

$$11111111111Z4Z3Z2Z10 \text{ (i.e. } A0 = 0)$$

the most significant byte (for A0 = 0) and the least significant byte (for A0 = 1) of the interrupt subroutine address. Table XII shows, for each interrupt level the vector $Z4Z3Z2Z1$ and the two interrupt addresses which should, in turn, contain the most significant byte and the least significant byte of the interrupt subroutine address corresponding to the interrupt level. Thus, if we wish to place at address C410 the interrupt subroutine corresponding to the IN3 input, the memory location FFEE should contain C4 and the memory location FFEF should contain 10.

Table XII. Interrupt addresses for the MOTOROLA 6828 controller

Priority	Input	Vector Z4	Z3	Z2	Z1	Interrupt address (in hexadecimal)	Interrupt addresses contain the address of:
Highest	$\overline{IN7}$	1	0	1	1	FFF6 and FFF7	I/S for priority 7
	$\overline{IN6}$	1	0	1	0	FFF4 and FFF5	I/S for priority 6
	IN5	1	0	0	1	FFF2 and FFF3	I/S for priority 5
	$\overline{IN4}$	1	0	0	0	FFF0 and FFF1	I/S for priority 4
	$\overline{IN3}$	0	1	1	1	FFEE and FFEF	I/S for priority 3
	$\overline{IN2}$	0	1	1	0	FFEC and FFED	I/S for priority 2
	$\overline{IN1}$	0	1	0	1	FFEA and FFEB	I/S for priority 1
Lowest	$\overline{IN0}$	0	1	0	0	FFE8 and FFE9	I/S for priority 0

I/S = Interrupt subroutine.

(4) Signals of the 6828. The 6828 pins are:

(a) The 8 interrupt request levels $\overline{IN0}$ to $\overline{IN7}$, the highest priority level being $\overline{IN7}$;
(b) The 4 address bus bits A4 A3 A2 A1;
(c) The 4 bits Z4Z3Z2Z1 of the vector transmitted by the interrupt controller to the ROM memory;
(d) The A0 address bit connected to the corresponding bit of the address bus;
(e) The R/W signal connected to the microprocessor R/W output;
(f) The E signal connected to VMA·ϕ_2;
(g) The $\overline{CS0}$ and CS1 signals. The interrupt controller should be enabled by FFF8 and FFF9. The A0, A1, A2, A3, and A4 bits are sent directly to the controller on the address bus. The other bits used are ANDed together and are linked, after inversion, to CS0. A NAND gate with eight inputs is entirely adequate. For a 2K byte ROM, the NAND gate will receive the inputs A15, A14, A10, A9, A8, A7, A6, and A5 (Figure 23). The CS1 signal is held at logic '1';
(h) The $\overline{IRQ}$ signal is the interrupt request addressed to the microprocessor if an interrupt input is activated which has a level equal to or greater than the mask setting;
(i) The $\overline{STRETCH}$ signal.

We have seen that the interrupt controller transforms the addresses FFF8 and FFF9 (which are deposited by the microprocessor on the address bus in the form of two other addresses, which we call interrupt addresses) by the modification of address bits A1 A2 A3 A4. This modification is, of course, not performed instantaneously and delays the moment when the address becomes enabled for ROM access. The 6828 controller then offers the possibility of prolonging the clock period in order to allow a correct read of the ROM when the latter requires significant decoding time. Note that this signal is not required for fast ROM memories. If necessary, the clock circuit linked to the 6800 should have a MEMORY READY input and the $\overline{STRETCH}$ signal will be sent on this input.

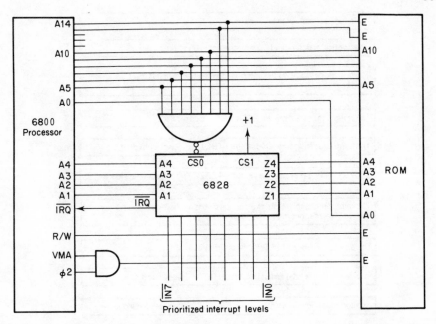

Figure 23. The 6828 interrupt controller in a microprocessor system with
MOTOROLA 6800

(5) Timing diagram for interrupt handling by the 6828. We recall that the only programming to be done consists of enabling interrupts and programming of the mask register with the four address bits A4 A3 A2 A1. This is done by a write instruction, the accumulator contents being unaffected. The sequence followed by the microprocessor is shown in Figure 24.

(6) Interrupt subroutine. The execution of an interrupt subroutine of level j, that is, corresponding to input $\overline{INj}$, should not be interrupted by any interrupt of lesser priority; but it could, however, be interrupted by an interrupt of higher priority. This effect is obtained by loading the mask with j + 1 and by granting the interrupt request of level j, followed by the enabling of new interrupts by the CLI instruction. Let us recall that granting an interrupt request is done automatically by the reading of data from the PIA, or the ACIA, when used as input devices. For those input/output devices requiring the clearing of an 'interrupt request' stored in a flip-flop, it is sufficient to assign a specific 'CS ADDRESS' to the flip-flop and to send onto the CLEAR input of this flip-flop the signal:

'FLIP-FLOP CS ADDRESS' · 'PERI WRITE'

The clearing is then performed by a write instruction to the address assigned to the flip-flop. The data placed on the data bus by this instruction will be of no consequence, since it is not used.

54

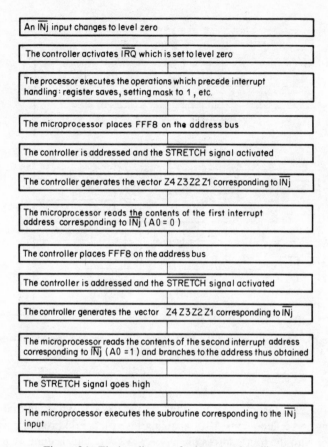

Figure 24. Timing diagram for interrupt handling

At the end of an interrupt subroutine, one must restore the initial value of the mask (1000, for example, if eight interrupt levels are used). The interrupt subroutine of level j is then of the following form:

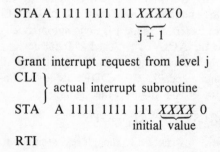

Grant interrupt request from level j
CLI ⎱
     ⎰ actual interrupt subroutine
STA   A 1111 1111 111 $\underbrace{XXXX}$ 0
                      initial value
RTI

Note. If the interrupt subroutine simply consists of reading data from a PIA,

CLI is not required and the interrupt subroutine reduces to three instructions:

LDA A PIAYD   (Y = A or B)
STA A MEM   (memory region required for the automatic
                      restoration of context)
RT1

(7) Switching function of the 6828 in a microprocessor system

Note. When the 6828 controller is not addressed (address other than FFF8 or FFF9) it allows address bits A4, A3, A2, and A1 to go through normally. The circuit therefore mainly plays the role of a selector with eight inputs and four outputs, as shown in Figure 25.

(8) Extension of the number of interrupt levels. The 6828 is not designed to be cascaded for handling more than eight interrupt levels. It is, however, possible to conceive a scheme allowing up to 56 interrupt levels (Figure 26).

The principle behind this extension consists of controlling seven 6828 controllers by an eighth 6828. Each of the seven 6828 slaves sends its IRQ output to an input of the 6828 master, except for the input IN4, which should not be used and is therefore set to level '1'. In fact, this input gives the combination $Z3 = Z2 = Z1 = 0$ for the 6828 master. Now this configuration forms the 000 address of a multiplexer, addressed relative to channel 0 which serves to send the address bits A5, A6, and A7 to the ROM when the microprocessor is not busy servicing an interrupt. In this case, the decoded function FFF8, or FFF9, has the value 0, which fixes the address of the multiplexer at 000.

When an interrupt is activated on one of the 6828 slaves, which are themselves always enabled, the $\overline{IRQ}$ activates the corresponding input of the 6828 master. The latter then activates the $\overline{IRQ}$ of the microprocessor, which, a little later, sends

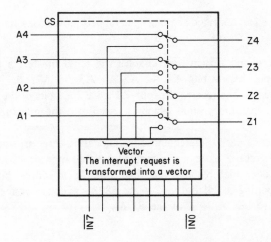

Figure 25. Basic function of the 6828 controller

56

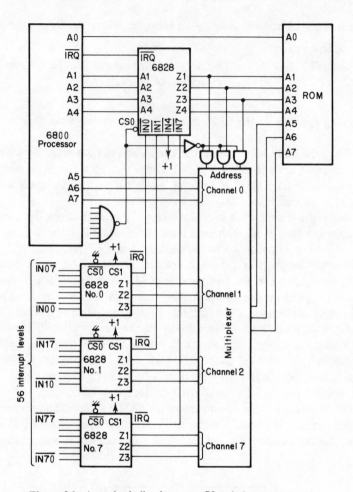

Figure 26. A method allowing up to fifty-six interrupt levels

the FFF8 address, and this in turn enables the 6828 master; a unique ROM address is then put out on bits A1 A2 A3 A4 A5 A6 A7:

The A1 A2 A3 A4 bits receive the four $Z4$ $Z3$ $Z2$ $Z1$ bits of the 6828 master. These four bits constitute a code which is specific to the interrupt level of the activated 6828.

The multiplexer is easily implemented by allocating three tri-state buffers per 6828 slave. These three buffers are enabled by the appropriate corresponding output of a decoder which receives the three multiplexer address bits. The buffer outputs corresponding to $Z1$ outputs of the 6828 slaves are connected together and then linked to bits Ai + 4 of the ROM.

II.4. Input/output by direct memory access

A peripheral-to-memory data transfer requires the reading of data by the microprocessor and then the writing to memory of the data just read. In the same way, a memory-to-peripheral transfer requires a read and then a write.

Thus, a transfer requires 10 to 15 clock periods for the processor, to which further synchronization periods are added. When there is a significant amount of data to be transmitted, this is too slow. To speed it up one suppresses transfers via the microprocessor accumulator: this is known as *direct memory access*. Numerous techniques of direct memory access exist: three are very well known, and, of these, two are of particular interest.

II.4.1. Direct memory access techniques

II.4.1.1. Burst mode DMA (by halting the microprocessor). This is the easiest one to use. The peripheral requiring the memory communicates a 'transfer request' to the DMA circuit. This circuit echoes the request to the microprocessor by its 'DMA request' signal. The current instruction is completed, which could take up several clock periods, and then the microprocessor informs the DMA circuit (via the 'DMA acknowledge' output) that it is placing the data bus, the address bus, and the memory-read and memory-write signals in a high impedance state, thus disconnecting itself from the buses and the two read and write signals. The DMA circuit now sends to the peripheral the 'transfer granted' information and then takes control of operations in order to ensure a memory-peripheral transfer, or vice-versa, at maximum speed, determined only by the memory-cycle time. Thus, with a memory having a cycle time of 500 ns, the transfer could be carried out at the maximum speed of 2 MHz. The memory address and the memory-read and memory-write signals are now generated by the DMA controller. The I/O transfer then consists of a block of data comprising N words. The number N is loaded in advance into an 'address register', the contents of which are incremented by one unit after each word transfer (one byte for 8-bit microprocessors). When the content of the 'byte counter' is equal to zero, the DMA controller ceases to activate the 'DMA request' signal, which has been active during the whole DMA transfer. As a result, the transfer is halted. Together, the 'address register', the 'word counter', the 'transfer request' signal, and its 'transfer granted' reply constitute a channel. This latter reply is made by the DMA controller following authorization from the microprocessor.

The DMA controller can have one or more channels; often, the number is four. In the case of several channels, it would be necessary, of course, to establish a priority hierarchy for several simultaneous transfer requests. This first technique, the most simple, is possible with any microprocessor having a 'direct memory access request' input, which, when enabled, causes the switching of the data bus, the address bus, and the memory-read and memory-write signals to a high impedance state. Such is the case with the HOLD input of the INTEL 8080A and the HALT input of the MOTOROLA 6800.

II.4.1.2. DMA by cycle-stealing. In this process the microprocessor is not stopped: its operation is simply suspended for one cycle in every n microprocessor cycles. There is, as it were, an apparent simultaneity in the operation of the

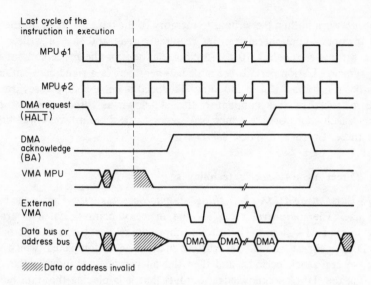

Figure 27. Burst-mode DMA by halting the microprocessor

microprocessor together with memory access by the peripherals. The only notice-able effect is that the general operation of the microprocessor is slowed down. This technique permits a transfer rate of one word per stolen cycle (one byte for 8-bit microprocessors), or, in effect, one word every two or three microprocessor cycles. The burst-mode DMA technique, on the other hand, allows the transfer of one word per microprocessor cycle and is thus two or three times faster, as well as being simpler, but pays the price of totally halting the microprocessor's execution (Figure 27).

What, then, is the principle of cycle-stealing? Let us recall that the burst-mode technique, involving halting of the microprocessor, is based on placing the address bus, the data bus, and the read and write signals at high impedance. The clock is in no way affected and continues to alternate between 0 and 1, but the microprocessor can do nothing about it. The cycle-stealing technique consists of suspending the microprocessor operation for one or more clock periods and placing the address bus, the data bus, and the read and write signals at high impedance during this time. Thus, in the case of the MOTOROLA 6800, this suspension is carried out by prolonging the duration of state '1' of the $\phi1$ clock and by setting the address bus and the read/write signal to a high impedance state. This command is carried out simply by setting the TSC (THREE STATE CONTROL) signal to '1'. As long as $\phi1$ has the value 1, the data bus is at high impedance. The 6800 is dynamic, therefore the prolonging of $\phi1$ at state '1' should not exceed a few μs. In the 6800, the direct memory access request is sent to the DMA REQUEST input of the 6875 clock circuit. This asynchronous request is synchronized by the circuit and increases $\phi1$ by one to four cycles (maximum value), depending on the duration at level zero of the DMA REQUEST input. The 6875 responds by sending the synchronous DMA GRANT signal, which, on the one hand, is sent to the DMA controller and, on the other, to the TSC (THREE STATE CONTROL) input of the 6800, which in turn sets the address bus and the read/write (R/W) signal to high impedance. Prolonging $\phi1$ means keeping $\phi2$ at state '0' and, consequently, keeping the data bus at high impedance.

Holding $\phi1$ high and $\phi2$ low should not last longer than 4.5 µs for a 1 MHz clock, which requires that the TSC signal should not last longer than 3 µs. The 1.5 µs is the time required for the microprocessor to take over the control of the bus. The 3 µs TSC allows two single-byte DMA transfers.

The cycle-stealing DMA technique is illustrated in the timing diagram of Figure 28, where we show two successive DMA requests, each allowing the transfer of two bytes. To do this, the signal sent on TSC is synchronized on the rising edge of $\phi1$, has a duration equal to three clock periods, or 3 µs, and is activated again after five clock periods, i.e. at the end of 5 µs. Using this technique, it is perfectly possible to transfer just one byte via a DMA request: for this, we only need the TSC signal to be at level '1' for two, instead of three, clock periods, and for it to be re-activated at the end of four clock periods, instead of five. One may perform as many successive DMA requests as one wishes. It is the DMA REQUEST signal, as generated by the DMA controller, which starts and stops the DMA transfer; in co-ordination with the peripheral, of course.

Let us return to the timing diagram of Figure 28. Contrary to what is normally found in books (or other documentation) about direct memory access by cycle-stealing, we have, for both the address and data buses, separated the information generated by the microprocessor from that generated by the DMA controller. In fact, this conforms more to what occurs in reality and greatly facilitates an understanding of the process, since we can see at a glance the overall division of tasks and, consequently, the division of the buses between the microprocessor and the DMA controller.

This technique, then, allows the transfer either of a byte every 4 µs, or two bytes every 5 µs. Thus, the microprocessor can execute a cycle every 4 µs in the first case and every 5 in the second case. It is therefore slowed down very substantially, but without coming to a complete halt.

II.4.1.3. Multiplexed (or transparent) DMA. This is the most efficient method, since it is almost as fast as the burst-mode DMA technique but with the incidental advantage of not stopping the microprocessor. There is a real simultaneity, which is, however, only possible at the price of having fast memories. The principle is based on the fact that the microprocessor only accesses the memory when necessary, and then only during one part of a cycle. In theory, therefore, we can let the DMA controller have access to the same memory during the other part of the cycle. This, of course, requires that a memory read or write be finished during this other part of the cycle. If this does not happen, it is necessary to slow down the clock frequency. In practice, the microprocessor has two anti-phased clocks $\phi1$ and $\phi2$, so that no recovery is possible. Clearly, this implies that the duration of $\phi1$ and $\phi2$ at level '1' is less than half a clock cycle. Let us suppose that the microprocessor has access to RAM memory while $\phi1$ is at level '1' and that the DMA controller has access to the same memory while $\phi2$ is at level '1'. The

60

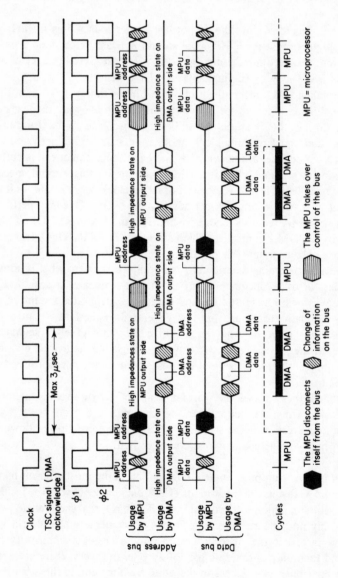

Figure 28. Time-sequence diagrams of a DMA transfer by cycle-stealing

61

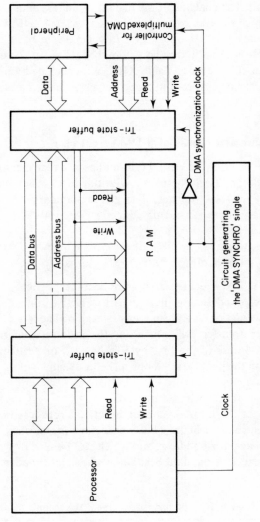

Figure 29. Diagram showing the principles of multiplexed DMA

address and data buses and the read and write signals should then be connected alternately to the microprocessor or to the DMA controller. In order to achieve this, tri-state buffers are inserted; on the one hand, between the microprocessor and the memory and, on the other, between the memory and the DMA controller (with its peripheral). The enabling of the one set of buffers entails an inhibiting of the other. For this, we create a signal (which we call 'DMA SYNCHRO'), which has a frequency equal to $\phi1$ or $\phi2$, but a cycle ratio equal to 1 (i.e. duration at level '1' is equal to duration at level '0'). Figures 29 and 30 show the block diagrams for this (see also Table XIII). We conclude by pointing out that shared access to memory, by two microprocessors, can be carried out using the same principle.

II.4.2. Architecture and signals of a DMA controller

In this section we shall try to describe in outline a direct memory access controller, usually called a DMA controller. With this in view, we shall describe the different stages of a DMA transfer, then give a summary and analysis of the operations necessary for a satisfactory direct memory access transfer.

II.4.3.1. Different stages of a DMA transfer. Whatever DMA technique is adopted, a DMA transfer always requires six stages:

(1) Initialization of DMA controller by a RESET to switch it on. Setting the registers to zero and setting the signals to inactive states.
(2) Writing of information to a given memory region. The latter region, reserved for this sort of transfer, will contain all the necessary information:
    (a) Memory address of the first byte to be read or written;
    (b) Address on the peripheral (floppy disk, for example) of the first byte to be read or written;
    (c) Number of bytes to be transferred.
(3) Programming of the DMA controller by the microprocessor. At this stage, the DMA controller behaves like a collection of registers, which can be selected by means of an address, and which can be read or written. Information is transferred via the data bus. Some of this information will have been

Table XIII. Comparison of three DMA techniques

Technique	Max. speed of DMA transfer	Microprocessor operation	Complexity of hardware
Microprocessor halt (burst mode)	1 byte per clock cycle	Halted	Low
Cycle-stealing	2 bytes for every 5 clock cycles	2 clock cycles every 5	Medium
Multiplexed DMA	1 byte per clock cycle	Unchanged	Very high

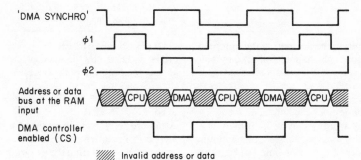

'DMA SYNCHRO'

$\phi 1$

$\phi 2$

Address or data
bus at the RAM
input

DMA controller
enabled (CS)

▨ Invalid address or data

Figure 30. Time-sequence for multiplexed DMA

pre-loaded into the memory region we have just referred to. The DMA controller functions as a 'slave'.

(4) Initialization of a DMA transfer: a transfer request is transmitted from the peripheral, which transmits it to the DMA controller; this, in turn, transmits it to the microprocessor, which then accepts it.

(5) Execution of a DMA transfer. This transfer is carried out by using one of the techniques discussed above: burst mode, cycle-stealing, multiplexed DMA.

(6) Halting the DMA transfer. When the transfer of all necessary bytes has been completed, an 'end of DMA' status bit is set to '1' in the DMA controller and, for some controllers, an 'interrupt request' output is activated. The microprocessor is thus informed of the end of the DMA transfer by a test of the status bit, or by an interrupt.

II.4.2.2. Registers and signals of a DMA controller. In Table XIV we have assembled the main operations which should be executed for the correct functioning of a direct memory access transfer. For each function we have indicated the consequences as regards DMA controller internal registers and signals. Let us recall that, for each channel, an 'address register' and a 'byte counter' are needed.

Together, the registers and signals, shown as necessary in Table XIV, are displayed in the block-diagram of Figure 31, where we have taken as an example a four-channel DMA controller. It should be pointed out that the three DMA techniques which we have mentioned will rarely be all supported by the same DMA controller.

II.4.3. Programming a DMA transfer

Before carrying out a DMA transfer it is necessary to write in the memory region assigned to this DMA transfer all the information required for the transfer. This includes:

(1) The memory address of the first byte to be transferred;
(2) The peripheral address of the first byte to be transferred (for a disk, this address will be the track number and the sector number).
(3) The number of bytes to be transferred;
(4) Transfer code: peripheral read or write.

Table XIV. Functions, registers, and signals of a DMA controller

Function	Circuit or signal required for the realization of this function
Remembering the position of the first read or write for each channel, followed by automatic incrementing of this address at each read or write	ADDRESS REGISTER (to be initialized by the microprocessor during the programming phase)
Remembering, for each channel, the number of words (or bytes for 8-bit microprocessors) to be transferred, and counting the number of bytes remaining to be transferred	BYTE COUNTER More precisely, what is meant here is a byte down-counter (to be initialized by the microprocessor during the programming phase)
Initialization of the DMA controller registers	RESET signal
Dialogue between the microprocessor and the controller to signal the DMA request and the end of the DMA transfer	'TRANSFER REQUEST' signal transmitted by the peripheral to the DMA controller 'DMA REQUEST' signal transmitted by the DMA controller to the microprocessor in response to a 'transfer request' 'DMA ACKNOWLEDGE' signal transmitted by the microprocessor to the DMA controller in response to a 'DMA request' 'END OF DATA' signal and 'END OF TRANSFER' signal
Determining the operating mode of the DMA controller from a command word sent by the microprocessor to the DMA controller	COMMAND REGISTER 'DMA WRITE REG.' signal DATA BUS
Controlling the status of operations executed by the DMA controller (by reading the status word)	STATUS REGISTER 'DMA READ REG.' signal DATA BUS
Microprocessor access to one of the DMA controller registers	Several ADDRESS BITS for selecting 1 register out of 10 CS or $\overline{\text{CS}}$ signal to enable or inhibit the DMA controller
Input transfer: reading of a peripheral byte and writing of this byte to memory at the address supplied by the address register	'DIRECT PERI READ' signal emitted by the DMA controller 'DIRECT MEMORY WRITE' signal emitted by the DMA controller
Output transfer: reading of a byte from memory, at the address supplied by the address register, and writing of this byte to the peripheral	'DIRECT MEMORY READ' signal emitted by the DMA controller 'DIRECT PERI WRITE' signal emitted by the DMA controller
Sequencing of the different operations executed by the DMA controller	CLOCK signal

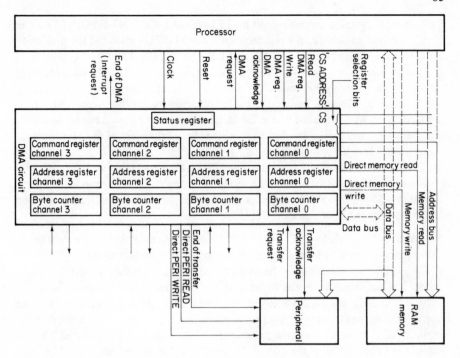

Figure 31. The DMA controller registers and signals

An input transfer is a peripheral-read and therefore a memory-write, which, for the DMA controller, means programming a write operation. In contrast, an output transfer is a write to the peripheral, and a read from the memory, which, for the DMA controller, means programming a read. The transfer is carried out on the initiative of the microprocessor.

The microprocessor carries out the programming of the peripheral starting from data in memory. Subsequently, it sends a read or write command to the peripheral. In response to this request, the peripheral addresses a direct memory access request to the DMA controller. Thus, the DMA transfer is initiated. We know that this direct memory access request is echoed to the microprocessor, which responds by a DMA acknowledge, and the actual transfer begins. This DMA request is maintained during the whole transfer. When the byte counter reaches the value zero, the DMA controller de-activates the DMA request, which signals end of transfer to the microprocessor; the microprocessor takes over the control of the bus and, if necessary, sends a halt command to the peripheral (a disk, for example).

II.4.4. Application to the INTEL DMA controller (the 8257 circuit)

II.4.4.1. 8257 registers. This circuit uses the burst-mode DMA (microprocessor halt) technique. It consists of four channels. A 16-bit address register, designated by DMA ADDRESS REGISTER, is assigned to each channel, as well as a 14-bit byte counter, designated by TERMINAL COUNT REGISTER. The 8257 also has an 8-bit status register called the STATUS REGISTER and an 8-bit command register called the MODE SET REGISTER. The status register has, for each channel, an 'end of DMA' status bit, which is set to 1 when the byte counter takes on the value zero. This status bit is reset to zero by a RESET or by the reading of a status register. This latter contains another status bit called UPDATE FLAG. It is used within DMA transfers having automatic block chaining. Between each block, the DMA takes over the parameters of the next block of data to be transferred. This updating is carried out during a cycle called UPDATE. It is signalled by setting the UPDATE FLAG bit to 1 (Figure 32).

The command register permits the selection of one of the many modes of operation allowed by the 8257. We note that these modes are relevant to the burst-mode DMA technique. These modes are:

(1) 'Auto-load' mode (AUTO LOAD) 2^7 bit $= 1$. The most frequently used mode in conjunction with burst-mode operation consists of transferring an N-byte block (the value $N - 1$ is initialized in the byte counter). To ensure that we operate in this mode, it is sufficient to set the 2^7 bit of the command register to zero. The 8257, however, usually allows the transfer of several successive blocks. For this, the corresponding parameters of the first block to be transferred are loaded into the registers of channel 2, while the parameters of the next block are loaded into the registers of channel 3. At the end of the transfer of the first block, the DMA controller puts into the registers of channel 2 the parameters stored in the registers of channel 3: this operation is called the UPDATE CYCLE by INTEL; it is indicated by the UPDATE CYCLE status bit of the status register, which then takes on the value 1. At the end of the UPDATE cycle, the transfer of the second block begins.

The parameters for the third block are then written in channel 3. At the end of the transfer of the second block, a new UPDATE cycle takes place, and the process continues thus until the end of the DMA transfer. This mode of operation is obtained by setting the 2^7 bit of the command register to 1.

(2) 'Stop at termination of count mode (TC STOP) 2^6 bit $= 1$. This is a classic method of ending a DMA transfer. When the byte down-counter reaches zero, the enable bit of the corresponding channel is reset to zero, which inhibits the DMA transfer and allows the end of transfer to be signalled to the

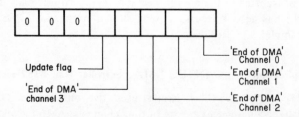

Figure 32. The 8257 status register

microprocessor. If this 2^6 bit is set to zero, it is the peripheral which should then signal end of transfer to the microprocessor.

(3) 'Extended write command' mode (EXTENDED WRITE) 2^5 bit $= 1$. The duration of $\overline{\text{MEMW}}$ and $\overline{\text{I/OW}}$ is prolonged by the fact that the rising edge of these signals occurs early in the DMA cycle. Such a prolongation is required for certain peripherals.

(4) 'Rotating priority' mode (ROTATING PRIORITY) 2^4 bit $= 1$. When several channels are used, the problem arises of prioritizing the direct memory access requests. A first solution (offered by INTEL in the 8257) is a fixed priority: the lower the number, the higher the channel priority (channel 0 having the highest priority). This solution is obtained by setting the 2^4 bit to zero. The other solution offered by the 8257 is a rotating priority. The channel which has just been serviced takes the lowest priority and the numbers of the other three channels determine their priority among the remaining three. This mode is obtained by setting the 2^4 bit to 1.

II.4.4.2. The 8257 signals

A0 to A7	Address bits. A0 to A3 are bi-directional
DMA REG. read	} $\overline{\text{I/OR}}$ bi-directional signal
Direct peripheral read	
DMA REG. write	} $\overline{\text{I/OW}}$ bi-directional signal
Direct peripheral write	
Direct memory write	$\overline{\text{MEMW}}$
Direct memory read	$\overline{\text{MEMR}}$
DMA request	HRQ
DMA acknowledge	HLDA
Reset	RESET
Clock	CLK
Transfer request	DRQ } Each channel has these two signals
Transfer acknowledge	$\overline{\text{DACK}}$ (DRQ_0 and DACK_0 for channel 0)
Memory ready	READY
End of DMA	TC
End of transfer	TC

The 8257 has three further signals

MARK   This output signals the 128th transfer. The number 128 arises from the fact that one sector of a floppy disk usually contains 128 bytes.

AEN   This output signal is generated by the output controller when the latter receives the DMA acknowledge signal from the microprocessor. The AEN signal is sent on the BUSEN input of the 8228, which sets the data bus and the command signals to high impedance.

ADSTB   The 8257 has only eight address bits. The most significant byte of the address is generated on the data bus and should be memorized in a tri-state latch; for example, the 8212. The ADSTB signal serves as command for the memorization of data by the 8212.

Figure 34 gives the block-diagram for interfacing the 8257 to the 8085A microprocessor. For the latter, the address should be demultiplexed and the signals $\overline{\text{MEMR}}$, $\overline{\text{MEMW}}$, $\overline{\text{I/OR}}$, $\overline{\text{I/OW}}$ created. For the 8080A, interfacing is immediate.

II.4.4.3. Operations of the 8257.   The INTEL DMA controller has three functions:

(1) Peripheral read (transfer from peripheral to memory);
(2) Peripheral write (transfer from memory to peripheral);
(3) Verification: this mode allows the control of bytes read or written in memory.

The choice of one of these three functions is made by programming bits 14 and 15 of the byte counter when it is being initialized (Table XV).

II.4.4.4.   Programming the 8257

(1) Initialization of the channel address register.   Since this is a 16-bit address, two successive single-byte writes are required. The DMA controller, through an internal flip-flop, automatically assures the allocation of the first byte to the eight least significant bits, and of the second byte to the eight most significant bits of the address register. No interrupt request should reach the microprocessor between the writing of the first byte and that of the second byte. It will be necessary to inhibit interrupts during register initialization if the application functions in interrupt mode.

(2) Initialization of the byte counter.   The problem is identical to the one we have just described for the initialization of the address register. Recall that this second initialization determines the choice of DMA function by using bits 14 and 15. If there are N bytes to be transmitted, the binary value corresponding to $N - 1$ should be encoded on the 14 least significant bits.

(3) Sending the command word. This is shown in Figure 33.

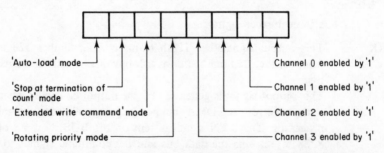

Figure 33. The 8257 command register (MODE SET REGISTER)

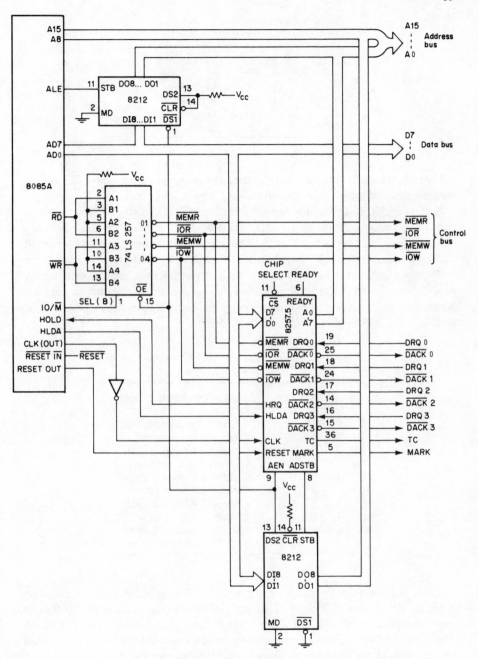

Figure 34. Interfacing the 8257 to the 8085A

II.4.4.5. Addressing and register selection in the 8257. The 8257 is, of course, addressed by a $\overline{CS}$ ADDRESS signal sent on the $\overline{CS}$ input. As regards the selection of an 8257 counter or register, this is carried out by the selection bits A0 to

Table XV. Programming   the   8257
operations

Bit 15	Bit 14	Operation
0	0	Verification
0	1	Peripheral write
1	0	Peripheral read
1	1	Illegal

A3, which are used as input signals during the programming of the 8257 and as output signals during DMA transfers.

Using the A0 to A3 bits for register selection makes it impossible to use one of them as a linear selection bit for I/O device addressing when the 8257 is used.

Loading an address register or byte counter requires two successive writes to the same address: the 8257 is responsible for sending the first item of data into the LSB (least significant byte) section of the register or counter, and the second item of data into the MSB (most significant byte) section of the register or counter. Remember that, during the programming of the 8257, interrupts should be disabled. Table XVI gives the addressing details.

Table XVI. Addressing   the   8257   registers   and counters

A3	A2	A1	A0	Registers or counters chosen
0	0	0	0	Channel 0 address register
0	0	0	1	Channel 0 byte counter
0	0	1	0	Channel 1 address register
0	0	1	1	Channel 1 byte counter
0	1	0	0	Channel 2 address register
0	1	0	1	Channel 2 byte counter
0	1	1	0	Channel 3 address register
0	1	1	1	Channel 3 byte counter
1	0	0	0	Command register (write)
1	0	0	0	Status register (read)

II.4.4.6. An example of 8257 programming. Let us display on a memory-mapped VDU screen 256 bytes situated at a starting address of 2000 in a microprocessor system RAM. These 256 bytes correspond to 16 lines of 16 characters. A DMA controller is then employed to read out the RAM and to send the 16 bytes of the line to be displayed to a buffer situated in the CRT controller. The role of this latter controller is to send appropriate signals for display of the text to the CRT circuits.

The 256-byte block should be read by the DMA controller and shown on the screen at least twenty-five times per second to prevent image-flickering. This

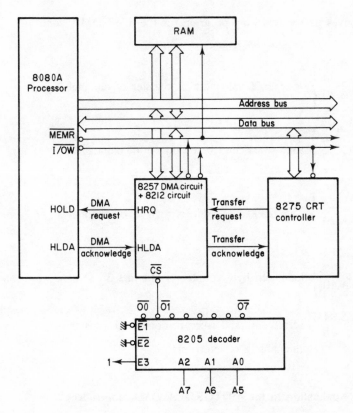

Figure 35. Example of the use of the 8257 DMA controller

means that the DMA transfer of this block should be repeated without stopping: here we have a typical example of operation in the 'auto-load' mode. The parameters of this block will then be loaded into channels 2 and 3.

Let us enable the 8257 via the $\overline{O1}$ output of the 8205 decoder shown in Figure 35, which receives on its inputs the address bits A5, A6, and A7. We then have the following addresses:

for the address register of channel 2   00100100 or 24 hexadecimal
for the byte counter of channel 2   00100101 or 25 hexadecimal
for the address register of channel 3   00100110 or 26 hexadecimal
for the byte counter of channel 3   00100111 or 27 hexadecimal
for the command register   00101000 or 28 hexadecimal

In addition:

address register contents = 2000 hexadecimal.
byte counter = 0100000011111111 or 40FF hexadecimal
command word = 10000100 or 84 hexadecimal

This gives us the following program for the 8257 DMA controller:

```
DI                  disable interrupts
MVI     A,00 ⎫
OUT     24   ⎪
MVI     A,20 ⎬ load 2000 into address register of channel 2.
OUT     24   ⎭
MVI     A,FF ⎫
OUT     25   ⎪
MVI     A,40 ⎬ load 40FF into byte counter of channel 2
OUT     25   ⎭
MVI     A,00 ⎫
OUT     26   ⎪
MVI     A,20 ⎬ load 2000 into address register of channel 3
OUT     26   ⎭
MVI     A,FF ⎫
OUT     27   ⎪
MVI     A,40 ⎬ load into byte counter of channel 3
OUT     27   ⎭
MVI     A,84 ⎫
OUT     28   ⎬ send command word to command register
EI                  re-enabling of interrupts
```

II.4.5. Application to the MOTOROLA DMA controller

II.4.5.1. The 6844 registers. The MOTOROLA 6844 DMA controller can manage four channels. Each channel has:

(1) A 16-bit address register called ADDRESS REGISTER;
(2) A 16-bit byte counter called BYTE COUNT REGISTER;
(3) An 8-bit command register called CHANNEL CONTROL REGISTER.

This latter register is also used as a status register.

In addition to these twelve, the 6844 has three other registers common to the four channels:

(1) A priority register called PRIORITY CONTROL REGISTER;
(2) An interrupt register called INTERRUPT CONTROL REGISTER;
(3) A chaining register called DATA CHAIN REGISTER.

These registers must, of course, be programmed.

However, each of the three registers assigned to the respective channels is a 16-bit register. It requires, therefore, two writes to the DMA controller: the most significant byte (A0 = 0) and the least significant byte (A0 = 1). Five address bits A0, A1, A2, A3, and A4 are required for selecting a register or a half-register. Table XVII gives the hexadecimal address for each location. In addition the five

Table XVII. Addressing the registers of a MOTOROLA 6844 DMA controller

	Channel	Register	Byte	Hexadecimal address (least significant byte)
Address register and byte counter	Channel 0	Address register	MSB	0
			LSB	1
		Byte counter	MSB	2
			LSB	3
	Channel 1	Address register	MSB	4
			LSB	5
		Byte counter	MSB	6
			LSB	7
	Channel 2	Address register	MSB	8
			LSB	9
		Byte counter	MSB	A
			LSB	B
	Channel 3	Address register	MSB	C
			LSB	D
		Byte counter	MSB	E
			LSB	F

	Register	Hexadecimal address (least significant byte)
Command registers	CHANNEL 0 COMMAND REGISTER	10
	CHANNEL 1 COMMAND REGISTER	11
	CHANNEL 2 COMMAND REGISTER	12
	CHANNEL 3 COMMAND REGISTER	13
	PRIORITY CONTROL REGISTER	14
	INTERRUPT CONTROL REGISTER	15
	DATA CHAIN REGISTER	16

selection bits should, of course, be addressed by their chip-select signal, designated $\overline{CS}$/Tx AKB, emanating from the chip.

The contents of the address registers and of the byte counters will be grouped together at contiguous addresses to allow these addresses to be loaded using an index register. The programming of each command register is performed as shown in Figure 36.

Bit 0 determines the type of DMA transfer, (peripheral read or peripheral write). Bits 1 and 2 permit the choice of one DMA technique from the three (Figures 37 and 38):

(1) DMA transfer by cycle-stealing starting with a $\overline{HALT}$ input (bit 1 = 0, bit 2 = 0). Each stolen cycle allows the transfer of one byte.
(2) Burst-mode DMA transfer; a byte transfer immediately follows a preceding byte transfer; this continues until the down-counter has reached the value zero. The DMA request is addressed to the $\overline{HALT}$ input. One clock cycle is lost between two DMA cycles.

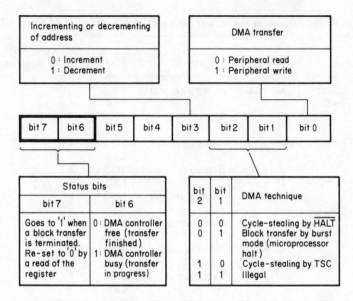

Figure 36. Programming a command register assigned to a channel
(CHANNEL CONTROL REGISTER)

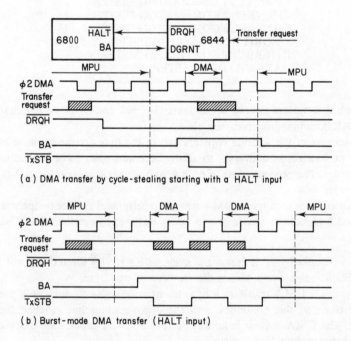

(a) DMA transfer by cycle-stealing starting with a $\overline{\text{HALT}}$ input

(b) Burst-mode DMA transfer ($\overline{\text{HALT}}$ input)

Figure 37. DMA transfers starting with a $\overline{\text{HALT}}$ input

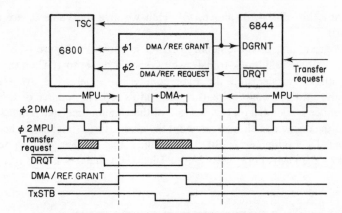

Figure 38. DMA transfer starting with a TSC input (cycle-stealing)

(3) DMA transfer by cycle-stealing starting with a TSC input (bit 1 = 0, bit 2 = 1). Each stolen cycle allows the transfer of one byte.

Bit 3 determines address-incrementing or address-decrementing. Bits 4 and 5 are not used. Bit 6 is a status bit, which is set to '1' at the beginning of a DMA transfer and back to 0 again at the beginning of the transfer of the last byte to be transmitted (the contents of the byte down-counter are then at zero). The technique used is irrelevant, and could be burst-mode transfer, transfer by cycle-stealing, or multiplex transfer.

Bit 7 (END OF DMA) is set to 1 when bit 6 returns to '0'. It is reset to zero by a read of the command register (which then becomes a status register). Bit 7 generates an interrupt if the corresponding channel has been enabled for interrupt mode during the programming of the interrupt register.

The object of the priority register is to enable (or inhibit), as well as to prioritize, the transfer requests for each channel. A transfer request received by a channel can only be handled if the RE (REQUEST ENABLE) bit of this channel is set at '1' in the priority register.

The programming of this register is carried out as shown in Figure 39. Bits 4, 5, and 6 are not used. We assign them the value zero. Bit 7 defines fixed or rotating priority. Let us explain this latter term with an example. If the channel just serviced is channel 1, it then takes the lowest priority. Afterwards it is channel 2 which takes the highest priority.

PRIORITY	highest			lowest
FIXED	0	1	2	3
ROTATING	2	3	0	1

(after channel 1 servicing)

The programming of the interrupt register consists of authorizing the channel to signal the end of a block transfer, via an interrupt on the IRQ/DEND output. Bit

7 is a status bit. Bits 4, 5, and 6, to which we give the value 0, are not used (Figure 40).

The programming of the chaining register is shown in Figure 41. When one wishes to chain several block transfers bit 0 should be set to 1. Then the contents of the address register and the byte counter for channel 3 are transferred respectively, into the address register and into the byte counter of the channel whose number is encoded on bits 1 and 2 of the chaining register. This channel is, of course, the one which should carry out the chained transfers; i.e., either channel 0, channel 1, or channel 2. Bit 3 determines the number of channels to be managed by the DMA controller: 2 if bit 3 has the value 0, 4 if bit 3 has the value 1.

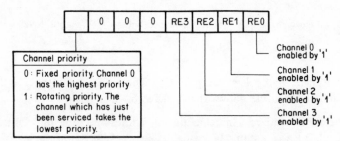

Figure 39. Programming the PRIORITY REGISTER

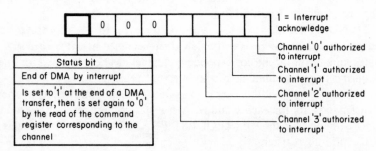

Figure 40. Programming the INTERRUPT CONTROL REGISTER

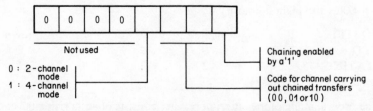

Figure 41. Programming the DATA CHAIN REGISTER

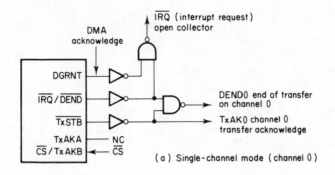

(a) Single-channel mode (channel 0)

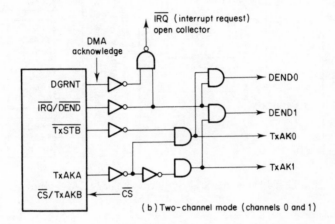

(b) Two-channel mode (channels 0 and 1)

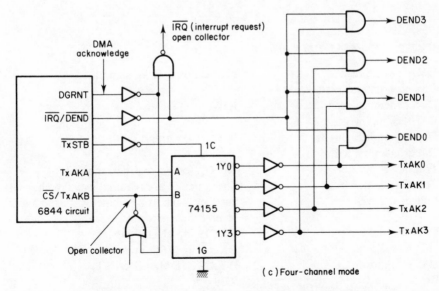

(c) Four-channel mode

Figure 42. Generation of 'TRANSFER ACKNOWLEDGE' and 'END OF TRANSFER' signals for the MOTOROLA 6844 controller

78

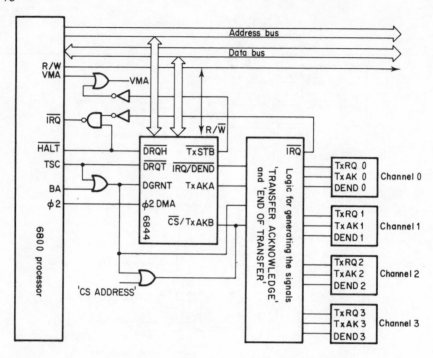

Figure 43. 6800 microprocessor system with 6844 DMA controller

II.4.5.2.   The 6844 DMA controller signals

DMA circuit read   bi-directional $R/\overline{W}$ signal
Direct peripheral read
Direct memory read $R/\overline{W} = 1$ read
DMA circuit write
Direct peripheral write $R/\overline{W} = 0$ write
Direct memory write
Transfer request   Tx RQ (one signal per channel)
Transfer acknowledge   These signals are required by each channel,
End of transfer   but they have to be created with the aid of
                                  several logic circuits.

DMA request $\overline{\text{DRQH}}$ for $\overline{\text{HALT}}$ input
                                  $\overline{\text{DRQT}}$ for TSC input
DMA acknowledge   DGRNT (DMA GRANT)
Reset $\overline{\text{RES}}$
Clock $\phi2$ DMA

In addition, the 6844 has three other signals:

(1) $\overline{CS}$/Tx AKB. This signal serves as a chip-select for addressing the DMA controller. When the latter carries out a transfer in a four-channel mode, $\overline{CS}$/Tx AKB becomes an output, which, when used with Tx AKA, helps to generate a transfer acknowledge, whose code is that of the channel in question.

(2) Tx AKA and $\overline{Tx\ STB}$. These two signals, linked to $\overline{CS}$/Tx AKB only in the four-channel mode, help to generate the transfer acknowledge signal for each channel.

(3) $\overline{IRQ}/\overline{DEND}$. This end of transfer signal, used as an interrupt request, helps to generate the end of transfer signal for each channel. These transfer acknowledge and end of transfer signals need to be generated (see Figure 42). If the peripheral does not require an end of transfer signal, then it would be pointless to create it.

Figure 43 gives the block diagram of a 6800 microprocessor system with the 6844 DMA controller. This latter is addressed by 'CS ADDRESS'.

Chapter III
Interfacing in a microprocessor system

In this chapter we shall study the main components most often used in microprocessor systems by giving the requirements for interfacing each of these circuits into a microprocessor system.

III.1. Interfacing CMOS circuits

CMOS technology is being used more and more: it is not uncommon to have to connect such a circuit to a microprocessor system and more especially to a parallel (or serial) interface, these being the two main means of communication between the microprocessor and the outside world, i.e. the industrial application. The leading manufacturers of microprocessors have designed their LSI circuits to be compatible not only with their own microprocessors, which is natural, but also with the most widely used logic families, i.e. TTL and CMOS.

For any technology family, several input and output values are defined. The designer has, in effect, to encompass the values that one could find in the most unfavourable case. These are:

VOH: output voltage for logic level '1'. The higher the output current, the lower this voltage becomes. It is defined for an output current called IOH generated by the circuit (CURRENT SOURCING).

VOL: output voltage for the logic level '0'. This level is practically independent of the current passing through the transistor junction or saturated MOS. This current, called IOL, is received by the circuit (CURRENT SINKING).

VIH: the input voltage which the circuit must receive to be in logic state '1'. The circuit receiving this VIH voltage consumes an input current, IIH, which is 100 μA for the majority of TTL circuits. As a kind of unit of value, one talks of an input equal to one TTL Load.

A TTL circuit consuming 200 μA will be considered as having an input of two TTL loads. For a CMOS circuit, this IIH current is almost zero on account of the very·high input impedance of MOS circuits of this type.

VIL: input voltage below which the circuit is in logic state '0'. The current taken by the input is called IIL. Again, this is practically zero for a CMOS circuit.

For each of these quantities, VOH, VOL, VIH, VIL, there exists a minimum value, a typical value, and a maximum value. Very often, the manufacturer just gives the most critical value; in some cases V min, in other cases V max. For the TTL family, these critical values are:

VOH = 2.4 V min; VOL = 0.4 V max
VIH = 2 V min; VIL = 0.8 V max

Under these conditions, the circuit is guaranteed to take on the state imposed upon it with a security safety equal to

VIL – VOL = 0.8 – 0.4 = 0.4 V for level '0' and
VIH – VOL = 2.4 – 2 = 0.4 V for level '1'.

This value of 0.4 is the noise-immunity. This immunity does not have to be identical at the low and high voltage levels.

For the CMOS family, which is fed by +5 V, the critical values are:

VOH = 4.99 V min; VOL = 0.01 V max
VIH = 3.5 V min; VIL = 1.5 V max

These values show CMOS logic to have the greater noise-immunity. The very high level of VOH is due to the fact that the IOH current is practically zero. It is convenient to represent these values diagramatically (see Figures 44 and 45).

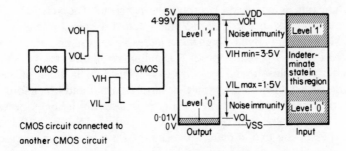

Figure 44. CMOS–CMOS interface in the most unfavourable
case

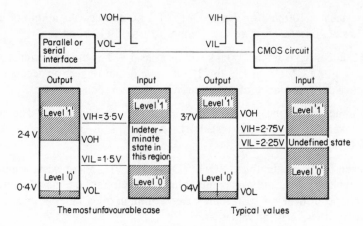

Figure 45. TTL–CMOS interface

Figure 44, which illustrates the connection of two CMOS circuits in the most unfavourable case, shows that interfacing does not really pose any problems. Figure 45 shows the same picture in the case of a parallel (8255 or PIA) or serial (8251 or ACIA) interface to TTL compatible outputs linked to a CMOS circuit. Having looked at the most unfavourable case, we shall now consider typical values.

If, in the case of typical values, there is a noise-immunity of

2.25 − 0.4 = 1.85 V at the low level and
3.7 − 2.75 = 0.95 V at the high level

then, applying these to the most unfavourable case, the CMOS circuit will not be set to logic level '1' since the voltage that it receives (2.4 V) is below that required (3.5 V). Of course, the chances are that the situation will not be so extreme; nevertheless, it is unthinkable that we should be satisfied with such an interface for a production run. But how do we solve the problem? The solution consists in adding a pull-up resistance to the +5 V, the value of the resistance being between 5 and 12 kΩ in general. Such a high value increases the rise and decay times, and therefore reduces the operating speed. This pull-up resistance raises the VIH level, which comes very close to +5 V. It has to be placed at the input of the CMOS circuit, which is attached to the parallel or serial interface and which forms part of the microprocessor system. Note that this resistance is only necessary if VIH > VOH. To know whether this is so, it suffices to consult the technical characteristics of the two circuits with regard to connecting one to the other.

When a parallel or serial interface is linked to a CMOS circuit, which functions with a supply voltage greater than +5 V, a level translator circuit is required. This circuit can be an open collector TTL circuit, a fast comparator, or a transistor.

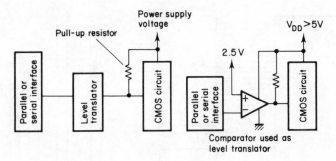

Figure 46. Interfacing a CMOS circuit to a level translator

Again, the pull-up resistance should be placed at the input of the CMOS circuit. Figure 46 shows the interfacing required in this case.

III.2. Bus buffering

A microcomputer board consists of a small number of LSI circuits and, more particularly, one or more input/output interfaces, a RAM, and an EPROM (or a ROM). But, often, we need to extend the possibilities of the microprocessor system by the addition either of memory or of one or more input/output facilities.

In this case it is necessary to boost the output of the buses because they cannot feed an unlimited number of circuits. In fact, each circuit connected to the bus has a drain current when it is not active and an input current when it is active. Moreover, it has an input capacity and the capacities of all the circuits connected to a bus add up to form an output capacity for that bus. This can perturb the functioning of the microprocessor system by imposing excessive rise times. Two solutions are possible: to buffer the bus either inside the microcomputer, or outside; that is, at the level of the industrial application.

III.2.1. Buffering the bus on a microcomputer board

The makers of microcomputer kits or boards generally foresee the possibility, if it has not already been done, of buffering the buses, at a position just after the processor outputs.

Figure 47 shows the placing of the bus buffers. The address bus and the command bus require unidirectional buffers. If the system dos not permit direct memory access the buffers can be permanently enabled. In this case, we shall have two enabling signals:

ABE (address bus enable) = 1
CBE (command bus enable) = 1

In the more general case, where direct memory access has to be provided, the

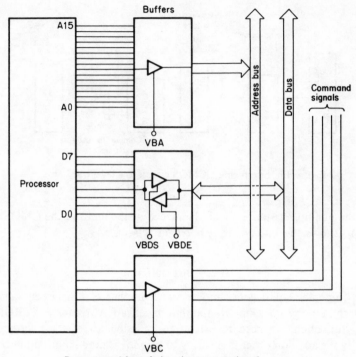

Processor and bus of the microcomputer board

Figure 47. Bus-buffering on a microprocessor board

unidirectional buffers remain permanently enabled, except when direct memory access is required. In this latter case, ABE and CBE should be connected to the complement of the 'DMA authorization' signal.

The data bus requires bi-directional buffers. The direction of transfer of the data is determined by the operation to be carried out: read or write. Moreover, in the case of direct memory access, the data bus buffers, whatever their direction, have to be in a high impedance state. In Figure 47, then, we have two enabling signals:

DBEO: data bus enabled for output
DBEI: data bus enabled for input

Table XVIII gives the details of the various command signals in Figure 47 for the 8080A, the 6800, and the 8085.

The wiring necessary to buffer the buses on a microcomputer board is always provided by the manufacturer if the need for these buffers has been foreseen. This wiring can only be provided by the user if he constructs the microcomputer board himself.

Table XVIII. Buffering the buses for the 8080A, the 6800, and the 8085

Buffering the buses on a microprocessor board

Microprocessor	Address bus enable ABE	Command bus enable		Data bus enable	
		CBE	Command signals	On input: DBEI	On output: DBEO
8080A INTEL	AEN	AEN	$\overline{MEMR}$ $\overline{MEMW}$ $\overline{I/OR}$ $\overline{I/OW}$ $\overline{INTA}$	AEN.DBIN	AEN.$\overline{DBIN}$
6800 MOTOROLA	BA + $\overline{TSC}$	BA + $\overline{TSC}$	R/W VMA φ2	BA + $\overline{TSC}$ DBE.VMA.R/$\overline{W}$	BA + $\overline{TSC}$ DBE.VMA.$\overline{R/W}$
8085 INTEL	AEN	AEN	Multiplexed mode / Demultiplexed mode $\overline{RD}$ / $\overline{MEMR}$ $\overline{WR}$ / $\overline{MEMW}$ IO/$\overline{M}$ / $\overline{I/OR}$ $\overline{I/OW}$	AEN.$\overline{RD}$	AEN.$\overline{WR}$

DBIN: Signal generated by the 8080A for a read operation. It determines the direction of the transfer.

AEN: This signal is generated by the INTEL DMA controller when one is performing direct memory access.

VMA: Signal generated by the 6800 when it has a valid address on the address bus.

φ2: Clock. The logical product VMA.φ2 allows the data bus buffers only to be enabled for instructions requiring an address, and then only during the data transfer (φ2 = 1).

R/W: Read/write signal which determines the direction of the transfer for the 6800.

BA: Signal generated by the 6800 when the HALT input has been activated (burst-mode DMA or burst-mode refresh).

TSC: In the case of DMA or refresh by cycle-stealing, the request is addressed to the clock circuit; the response of this circuit (DMA or refresh authorization) is sent to the 6800 TSC input.

86

III.2.2. Buffering the buses when extending the microprocessor system

Suppose that we have to add extra programmable parallel interfaces to our system. In most cases, these will be on a printed circuit board rather than a microcomputer board. If the buses are not supported by buffers on the microcomputer board (the manufacturer does not always foresee this possibility) it is necessary to buffer the bus at the level of the industrial application. The same is true for the addition of further memory. When such extensions are necessary they are generally made by constructing an input/output extension board and/or a memory extension board. The problems arising are different and we shall treat them separately.

III.2.2.1. Input/output extension board.   Care must be taken to avoid the situation where one of the I/O ports forming part of the extension board puts its data onto the bus at the wrong time. For this reason the data bus buffer has to be enabled, in the I/O port-to-microprocessor direction, only when the I/O port is addressed for a read operation. This enabling should therefore be done by the logic function 'CS ADDRESS' · 'PERI READ'. In order to respond to this request a bi-directional buffer has two command inputs:

(1) A CS (or $\overline{CS}$) input which sets all the buffers to a high impedance state when the I/O port linked to the buffer is not addressed; and
(2) A MODE input which enables a given transfer direction when the buffer is addressed.

The most rational solution consists, then, in controlling the MODE input by means of the 'PERI READ' signal to ensure that the I/O port is only connected to the data bus for a read operation. By way of example, we show in Figure 48 the bi-directional DP8304B buffer produced by NATIONAL SEMICONDUCTOR.

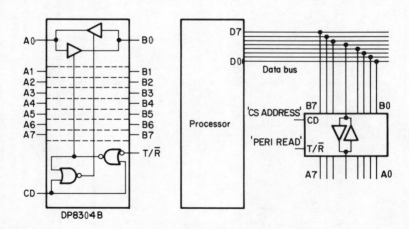

Figure 48. The bi-directional DP8304B buffer

The input playing the role of CS is a CHIP DISABLE (CD) input. This input, when it is at level '1', puts all the buffers in a high impedance state. We therefore have to connect onto CD our chip-addressing function, which we have called 'CS ADDRESS', after having complemented it to conform to CD which behaves like a $\overline{\text{CS}}$ input.

The MODE input is called TRANSMIT/RECEIVE (T/$\overline{\text{R}}$). A '1' on this input defines a transfer from A to B in Figure 48, where T/$\overline{\text{R}}$ = 'PERI READ'. Note that the TEXAS 74L5245 circuit is identical to the DP8304B circuit, replacing CD by $\overline{\text{G}}$ and T/$\overline{\text{R}}$ by DIR.

Suppose now that the input/output extension board consists of two I/O ports enabled by $\overline{\text{CS}}$. We shall apply the layout of Figure 48 first to the 8080A and then to the 6800 (Figure 49).

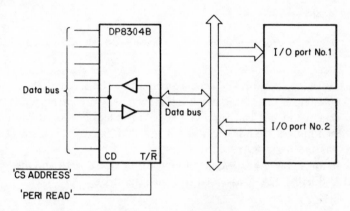

Figure 49. Bus-buffering for input/output extension board

(1) Application to the 8080A. Suppose the first I/O port is enabled by A4 and the second by A5. In this case the buffers have to be enabled if A4 = 0 (active level = level zero for the 8080A) or if A5 = 0. It follows that

$$\text{'CS ADDRESS'} = \overline{\overline{\text{A4}} + \overline{\text{A5}}} = \text{A4} \cdot \text{A5}$$

$$\text{T/}\overline{\text{R}} = \text{I/OR}$$

(2) Application to the 6800. Suppose that the I/O ports are enabled by outputs such as $\overline{\text{O4}}$ and $\overline{\text{O5}}$ shown in Figure 5. We then have

$$\text{'CS ADDRESS'} = \overline{\overline{\text{O4}} + \overline{\text{O5}}} = \overline{\text{O4}} \cdot \overline{\text{O5}}$$

$$\text{T/}\overline{\text{R}} = \text{R/W}$$

III.2.2.2. RAM extension board. The same care needs to be taken as with an input/output extension board: we must only enable the data bus buffer in the memory to data bus direction when memory is addressed by a read operation. It is sufficient, therefore, to replace 'PERI READ' by 'MEMORY READ'. Figure 50

88

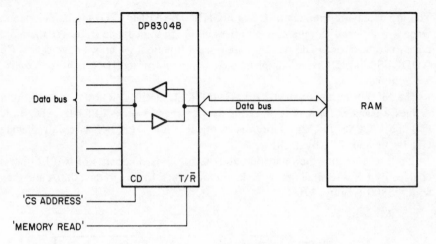

Figure 50. Buffering of the data bus for a RAM extension board

gives the layout for such a RAM extension board. In the diagram, the address bus and the command signals have not been shown: they are permanently enabled. We note that if the bus can support the RAM extension board without being buffered, then buffers are not necessary. The RAM extension is connected in the same way as the basic RAM.

We shall now apply the schematic of Figure 50 to the 8080A and the 6800. For the INTEL 8080A (RAM assumed to be addressed by A15 = 1)

$$CD = \overline{A15}$$
$$T/\overline{R} = MEMR$$

For the MOTOROLA 6800 (RAM assumed addressed by $\overline{A15}. \overline{A14}.$ WMA. $\phi2$)

$$CD = \overline{\overline{A15}. \overline{A14}. VMA. \phi2}$$
$$T/\overline{R} = R/W$$

III.2.2.2. ROM, PROM, and EPROM extension boards. The data bus buffer becomes unidirectional. The 'READ MEMORY' command is no longer necessary because these memories cannot be written to. We shall use as data bus buffer the NS DM81LS45 circuit already shown in Figure 8. By making $\overline{G_2} = 0$ we will have:

For the 8080A (ROM assumed enabled by A15 = 0)
$$\overline{G_1} = \text{'}\overline{CS} \text{ ADDRESS'} = A15$$
For the 6800 (ROM assumed enabled by A15. A14. VMA. $\phi2$)
$$G_1 = \text{'}\overline{CS} \text{ ADDRESS'} = \overline{A15. A14. VMA. \phi2}$$

$\overline{G_1}$ and $\overline{G_2}$ are the enabling inputs of the DM81LS95 (see Figure 8). For these extension boards it is, of course, possible to use buffers other than those we have chosen.

III.3. Memory interfacing

III.3.1. Synchronous and asynchronous memories

The concept of synchronous memory has appeared recently with the multiplexing of data and address buses in microprocessors such as the INTEL 8085 and 8048, and the INTERSIL IM6100. It then becomes necessary to latch the address in a register. But for this a latching command (STROBE) is needed, this command being, of course, produced by the microprocessor at an opportune moment – that is, when the address on the bus is valid. This bus will then be available, after the latching of the address, to serve as the data bus, for example. This concept of synchronous memory is valuable for all RAM, ROM, and EPROM memories, no matter whether the technology is bipolar, MOS, or CMOS. It is, however, particularly interesting for CMOS memories, for two reasons:

(1) Reduction of power consumption: a given memory is not interested in every address deposited on the address bus. In particular, a RAM is not concerned with addresses destined for the ROM or for the I/O ports. However, for each change of address, whether or not it is useful for the CMOS memory, there is

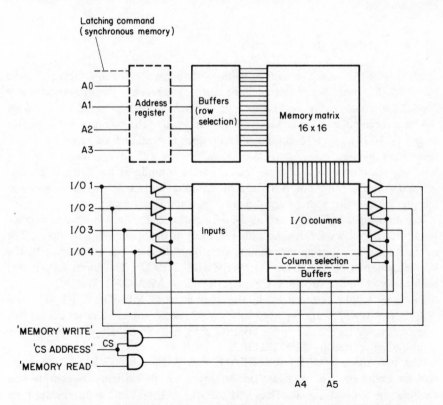

Figure 51. Interfacing a synchronous or asynchronous static memory

a consumption of energy since – for CMOS technology – current is used during transitions. By storing the CMOS memory address in a register, energy is not expended on changes of address which do not concern it.

(2) Greater speed: the cycle-time of a semiconductor memory is theoretically equal to the access time. In fact, this is not entirely accurate since it is necessary to maintain the address for between 20 and 50 nanosec after the access time in order to make use of the acquired data. With a static synchronous memory the next address can immediately be placed on the data bus, from the moment the address is latched, while the data corresponding to the stored address is read or written. The stabilization time of the address on the data bus disappears from the cycle time: there only remains the propagation time of the address, from its latching until the memory location is addressed, and the time necessary to pass the data across the output buffers in the case of a read operation.

Naturally, classical memories, which do not have this address register, have been called asynchronous memories. We shall call this latching command the *sampling signal*; this is the ALE (ADDRESS LATCH ENABLE) signal for the INTEL 8085 and 8084 and the LXMAR signal for the INTERSIL IM6100 microprocessor.

III.3.2. Interfacing static memories

III.3.2.1.   RAM memories with common input/output.   The interfacing of these memories does not pose any problem because it is direct and does not require any special components. Figure 51 shows the signals to be connected to a 256-bit RAM, structured into a memory of 64 4-bit words. The memory network is a matrix of 16 rows and 16 columns. The output information delivered by the 16 columns is directed to four outputs by a multiplexer with four channels each of 4 bits. The selection of one of these four channels is made by the two address bits A4 and A5. The only modification brought about by a synchronous memory is the presence of the address register and the sampling signal.

The data input buffers as well as the data output buffers are integrated into the RAM chips since we are dealing with a memory with common input/outputs. The tri-state buffers depositing the memory data onto the data bus are enabled by the logic function 'CS ADDRESS' · 'MEMORY READ'. The input buffers are enabled by the logic function 'CS ADDRESS' · 'MEMORY WRITE'.

For the 6800 microprocessor the two signals 'MEMORY READ' and 'MEMORY WRITE' are replaced by R/W.φ2. Also, it is more practical for this microprocessor to use memories controlled by a R/W signal; in particular, the memories suggested by MOTOROLA.

The two signals 'MEMORY READ' and 'MEMORY WRITE', however, are not both required. A single one of these signals suffices; its complement forming the second signal. Thus, 'MEMORY READ' could be replaced by 'MEMORY WRITE'. Since these signals are ANDed with 'CS ADDRESS', the tri-state buffers are never enabled at the wrong times.

III.3.2.2. RAM memories with separate inputs and outputs. The memory is linked to the data bus by an intermediate tri-state bi-directional buffer controlled in the same way as the bi-directional buffer which forms the input and output buffers in Figure 51. Memory transfer to the data bus will be enabled by 'CS ADDRESS' · 'MEMORY READ'; data bus transfer to the memory will be enabled by 'CS ADDRESS' · 'MEMORY WRITE' or 'CS ADDRESS' · $\overline{\text{MEMORY READ}}$'. There exist tri-state bi-directional buffers for which the output from each output buffer is connected to the input of the corresponding input buffer. As with the majority of bi-directional buffers we again find two command signals: one is the CHIP SELECT, the other is the MODE input which fixes the direction of transfer. Figure 52 shows the interfacing of two RAM chips of 2^n 4-bit words to the data bus via two INTEL 8216 bi-directional buffers.

The 8216 $\overline{\text{CS}}$ input receives the signal '$\overline{\text{CS}}$ ADDRESS'. The input $\overline{\text{DIEN}}$ (DI ENABLE) enables the transfer of DI to DB when at its zero level. This transfer corresponds to a memory read and the $\overline{\text{DIEN}}$ input has to receive the 'MEMORY READ' signal.

III.3.3. Interfacing ROM, PROM, and EPROM memories

Since these memories are not read, the problem of separate inputs and outputs does not arise. The 'MEMORY WRITE' signal disappears and the 'MEMORY

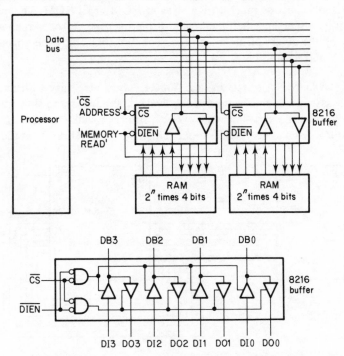

Figure 52. Interfacing two RAM chips to inputs and outputs via
two 8216 buffers

READ' signal is no longer necessary, the CS command being sufficient (it enables the output buffers of the memory). Figure 53 shows the interfacing of EPROM memory in the INTERSIL CMOS IM 6604 with the INTEL 8039 microsystem, the latter being the 8049 without ROM. This memory is synchronous and the latching command is the ALE signal. The data bus is therefore used for addresses and data.

III.3.4. Interfacing slow memories

III.3.4.1 The MEMORY READY concept. When the microprocessor executes a memory read or memory write this operation must have a maximum duration, depending on the microprocessor clock, of the order of 400 to 500 nanosec in general for 1 MHz working. If the memory access time is greater than this maximum duration, it is necessary to cause the microprocessor, or its clock, to stop or to slow down momentarily. In order to do this we have to create, using external logic, a MEMORY READY signal. This signal will be enabled for every read or write operation that is generated and will maintain itself in that state for a sufficient time to allow the memory to be read or written. It is this active state which will intervene in the microprocessor system to suspend, momentarily, the normal microprocessor sequencing. The MEMORY READY signal can be generated by a monostable triggered by the memory 'CS ADDRESS' signal. This principle applies just as much to RAM as to ROM or EPROM. The method of momentarily suspending the functioning of the microprocessor is fundamentally governed by the design of the microprocessor. We shall study these methods for the 8080A and for the 6800.

III.3.4.2. Application to the INTEL 8080A. It is very easy with the INTEL 8080A to assign a supplementary clock cycle (500 nanosec) to slow memory in order for it to finish its read or write cycle. It suffices to link the READY input of the microprocessor to its WAIT output. The first test of READY, at the T_2 state

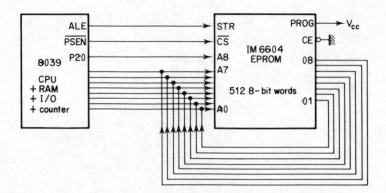

Figure 53. Interfacing the synchronous IM 6604 EPROM to the INTEL 8039 micro-system

of a FETCH cycle, gives READY = 0 since the normal state of WAIT is 0. The microprocessor then goes into the WAIT state, setting this output at 1. The second test of READY gives READY = WAIT = 1. The microprocessor then leaves the WAIT state and this output returns to 0, a value which causes the microprocessor to pass to the WAIT state at the next FETCH cycle. This very simple solution has the disadvantage of creating a WAIT state for all FETCH cycles and therefore for all memory cycles, whether accessing RAM or ROM, as well as for input/output cycles. The operating speed of the microprocessor is diminished by at least 20 per cent.

To diminish the speed of the microprocessor only when it accesses slow memory, we create a 'MEMORY READY' signal by a monostable and send it to the READY input of the 8080A. The monostable is triggered by the SYNC signal when slow memory is addressed. The SYNC signal is generated by the 8080A at the beginning of every microprocessor cycle, before the READY test.

III.3.4.3. Application to the MOTOROLA 6800. The transfer of data in the case of a memory read or write operation is made when the $\phi2$ clock is in state '1'. It is possible to keep $\phi2$ in the state '1' and $\phi1$ in the state '0' long enough for correct functioning of the memory. To do this, and to also allow interfacing with dynamic memories, MOTOROLA have designed a clock circuit where either $\phi1$ or $\phi2$ can be prolonged on command. Two situations are then possible: the extension of $\phi2$ by half a clock period, or the extension of $\phi2$ by a time determined by a monostable. The first solution is sufficient for the majority of existing memories which are slighltly too slow for the microprocessor. In this case we create a MEMORY READY signal with the aid of a flip-flop, whose output Q, normally in state '1', passes to state '0' on the rising edge of the signal '$2f_0$' · '$4f_0$' if CS ADDRESS = 1 and $\phi2 =: 0$; this output returns to state '1' on the next rising edge of the signal '$2f_0$' · '$4f_0$'. We have thus slowed down $\phi2$ by half a clock period. If this extension of $\phi2$ is not sufficient for the memory the signal which we have just created triggers a monostable, the duration of which is determined as a function of the cycle time of the slow memory. Instead of linking S_1 to the 6875 MEMORY READY, we link S_2 to this input. In Figure 54 we have put together the interfacing schematics as well as the timing sequences for the 8080A and the 6800.

III.3.5. Interfacing dynamic memories

III.3.5.1. The need for refreshing. Static memories are very easy to use. However, dynamic memories allow one an integration density which is four times greater, as well as having a smaller power consumption. On the other hand, these dynamic memories require refresh logic which is not always simple. But here again technology progresses rapidly and single-chip refresh controllers do exist: the INTEL 8202, for example. Dynamic memories are very effective for building memory boards of at least 16K bytes, starting with integrated memories of 16K times 1 bit, or even 64K times 1 bit.

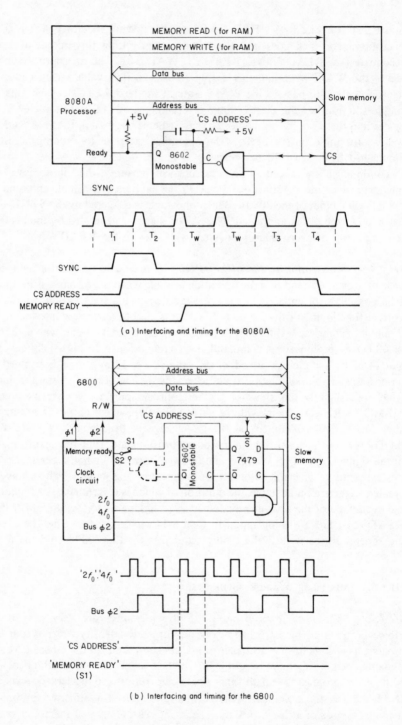

(a) Interfacing and timing for the 8080A

(b) Interfacing and timing for the 6800

Figure 54. Interfacing a slow memory

In a MOS dynamic memory, the elements of bit storage are the mass-array of capacitances in MOS. The voltage at the terminals of such a capacitance discharges itself and, moreover, the MOS input current, low though it is, charges this capacitance at constant current thereby modifying the previously stored voltage. This latter then decays more and more strongly with time, so that it is necessary to regenerate the initial voltage, a logic '0' or a logic '1', about every 2 or 3 msec, depending on the memory. This regeneration of data is carried out by a simple read operation which always involves one or two stages of amplification so as to automatically restore the memorized value. Of course, the memory outputs must not be connected to the data bus of the microprocessor system during this operation. This limited read cycle is called a refresh cycle.

A dynamic memory is basically composed of a matrix of N rows of cells (forming N rows and N columns). There are 64 rows of 64 cells for a 4096-bit memory; 128 rows of 128 cells for a 16,384-bit memory. Starting with this square matrix, the memory is structured to form a memory of N^2 1-bit words – giving 4096 or 16,384 1-bit words (in the cases mentioned). How is this structuring carried out? Quite simply by selecting one row from N, by means of n address bits ($N = 2^n$, giving $n = 6$ for $N = 64$ and $n = 7$ for $N = 128$) and also by selecting an input or output bit which amounts to selection of one column from N, again by n address bits. The refresh cycle is obtained by selecting a row without selecting a column and then sending a read command.

Normal functioning of the memory will thus be regularly suspended for refreshing all the rows of N cells one after another (Figure 55). For this, we

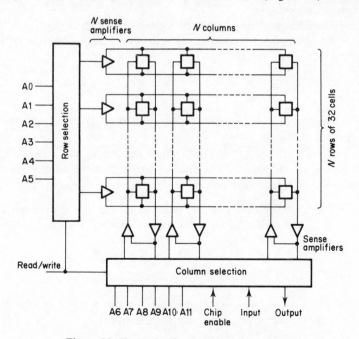

Figure 55. Example of memory organization

obviously require a row counter followed by an address multiplexer which sends out, in the address, the following memory-row selection bits:

(1) The corresponding bits of the address bus in the case of a read or write cycle; and
(2) The bits of the row counter in the case of a refresh cycle.

III.3.5.2. Study of refreshing

(1) The principle of refreshing. In order not to increase the number of pins on integrated circuits of 16K or 64K times 1 bit, memory manufacturers have adopted the solution of address multiplexing. The row address and column address are sent to the memory one after the other along the same wire. Of course, this can only be done by memorizing, at the very least, the first address sent, and this requires sending the memory a storage command for memorizing the new address. This command, also called a sampling signal, is denoted by RAS (ROW ADDRESS STROBE) and is active at level zero, so that the precise notation is $\overline{RAS}$.

A second storage command is sent to the memory when the column address is stable. This command is denoted by $\overline{CAS}$ (COLUMN ADDRESS STROBE) and is also active at level zero.

It follows that the address multiplexer, in effect, receives three addresses:

(a) the row address
(b) the column address $\left.\right\}$ in the case of a read or a write cycle
   (these two addresses being furnished by the microprocessor).
(c) The refresh address, in the case of a refresh cycle (this address is furnished by a refresh counter).

In order to select one type of address from the three this multiplexer has two MODE inputs:

(a) The REF (refresh) input which for a '1' value puts the refresh address onto the multiplexer outputs; and
(b) the ROW/$\overline{COL}$ (row/column) input, which denotes by the value '1' the row address, and by the value '0' the column address, on the multiplexer output, for the case of a read or write cycle.

REF	ROW/$\overline{COL}$	Address on the multiplexer output
0	0	Column address
0	1	Row address
1	X	Refresh address

$X = 0$ or 1

A refresh clock is required to trigger refresh cycles at the rate of 128 every 2 ms for a 16K memory. This clock can be obtained:

(a) Either by a programmable timer of the INTEL 8253 or MOTOROLA 6840 type;

(b) Or by an astable;

(c) Or by the output from one of the divisions of the rate generator used when there is a serial interface;

(d) Or by the microprocessor clock after suitable frequency division.

Each pulse from the refresh clock constitutes a *refresh request* addressed to the processor (either to the microprocessor itself or to its clock circuit). The processor then sends in return a *refresh acknowledge*. This signal:

(a) Increments the refresh counter;

(b) Gives the value '1' to the REF input mode;

(c) Triggers a memory read;

(d) Grants the refresh request.

During each refresh cycle the $\overline{\text{CAS}}$ memory input is not used and the memory output must not be enabled. These considerations have led memory manufacturers to enable the memory output by the signal CAS · READ. For the majority of dynamic memories, the READ and WRITE commands are realized by a single signal $\overline{\text{WRITE}}$, often denoted by $\overline{\text{WE}}$ (WRITE ENABLE), or $\overline{\text{WRITE}}$ (Figure 56).

The three signals $\overline{\text{RAS}}$, $\overline{\text{CAS}}$, $\overline{\text{WE}}$ must, of course, be sent at appropriate times in conformity with the timings of Figure 57. These signals are generated by a special circuit, or by the refresh controller when such a circuit is used.

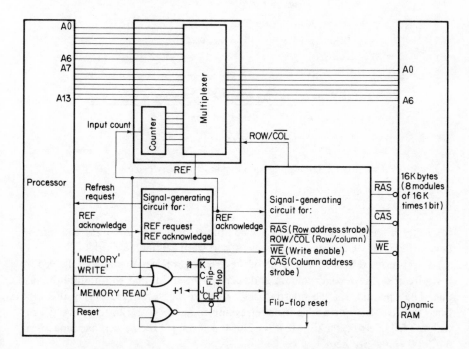

Figure 56. Refreshing a dynamic memory via multiplexed addressing

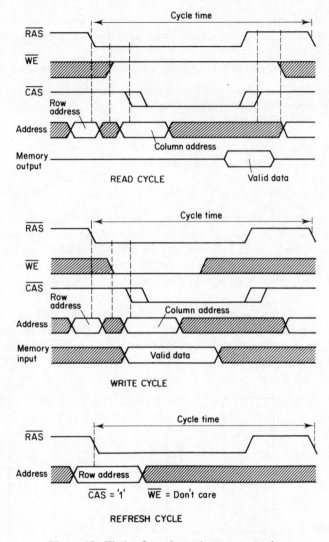

Figure 57. Timing for a dynamic memory cycle

(2) Refresh techniques. The way in which the signals *refresh request* and *refresh acknowledge* are generated determines the refresh technique used.

(a) Burst-mode refresh. The refresh of the first column is immediately followed by the refresh of the second column and then by the third, and so on, until the last one. The operation of the microprocessor has to be suspended during this time since the RAM is not usable. For refreshing a memory of 128 rows every 2 ms with a 2 MHz clock, the time lost is $128 \times 0.5 = 64$ μs. The percentage time lost is $64/2000 = 3.2$ per cent.

(b) Distributed refresh (by cycle-stealing). In this technique the refresh of the 128 rows is distributed over the 2 ms; one row being refreshed every 15.5 µs. The operation of the microprocessor has to be suspended during each refresh cycle. The refresh requests are asynchronous with respect to the microprocessor clock, as for burst-mode refresh. This technique is similar to direct memory access by cycle-stealing.

In this technique the refresh requests and the memory cycle requests, arising from the microprocessor and the DMA controller, if there is one, are addressed to arbitration logic which gives priority to refresh requests. This arbitration logic generally plays the role of refresh controller. Certain functional limits are imposed by situations which modify the normal operation of the microprocessor: RESET, HALT state, WAIT state, for example on the 8080A.

Note. The first two techniques provide an *asynchronous refresh* with refresh requests being considered as real-time events. In consequence, a dynamic memory refreshed by one or other of these techniques is independent of the microprocessor used. The only precaution to take is to examine carefully, for the given microprocessor, the limits imposed by certain situations where the minimal acceptable refresh cycle rate can no longer be assured.

(c) Transparent refresh (hidden, or synchronous refresh). The idea of this technique is to refresh a RAM line at a moment when the microprocessor is not using the RAM. For every microprocessor there exists one or more clock periods during which the RAM cannot be addressed. It suffices, then, to effect a refresh cycle during this time. In contrast to the first two techniques, this third requires a synchronous refresh request, generated by a synchronization circuit specific to the microprocessor. The latter is not slowed down in operation and takes no notice of the refresh (hence the terms 'transparent' and 'hidden').

This technique, attractive in principle, has its limitations like the first two techniques. Anything which momentarily inhibits that microprocessor state or cycle during which a row of RAM is refreshed clearly hinders refreshing and can therefore destroy the contents of the memory. Thus, for the INTEL 8080A, the T4 state of a FETCH cycle is the one which allows a refresh cycle. Now, this T4 state ceases to exist in the following situations:

(1) Pressing the RESET button;
(2) The READY input is at level '0' (WAIT state). This input is used for some slow memories or for a stepwise operation;
(3) The HOLD input is at level '1'; used, for example, for a direct memory access;
(4) The microprocessor HALT state (TWH) following the execution of the HLT instruction.

III.3.5.3. Refresh implementation. Refreshing of dynamic memories can actually be affected without difficulty as a result of the systems developed by the memory manufacturers. A refresh controller, such as the INTEL 8202, guarantees almost all functions which refreshing requires. Moreover, in 1979, the first memory with internal refresh appeared; this is the MOTOROLA MCM 6664 which is a 64K memory. Refreshing is transparent to the user for whom the sole constraint is that the technique of transparent DMA should not be used.

III.3.5.4. Study of the INTEL 8202 refresh controller. The INTEL 8202 circuit provides for refreshing a dynamic memory constructed from integrated circuits of 4K times 1 bit, or 16K times 1 bit (for example, the INTEL 2117 memory, the MOTOROLA MCM 6616, or the NS MM 5290) or 64K times 1 bit. This refresh is normally performed in an asynchronous manner without the user having to worry about RESET and DMA transfer functions. It is also possible to effect the refresh in transparent mode. For this, the user employs an input (REFRQ/ALE) on which synchronous refresh requests will be sent by external logic. In addition to this optional mode, the user can consider the dynamic memory as a static memory since the controller manages the arbitration of priority between refresh requests, which it generates itself, and memory cycle requests (read or write) sent by the microprocessor. Arbitration of requests is carried out on the basis of 'first come, first served'. When a read or write command is sent to the 8202 while it is executing a refresh cycle, the microprocessor has to wait until the end of execution of the command. This wait is accomplished by means of the MEMORY READY concept that we introduced in the context of slow memories. The 8202 then generates the signal $\overline{\text{XACK}}$ (Transfer acknowledge) which changes to level '0' when the memory cycle is terminated. The refresh itself is effected by 'RAS ONLY' cycles; that is, by activating only one $\overline{\text{RAS}}$ integrated circuit input, or more exactly one $\overline{\text{RAS}}$ input common to a row of N integrated circuit memories for N-bit words ($N = 8$ with 8-bit microprocessors). The 8202 has 4 $\overline{\text{RAS}}$ outputs: each output is assigned to one row of 8 integrated circuits (for 8-bit words) of 16K times 1 bit, for the case where the dynamic memory is constructed from such integrated circuits, and has a total capacity of 64K words. The selection of one 16K module from the 4 is made by two address bits B0 and B1 connected, respectively, to A14 and A15. Capacities of 16K, 32K, or 48K are possible with the 8202 (Figure 58). It suffices for these cases to disable the memory read or write commands for the unused address field by putting the $\overline{\text{PCS}}$ input (PROTECTED CHIP SELECT) at '1'. Thus, if we want to construct a dynamic memory of 48K or 32K words located in the higher part of the address space, we have to send, on the $\overline{\text{PCS}}$ input, the address function $\overline{\text{A15} + \text{A14}}$ for 48K, or $\overline{\text{A15}}$ for 32K. In effect, one must disable the 8202 for the configuration A15 = 0, A14 = 0 in the case of a 38K RAM, and for the configuration A15 = 0 in the case of a 32K RAM.

III.4. Interfacing a programmable timer

We know that a microprocessor can easily carry out one timing loop or several overlapping loops if necessary. This function is rather common in industrial applications: for example, pulses of minimal duration for motor commands, searching for a recorded item on a floppy disk, etc. However, when a microprocessor is carrying out a timing operation it cannot do anything else. The solution to this consists in having the task carried out by a specialized circuit, generally known as a PROGRAMMABLE TIMER. When the microprocessor wishes to start timing it will initialize the programmable timer by sending it a

101

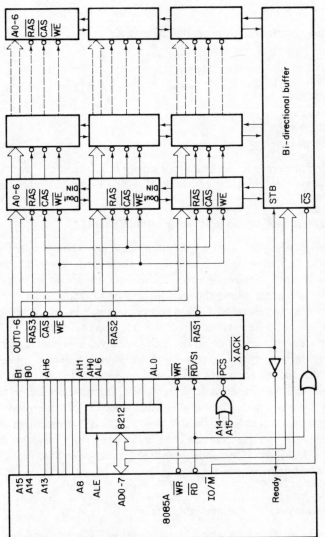

Figure 58. 48K dynamic memory managed by an 8202 controller

command word. This then takes charge of the timing function and will signal the end of execution by triggering an interrupt. A programmable timer also carries out several other functions which we shall now look at.

III.4.1. Usual functions of a programmable timer

This circuit can be programmed so that it forms:

(1) An astable;
(2) A monostable;
(3) A clock circuit;
(4) An event counter; and
(5) A pulse generator

and can sometimes serve for measuring or comparing frequencies and widths of pulses – as is the case with the MOTOROLA 6840 programmable timer.

III.4.2. Registers and signals of a programmable timer

Such a circuit basically consists of programmable counters (or more often of down-counters, i.e. decrementers), of which there are generally three. The programming of each down-counter is carried out by means of a command register. A status register allows the microprocessor to read certain information from within the timer-generator. Each down-counter can be connected either to the internal clock or to an external clock, which we shall denote by EXT. CLK followed by the number of the down-counter. It receives an enabling signal input for counting or decrementing called GATE. Each down-counter has, of course, an output on which the programmed signal will be generated. Like other chips, a programmable timer has one or more 'CS-chip select' inputs. In order to address a register or a down-counter in the chip, several selection bits are required.

The programmable timer has to be able to signal the end of execution of a function by causing an interrupt. In addition timer-generators have an interrupt request output. In Figure 59 we show the standard registers, down-counters, and signals of a programmable timer.

III.4.3. Programming a programmable timer

Programming is carried out by writing a command word in the command register associated with a down-counter and by loading this down-counter with an appropriate value. This is done for each down-counter used and, in general, on each occasion that it is used.

III.4.4. Application to the INTEL programmable timer

III.4.4.1. The 8253 registers. This circuit has:

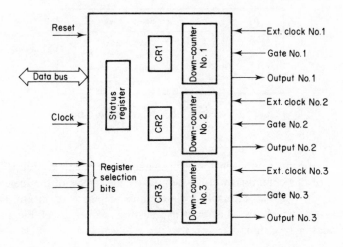

Figure 59. Registers and signals of a programmable timer

(1) Three 16-bit down-counters, numbered 0, 1, and 2, which can be read and written.
(2) One command register which can only be written to.

Addressing a counter or a command register is carried out by means of two chip-select bits A0 and A1, linked, of course, to the corresponding bits of the address bus (Figure 60).

III.4.4.2. The INTEL 8253 signals

1 chip select bit		$\overline{CS}$ (ADDRESS)
2 register select bits		A0 and A1
8 data bus bits		D0 and D7
EXT. CLK	No. 1	CLK 0 (CLOCK 0)
GATE	No. 1	GATE 0
OUTPUT	No. 1	OUT 0
EXT. CLK	No. 2	CLK 1
GATE	No. 2	GATE 1
OUTPUT	No. 2	OUT 1
EXT. CLK	No. 3	CLK 2
GATE	No. 3	GATE 2
OUTPUT	No. 3	OUT 2
READ		$\overline{RD}$ linked to $\overline{I/OR}$
WRITE		$\overline{WR}$ linked to $\overline{I/OW}$

III.4.4.3. Programming the 8253. Programming the 8253 counter is carried out by means of a command word in the command register. Bits 6 and 7 of this command word allow it be connected to any one of the three down-counters. A

104

A1	A0	Selected register
0	0	Down-counter No. 0
0	1	Down-counter No. 1
1	0	Down-counter No. 2
1	1	Command register

Figure 60. Selection of registers or down-
counters in the 8253

command word must be given for each of the down-counters used (Figure 61).
The layout of this command word is defined by the means of the table shown in
Figure 62. This shows that each down-counter can be used in any one of six
possible modes, which are illustrated by the time sequences of Figure 63.

These possibilities, or modes, are:

(1) Counter or timer (mode 0);
(2) Resettable monostable (mode 1);
(3) Divide-by-n (mode 2);
(4) Astable (mode 3);
(5) Generate a pulse after a program-determined delay (mode 4);
(6) Generate a pulse after a delay determined by the GATE signal (mode 5).

In order to use the 8253 as a counter it suffices to send the appropriate
command word to the command register, to set the GATE input at 1, if it is not
already so set, and to initiate down-counting by loading FFFF into the down-
counter. Each pulse arriving at the clock input decreases the counter contents by
one. When we wish to stop the count, we only need to read the counter contents
after having sent the command word indicated in Figure 61. The number of pulses
counted is given by the ones complement of the counter contents. If the number of
pulses to be counted exceeds the counter capacity this generates an interrupt each
time the value 0 is passed. This interrupt works by simply incrementing another
counter, which serves to increase the capacity of the down-counter. The complemented contents of the latter counter give the two least significant bytes of the
pulses counted.

Using the 8253 as a timer consists of loading n into the down-counter if the
timing period is to be $n \times T$ (T being the clock period). At the end of timing, the
down-counter generates an interrupt request which informs the microprocessor
that timing is finished. In the 'resettable monostable' mode the output changes

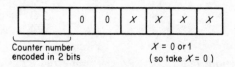

Figure 61. Command word preceding the
read of the down-counter contents

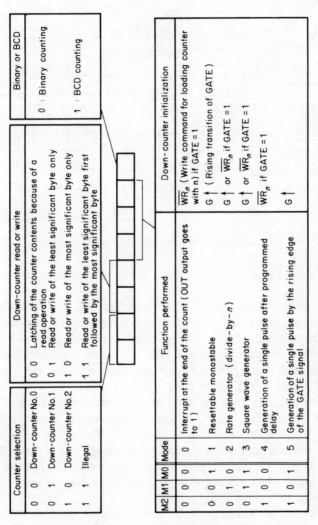

Counter selection

0	0	Down-counter No.0
0	1	Down-counter No.1
1	0	Down-counter No 2
1	1	Illegal

Down-counter read or write

0	0	Latching of the counter contents because of a read operation
0	1	Read or write of the least significant byte only
1	0	Read or write of the most significant byte only
1	1	Read or write of the least significant byte first followed by the most significant byte

Binary or BCD

0	: Binary counting
1	: BCD counting

M2	M1	M0	Mode	Function performed	Down-counter initialization
0	0	0	0	Interrupt at the end of the count (OUT output goes to 1)	$\overline{WR}_n$ (Write command for loading counter with n) if GATE = 1
0	0	1	1	Resettable monostable	G ↑ (Rising transition of GATE)
0	1	0	2	Rate generator (divide - by - n)	G ↑ or $\overline{WR}_n$ if GATE = 1
0	1	1	3	Square wave generator	G ↑ or $\overline{WR}_n$ if GATE = 1
1	0	0	4	Generation of a single pulse after programmed delay	$\overline{WR}_n$ if GATE = 1
1	0	1	5	Generation of a single pulse by the rising edge of the GATE signal	G ↑

Figure 62. Summary of command-word format for the INTEL 8253

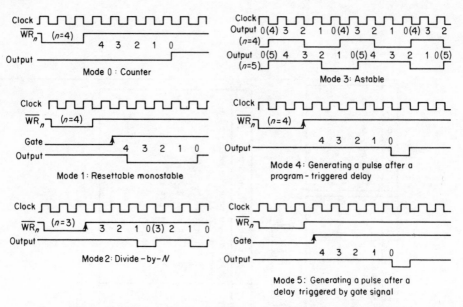

Figure 63. Timing diagrams of 8253 signals in different modes

to level 0 on the first falling edge of the clock following the transition from 0 to 1 of the GATE input.

This output resets to 1 when the down-counter takes on the value zero. Loading the down-counter while the output is at level zero has no effect on the duration of the monostable. By contrast, an active transition – that is, from 0 to 1 – of the GATE input, while the output is at level zero, resets the monostable back to its initial value. In other words, the down-counter takes on again the value with which it was loaded and the count starts again.

The 'divide-by-n' mode gives, on the down-counter output, a signal of frequency n times lower than that of the signal applied to the clock input of the counter.

The astable mode gives, on the outputs, a signal at level '1' for $n/2$ clock periods and at level '0' for the next $n/2$ clock periods, where n is the value loaded in the down-counter. When n is an odd number the output stays at level '1' for one clock period more than level '0'.

In mode 4 the down-counter generates, on its outputs, a single pulse whose duration is equal to one clock period, and it does this after a delay of n clock periods, where n is the value loaded in the down-counter.

Mode 5 is the same as mode 4, except that the delay is triggered by a positive transition of the GATE input.

Loading the number n into the down-counter can be done in three ways:

(1) By loading the least significant byte only;
(2) By loading the most significant byte only;
(3) By loading the two bytes, one after the other, beginning with the least significant byte.

The order of writing the command words into the command register, and the number n into the down-counter, is arbitrary provided that (a) on the one hand, the command word precedes the loading of a counter and (b) on the other hand, that the loading is carried out in accordance with what has been programmed into the command word.

The contents of a down-counter can be read by a simple read operation without disturbing its operation, with the sole proviso that this read operation be preceded by the writing of a particular command word. This command word has to have bits 4 and 5 at 0, whilst bits 6 and 7 must indicate the counter number (Figure 61). The values of bits 0, 1, 2, and 3 do not matter.

By way of example, we show two possible sequences for programming the three down-counters of an 8253. Obviously, these two sequences are not the only possible ones.

Possible programming sequence

Down-counter command word write	No. 0
Down-counter command word write	No. 1
Down-counter command word write	No. 2
Down-counter LSB write	No. 0
Down-counter MSB write	No. 0
Down-counter LSB write	No. 1
Down-counter MSB write	No. 1
Down-counter LSB write	No. 2
Down-counter MSB write	No. 2

Another possible programming sequence

Down-counter command word write	No. 1
Down-counter LSB write	No. 1
Down-counter MSB write	No. 1
Down-counter command word write	No. 0
Down-counter LSB write	No. 0
Down-counter MSB write	No. 0
Down-counter command word write	No. 2
Down-counter LSB write	No. 2
Down-counter MSB write	No. 2

III.4.5. Application to the MOTOROLA 6840 programmable timer

III.4.5.1. The 6840 registers. This circuit consists of:

(1) Three 16-bit down-counters numbered 1, 2, and 3. Each down-counter is made up of two 8-bit down-counters, the MSB (for the most significant), and the LSB (for the least significant), each having a specific address, so that a total of six addresses is required.
(2) Three 16-bit latches, one linked to each down-counter and possessing the counter's number. The binary number N which is to be written to the down-counter is, in fact, written to its latch. The contents of this latch are then

108

transferred to the corresponding down-counter at the appropriate time by an *initialization cycle*, which will often begin the execution of the particular 6840 function requested by the microprocessor. The latches are 'hidden' from the user and do not have specific addresses.

(3) Three 8-bit *command registers*, one for each down-counter, numbered from 1 to 3. However, these three registers only have two distinct addresses:
   (a) The address of command register No. 2;
   (b) The address of command registers Nos 1 and 3.
   The selection of one of the latter two is effected by the second bit of register No. 2.

This method of choosing a register, using one particular bit, has already been used by MOTOROLA in the PIA for selecting the data register and the direction register. The command registers can only be written to.

(4) One *status register* which can only be read. This is the reason why the address which is assigned to it is already used: it is that of command register No. 2 (Table XIX).

We have, therefore, ten registers or counters in all and only eight addresses. Addressing the 6840 is carried out by two chip-select bits $\overline{CS0}$ and CS1. Of course, these two bits receive our 'CS ADDRESS' signal. The selection of a register, or a down-counter, is made by three selection bits for registers RS0, RS1, and RS2 which will be connected, as indeed they must be, to the A0, A1, and A2 bits of the address bus.

Following from this, we note that use of the A2 bit means that it is no longer possible to address an interface or an input/output device by linear selection using the A2 bit.

Table XIX. Register and counter selection for the 6840

RS2	RS1	RS0	R/$\overline{W}$	Register or counter address
0	0	0	0	Command register No. 1 if bit 2 of command register No. 2 = 1 Command register No. 3 if bit 2 of command register No. 2 = 0
0	0	1	0	Command register No. 2
0	0	1	1	Status register
0	1	0	0 or 1	MSB for counter No. 1*
0	1	1	0 or 1	LSB for counter No. 1*
1	0	0	0 or 1	MSB for counter No. 2*
1	0	1	0 or 1	LSB for counter No. 2*
1	1	0	0 or 1	MSB for counter No. 3*
1	1	1	0 or 1	LSB for counter No. 3*

*In fact, a write operation to one of these six addresses only transfers the written data to the latch associated with the counter. By contrast, a read operation to one of these addresses yields either the MSB or LSB of the addressed counter.

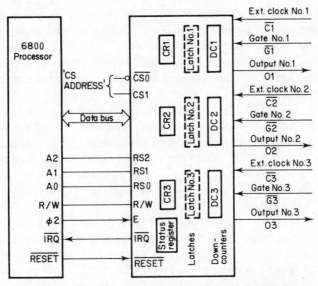

Figure 64. Registers and signals of the MOTOROLA 6840

III.4.5.2. The MOTOROLA 6840 signals

- Two chip select bits — $\overline{CS0}$ and CS1 ('CS ADDRESS')
- Three register select bits — RS0, RS1, and RS2 linked to A0, A1, A2
- Eight data bus bits — D0 to D7
- EXT. CLOCK — No. 1 — $\overline{C1}$
- GATE — No. 1 — $\overline{G1}$
- OUTPUT — No. 1 — O1
- EXT. CLOCK — No. 2 — $\overline{C2}$
- GATE — No. 2 — $\overline{G2}$
- OUTPUT — No. 2 — O2
- EXT. CLOCK — No. 3 — $\overline{C3}$
- GATE — No. 3 — $\overline{G3}$
- OUTPUT — No. 3 — O3
- EXTERNAL CLOCK — Pin linked to $\phi2$ of the microprocessor
- INTERRUPT REQUEST — $\overline{IRQ}$
- RESET — $\overline{RESET}$
- READ/WRITE — $R/\overline{W}$

The signal produced by using one of the down-counters is, of course, delivered to the OUTPUT pin of the down-counter.

III.4.5.3. Programming the 6840.
Programming the MOTOROLA 6840 programmable timer is carried out by means of a command word within the

command register for each counter used. The layout of the command word is defined by means of the table in Figure 65. This table is relatively complicated because the 6840 offers numerous possibilities.

The 0 bit of the command register, which MOTOROLA call CRX0 (where X is the number of the command register), has a different role for each of the three command registers.

For command register No. 1 (CR10), this 0 bit allows an internal reset. Writing a '1' into CR10 has the effect of loading each down-counter with the contents of the latch connected to it, of disabling the counter clocks, and of setting the down-counter outputs to zero, as well as the interrupt status bits. The contents of the down-counters and command registers are not affected by the internal reset. It is possible to write into the latches, or into the command registers, no matter what value the CR10 bit has.

For command register No. 2 (CR20) the 0 bit is used as a register select bit, for selecting either command register No. 1 (if CR20 = 1) or command register No. 3 (if CR20 = 0).

The 0 bit of command register No. 3 (CR30) is specific to down-counter No. 3. It enables and inhibits the division by 8 of the external clock of down-counter No. 3.

The 1 bit of the three command registers (CRX1) determines the choice of clock; either internal (that is, $\phi 2$) or external (where the signal is provided by the user).

The 2 bit determines the operating mode of the down-counter: the mode is 'one times 16 bits' (down-counter modulo 2^{16} pre-loaded with value N) if this bit is '0'; the mode is 'two times 8 bits' (two down-counters modulo 2^8 pre-loaded with the value L for LSB and M for MSB) if bit 2 is '1'.

Bits 3, 4, and 5, that is, CRX3, CRX4, and CRX5, program the functions to be executed by the down-counter. For the astable or monostable functions the programmed signal is furnished by the output OX; for example, O1 for down-counter No. 1. The value L, M, or N which we have just mentioned is loaded into the latch linked to the down-counter. This value can only be loaded into the down-counter by an *initialization cycle*. Whatever mode is chosen there are always many ways of triggering the initialization cycle. These depend on the mode chosen and are indicated in the command word layout table. The different possibilities are:

(1) Transition from level '1' to level '0' of the GATE input of the down-counter. This transition is denoted by G↓ in the table.
(2) Sending a write command to the latch linked to the down-counter. This command is denoted by W in the table.
(3) External or internal RESET, denoted by R in the table.

The first clock pulse arriving after the zero state of the down-counter (all bits at zero) triggers an initialization cycle. The contents of the latch are then transferred to the down-counter. In the case of the down-counter functioning in astable or monostable mode, at least two possibilities exist for triggering an initialization cycle. In this case, of course, the first one produced will generate the initialization cycle.

111

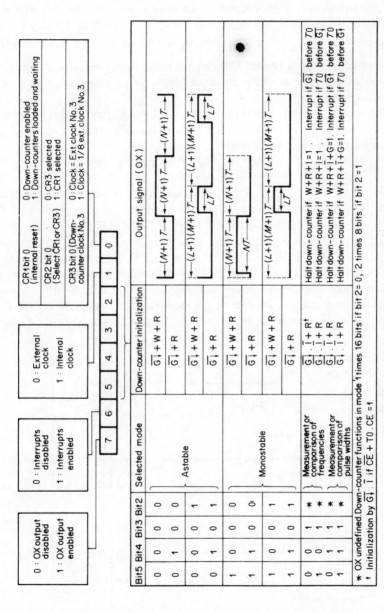

Figure 65. Format of the 6840 command word

112

Bit 6 of the command register (CRX6) enables or inhibits interrupt mode by setting the bit to '1' or '0', respectively.

Bit 7 of the command register (CRX7) enables or inhibits the OX output of the down-counter. Each output has an output capacity of two TTL loads.

In the table of Figure 65, certain abbreviations have been used as follows:

T: Down-counter clock period. This clock is active during negative transitions.

t_0:   This is the instant at which the down-counter initialization cycle becomes executed.

T_0:   This denotes the arrival time of the first clock pulse after the down-counter zero state (all bits at zero). A little less rigorously, the symbol is also used to characterize the down-counter zero state.

I: This represents an interrupt relating to the down-counter.

III.4.5.4.   TIME INTERVAL mode.   This mode deals with the measurement of either the frequencies or the widths of pulses. The initialization cycle for one of these functions is also affected by the INTERRUPT STATUS BIT. In effect, this cycle can only be accomplished for a counter if the latter has not set the INTERRUPT STATUS BIT to '1' in the status register. Figure 66 illustrates the techniques which permit measurement of the frequency or width of a pulse.

The counter latch is loaded with the maximum value. The negative transition of the signal whose frequency we want to measure (signal connected to the GATE input) starts a down-counter initialization cycle. This then counts down, and when

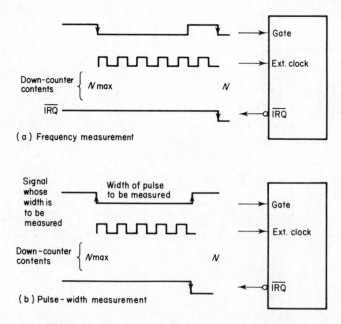

Figure 66. Frequency and pulse-width measurement

the next positive signal transition is produced the down-counter is stopped and the INTERRUPT STATUS BIT is set to one. The period T of the signal arriving at the GATE input is then

$$T = (N \text{ max} - N) \cdot T_0$$

N max is the down-counter value when all the bits are at '1'. N is the value contained in the down-counter when arrested by the positive transition of the GATE signal. T_0 is the period of the internal clock, if this has been selected, or of the external clock applied on the EXTERNAL CLOCK output, if the latter has been selected by the command word. We note that $N \text{ max} - N = \bar{N}$ (ones complement of N). By a simple calculation it is possible to show that

$$F = 1/T = 1/[(N \text{ max} - N) \cdot T_0]$$

For measuring pulse widths the principle is the same, except that it is a positive GATE signal transition which stops the count, sets the INTERRUPT STATUS BIT to '1', and finally triggers an interrupt.

III.5. Interfacing the AM 9511 arithmetic circuit

Microprocessors are not very advanced so far as arithmetic calculations are concerned. However, the ADVANCED MICRO DEVICES (AMD) company has developed a powerful arithmetic circuit called the AM 9511 which easily connects to a microprocessor. The circuit carries out arithmetic operations in both fixed-point and floating-point, as well as performing other trigonometric and mathematical functions.

III.5.1. AM 9511 circuit signals

(1) DB0 to DB7: these are the eight bits of the data bus. They enable the 9511 command and operation words to be sent, as well as allowing the reading of the status word and the result of an operation. We note that data transfers can be made with the AM 9511 circuit either in programmed mode or by direct memory access.

(2) CLK (CLOCK): the clock input;

(3) RESET: the 9511 initialization command.

(4) $\overline{CS}$: this enabling input supplements the $\overline{RD}$ and $\overline{WR}$ commands and enables communication with the data bus.

(5) $\overline{RD}$: the read command, active-low when $\overline{CS} = 0$

(6) $\overline{WR}$: the write command, active-low when $\overline{CS} = 0$

(7) $C/\bar{D}$ (COMMAND/DATA): this input is one bit of the selection register used in conjuction with $\overline{RD}$ and $\overline{WR}$.

(8) $\overline{PAUSE}$: this output is a status bit which permits an asynchronous data transfer between the microprocessor and the AM 9511 circuit. This output takes the value '0' as long as the transfer is incomplete.

(9) $\overline{END}$ (END EXECUTION): this output, active-low, indicates the end of

execution of the last programmed operation. This signal can be used to generate an interrupt request: it is reset to zero by a RESET or by $\overline{EACK}$.

(10) $\overline{EACK}$ (END ACKNOWLEDGE): this input command resets the END output to zero.

(11) SVREQ (SERVICE REQUEST): this output signals, by level '1', the end of execution of the previous command operation, whenever a service request has been programmed in the command word.

(12) SVREQ is reset to zero by a RESET or by $\overline{SVACK}$.

(13) SVACK: this input resets SVREQ to zero.

Table XX. Microprocessor – 9511 transfers

C/D	RD	WR	*Operation carried out*
0	1	0	Write a data byte to the 9511 stack
0	0	1	Read a data byte from 9511 stack
1	1	0	Write a command word
1	0	1	Read a status word

III.5.2. Programming the AM 9511 circuit

The AM 9511 can only carry out one operation at a time, and programming the device reduces to programming the desired operation as shown in the summary of Figure 67. The operation code is expressed in five bits.

Table XXI gives all the operations possible with the AM 9511 circuit, as well as the hexadecimal code for the command word, the required number of cycles, and the mnemonic for each command. This one table suffices to illustrate the power of the circuit. Each operation is a program in ROM, this program itself also being a sequence of micro-instructions also in ROM.

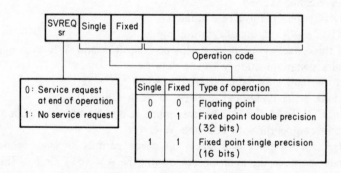

Figure 67. Summary of command-word format

Table XXI. List of possible operations using the AM 9511 circuit

Command mnemonic	Hex code (sr = 1)	Hex code (sr = 0)	Execution cycles	Summary description
16-bit fixed-point operations				
SADD	EC	6C	16–18	Add TOS to NOS. Result to NOS. Pop Stack
SSUB	ED	6D	30–32	Subtract TOS from NOS. Result to NOS. Pop Stack
SMUL	EE	6E	84–94	Multiply NOS by TOS. Lower result to NOS. Pop Stack
SMUU	F6	76	80–98	Multiply NOS by TOS. Upper result to NOS. Pop Stack
SDIV	EF	6F	64–94	Divide NOS by TOS. Result to NOS. Pop Stack
32-bit fixed-point operations				
DADD	AC	2C	20–22	Add TOS to NOS. Result to NOS. Pop Stack
DSUB	AD	2D	38–40	Subtract TOS from NOS. Result to NOS. Pop Stack
DMUL	AE	2E	194–210	Multiply NOS by TOS. Lower result to NOS. Pop Stack
DMUU	B6	36	182–218	Multiply NOS by TOS. Upper result to NOS. Pop Stack
DDIV	AF	2F	196–210	Divide NOS by TOS. Result to NOS. Pop Stack
32-bit floating-point primary operation				
FADD	90	10	54–368	Add TOS to NOS. Result to NOS. Pop Stack
FSUB	91	11	70–370	Subtract TOS from NOS. Result to NOS. Pop Stack
FMUL	92	12	146–168	Multiply NOS by TOS. Result to NOS. Pop Stack
FDIV	93	13	154–184	Divide NOS by TOS. Result to NOS. Pop Stack
32-bit floating-point derived operations				
SQRT	81	01	782–870	Square Root of TOS. Result to TOS
SIN	82	02	3796–4808	Sine of TOS. Result to TOS
COS	83	03	3840–4878	Cosine of TOS. Result to TOS
TAN	84	04	4894–5886	Tangent of TOS. Result to TOS
ASIN	85	05	6230–7938	Inverse Sine of TOS. Result to TOS
ACOS	86	06	6304–8284	Inverse Cosine of TOS. Result to TOS

Table XXI   *continued*

Command mnemonic	Hex code (sr = 1)	Hex code (sr = 0)	Execution cycles	Summary description
32-bit floating-point derived operations – continued				
ATAN	87	07	4992–6536	Inverse Tangent of TOS. Result to TOS
LOG	88	08	4474–7132	Common Logarithm of TOS. Result to TOS
LN	89	09	4298–6956	Natural Logarithm of TOS. Result to TOS
EXP	8A	0A	3794–4878	e raised to power in TOS. Result to TOS
PWR	8B	0B	8290–12032	NOS raised to power in TOS. Result to NOS. Pop Stack
Data and stack manipulation operations				
NOP	80	00	4	No Operation. Clear or set SVREQ
FIXS	9F	1F	90–214 ⎫	Convert TOS from floating point
FIXD	9E	1E	90–336 ⎭	to fixed point format
FLTS	9D	1D	62–156 ⎫	Convert TOS from fixed point
FLTD	9C	1C	56–342 ⎭	format to floating point format
CHSS	F4	74	22–24 ⎫	Change sign of fixed point operand
CHSD	B4	34	26–28 ⎭	on TOS
CHSF	95	15	16–20	Change sign of floating point operand on TOS
PTOS	F7	77	16 ⎫	
PTOD	B7	37	20 ⎬	Push stack. Duplicate NOS in TOS
PTOF	97	17	20 ⎭	
POPS	F8	78	10 ⎫	
POPD	B8	38	12 ⎬	Pop stack. Old NOS becomes new TOS. Old TOS rotates to bottom
POPF	98	18	12 ⎭	
XCHS	F9	79	18 ⎫	
XCHD	B9	39	26 ⎬	Exchange TOS and NOS
XCHF	99	19	26 ⎭	
PUPI	9A	1A	16	Push floating point constant π onto TOS. Previous TOS becomes NOS

TOS = Top of stack.
NOS = Next on stack.

III.5.3.   Interfacing the AM 9511 to the INTEL 8080A

When the signal $\overline{\text{EACK}}$ is grounded the $\overline{\text{END}}$ output generates, at the end of the operation, a pulse of smaller width than the clock pulse (Figure 68).

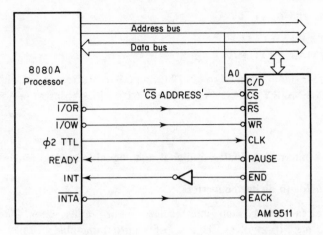

Figure 68. Interfacing the AM 9511 circuit to the INTEL
8080A with an interrupt request at the end of operation

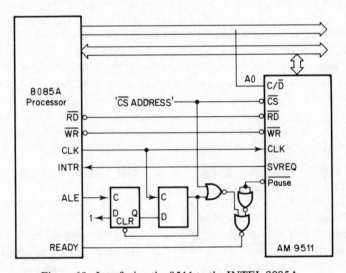

Figure 69. Interfacing the 9511 to the INTEL 8085A

III.5.4. Interfacing the AM 9511 to the INTEL 8085

With the 8085, the $\overline{\text{PAUSE}}$ signal cannot be sent directly to the 8085 READY
input and it is necessary to create a signal similar to that indicated in Figure 69.

III.5.5. Interfacing the AM 9511 to the MOTOROLA 6800

With the 6800 it is necessary to create the $\overline{\text{RD}}$ and $\overline{\text{WR}}$ signals starting with

118

VMA, R/W, and $\phi2$ (TTL):

$$\overline{RD} = \overline{VMA.\phi2\ TTL.R/W}$$
$$\overline{WR} = \overline{VMA.\phi2\ TTL.\overline{R/W}}$$

The PAUSE signal is linked to $\phi2$ TTL and $\overline{CS}$ to create a signal which is sent out on the MEMORY READY input of the 6800 clock so as to prolong the '1' state of $\phi1$.

III.6. Interfacing analog-to-digital and digital-to-analog converters

III.6.1. Analog-to-digital converters

We have already met such interfacing in our earlier book *The Use of Microprocessors*. It involves the use of a programmable parallel interface. However, there now exist analog-to-digital converters whose outputs can be set to a high impedance state. In this case the data bits of the converters can be connected directly to the data bus. However, for converters of more than 8 bits at least two successive read operations are necessary. As an example, we shall consider the interfacing of the ANALOG DEVICES AD 7550 converter. This 40-pin monolithic CMOS circuit is a 13-bit analog-to-digital converter (twelve bits plus sign) using the so-called 'quadruple ramp' technique. This consists of speeded-up double ramp integration with derivative correction. The conversion time is 40 ms.

To facilitate interfacing to an 8-bit microprocessor the manufacturer has provided, for the 13 data bits, two tri-state latches each having an output enable command. The commands are:

LBEN (LOW BYTE ENABLE) for enabling the least significant byte; that is, bits DB0 to DB7. These output bits are only valid when LBEN is at level '1'; and HBEN (HIGH BYTE ENABLE) for enabling the most significant bits DB8 to DB12. These bits are only valid when HBEN is at level '1'.

The 'end of conversion' signal, which is usually encountered with A/D converters, has the name $\overline{BUSY}$. When the voltage to be measured, as applied to the AIN input, exceeds full scale by at least $\frac{1}{2}$ LSB, a 'scale overrange' (OVRG) status bit is set to '1'. These three bits BUSY, $\overline{BUSY}$, and OVRG are themselves usually in a high impedance state. They are only enabled if a logic '1' is applied by an enabling command denoted by STEN (STATUS ENABLE) (Figure 70).

We shall now consider the sequence of operations to be performed in order to effect an analog-to-digital conversion. For this purpose we assign to each of the three enabling commands STEN, LBEN, and HBEN a CS address, which we denote by ASTEN, ALBEN, and AHBEN. The STRT signal can be connected either to the output of a parallel interface (to a C port bit in the INTEL 8255, or to one of the CA2, CB2 bits of the MOTOROLA PIA) or to another CS address (Figures 71 and 72).

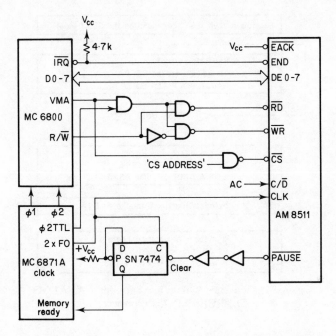

Figure 70. Interfacing the 9511 to the MOTOROLA 6800

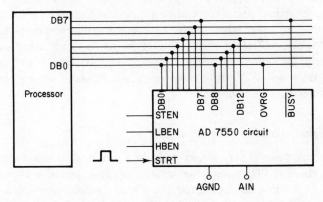

Figure 71. Interfacing the AD 7750 circuit to an 8-bit micro-processor

We then have

STEN = ASTEN · PERI READ
LBEN = ALBEN · PERI READ
HBEN = AHBEN · PERI READ
STRT = ASTRT · PERI WRITE where ASTRT is a CS address

120

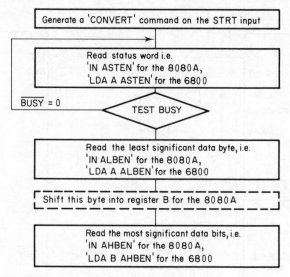

Figure 72. Conversion flowchart for the ANALOG
DEVICES AD 7550 converter

Note. If the industrial application requires several analog-to-digital converters
the 'end of conversion' status bits can be grouped in eights and connected to the
inputs of a tri-state buffer whose outputs are linked to the corresponding bits of a
data bus. A single address is then sufficient for reading the 'end of conversion'
status, namely, the address controlling the high impedance output of the buffers.
If the converters were AD7550 circuits the STEN inputs of these circuits would
be kept permanently at level '1'.

III.6.2. Digital-to-analog converters

Interfacing is carried out very simply with the aid of a latch which stabilizes the
numerical data at the D/A converter input. This latch, placed between the data
bus and the D/A converter inputs, requires a latching command which can either
be a CS ADDRESS or an output bit of a parallel interface (Figure 73).

When the D/A converter has more than 8 bits, three latches are required in
order to avoid spurious output voltages being generated between two genuine
programmed output voltages. In effect, a microprocessor write operation can only
affect 8 bits, the others remaining at the previous values, and this would generate a
false output magnitude. To avoid this, it is necessary to store the first 8 bits of the
new value in a preliminary latch and then, with a second microprocessor write
operation, to load all the bits into yet another latch which has as many bits as the
D/A converter. In practice, this latter latch will be made up of two 8-bit latches.

These three latches require two CS ADDRESSes – one for the intermediate

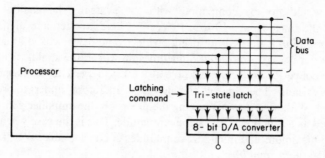

(a) Example of an 8-bit D/A converter

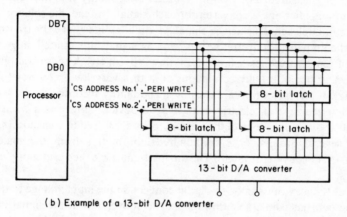

(b) Example of a 13-bit D/A converter

Figure 73. Interfacing a digital-to-analog converter

latch, the second for the other two latches. Two write instructions follow one after the other: the first has the address of the intermediate latch, which allows the loading of 13 bits into the digital-analog converter.

Readers who want detailed information about analog-to-digital or digital-to-analog conversion techniques should consult the author's *Pratique de l'Electronique (Practical Electronics)*, Vol. II, Masson.

III.7. Interfacing a data-acquisition circuit or board

III.7.1. Description of a data-acquisition chain

I/O transfers, as we have already made clear, constitute one of the most important functions of a microprocessor system. These transfers are either in the form of reading data or writing data. The 'data read' function is generally more complicated. In fact, the data to be read could be numerical information, compatible with the microprocessor I/O system, but they could also be analog signals, which, of course, would not be compatible with the system. The analog voltages, generally in the range from −10 to +10 V, must be converted into digital values. This transformation is carried out using an electronic device called an analog-to-digital converter or A/D converter. Sometimes, however, the analog signals at the input of the converter are very weak, or, at least, too weak to be measured with sufficient precision. The analog signals must therefore undergo preliminary amplification. With a view to optimizing the precision, the amplifier gain is, sometimes, defined as a function of the signal amplitude. This is the case when the ratio between the maximum and minimum amplitudes is considerable. We then have a *programmable gain amplifier*.

In an industrial process there are often dozens, or even several hundred, analog signals to be measured. For obvious reasons of economy it is not reasonable to provide an amplifier and a converter for each signal. Instead, the solution is to use an analog multiplexer. This device will allow each input signal to be transmitted in turn, to the amplifier–converter set-up. Analog signals are emitted, in general, by *sensors* of temperature, pressure, strain, flow, speed, etc. A sensor output should be an electric signal, usually continuous or with a very low frequency (often less than 1 Hz). If this is not the case the physical quantity recorded by the sensor has to be converted into an electric voltage by a device known as a *transducer*.

In industrial process control the sensors, possibly linked to transducers, may be situated several dozens, or even hundreds, of metres from the multiplexer–amplifier–A/D converter system. The analog signals are then sent along *transmission lines*.

In order to carry out analog-to-digital conversion the input voltage to the device has to be constant and stable throughout the conversion. If the signal variations are such that these conditions are not guaranteed, the input signal is sampled. This means that we take the value of the analog signal at the beginning of a very short time interval, memorize it, and then maintain this constant analog-value in a capacitor in such a way as to effect the A/D conversion. In Figure 74 the input signal $E(t)$ has been sampled four times, giving four constant and stable analog values $V1$, $V2$, $V3$, $V4$. $E(t)$ can be reconstituted by regenerating the four analog values. For this, the numerical values are entered into a digital-to-analog converter and the output of each converter is integrated.

The electronic device which carries out the sampling and holding is called a *sampler/holder*. It is placed between the amplifier and the A/D converter. The complete system of multiplexer, amplifier, sampler/holder, and A/D converter constitutes a *data-acquisition chain* (Figure 75).

Such a chain, however small, always exists in industrial process control. For this reason we think it useful to give some basic information about it. Moreover, data-acquisition boards have recently appeared which are compatible with the microcomputer boards of principal microprocessors. This compatibility applies both to the board layout and to the input/output signals of the data-acquisition board as regards connecting it to a microcomputer board. Data-acquisition circuits are also available where the chain is formed by a single hybrid or monolithic circuit.

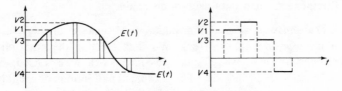

Figure 74. Sampling and holding of $E(t)$

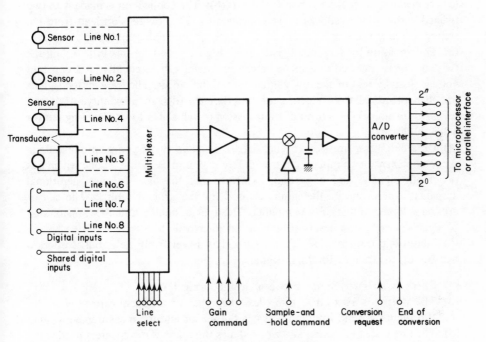

Figure 75. Data-acquisition chain

The control of each of the data-acquisition chain systems is carried out by signals sent from the microprocessor (conversion commands, for example) and by binary words, also furnished by the microprocessor (address of the multiplexer channel, for example). These operations handle the driving of the data-acquisition chain (which is also called the measurement chain). The examination, by the multiplexer, of each of its channels, with signal measurement on each channel constitutes an examination-cycle or measurement-cycle.

To understand better the interfacing of a data-acquisition circuit or board to a microprocessor we shall now give some basic information about each of the components of the chain. We shall not study the sensors themselves as this would be outside the scope of this book. On the other hand, we shall briefly describe transmission lines which are closely associated with the analog multiplexer.

124

III.7.2. Components of a data-acquisition chain

III.7.2.1. Transmission lines. Transmission of analog or logic signals is carried out using several types of link. We shall mention the main ones.

(1) Transmission by single wire (Figure 76(a)). A single wire is used, the return being made by the earth which acts like a capacitor of infinite capacitance. This form of transmission carries a great deal of noise. It is used very little and is only acceptable for signals of several volts.

(2) Transmission by twisted pair (Figure 76(b)). The connection is made with two twisted wires, which reduces noise considerably. The low-tension lead from the sensor to the measurement chain is connected to the analog multiplexer ground.

(3) Transmission by screened twisted pair (Figure 76(c)). In this type of link the twisted pair is enclosed in a metal screen maintained, theoretically, at a constant voltage, usually that of the low voltage side of the sensor. The transmitted signals are then protected from electrostatic interference (due to proximity of electric wires, for example). This form of transmission is well suited to low-level signals (of a few millivolts).

(4) Differential transmission (Figure 76(d)). The two twisted wires are linked via the multiplexer to two inputs of a true differential amplifier; that is, one which has two input signals, and a ground, (which is not the case for an operational amplifier, where one of the inputs is used for the ground return). The sensor ground is linked to that of the amplifier. This type of link permits the transmission of signals at very low levels (a few dozen microvolts).

(5) Fibre-optic transmission. This type of link is relatively new, but it offers a number of advantages for logic signals:

(a) There is no interference between neighbouring fibres.
(b) The weight is 10 to 100 times less than that of a copper wire.
(c) It provides ground-isolation between the sensor and the measurement chain.
(d) The line losses are small and this reduces the number of repeaters used when the lines are long.
(e) It permits undetectable transmission, in contrast to signals transmitted by copper wire, where an inductance loop allows the transmitted signals to be intercepted.
(f) In case of an accident, it does not carry dangerous voltages.

On the other hand, there are some problems with optic fibres:

(a) Solid covering around the fibres is required – although this is perfectly feasible to arrange.
(b) The cost is still high.
(c) Project designers are not yet familiar with this new product.

The future of optic fibres is very promising indeed. They will be used a great deal when technology makes possible what is called the 'digitized sensor', where the analog-to-digital conversion will be integrated within the sensor itself.

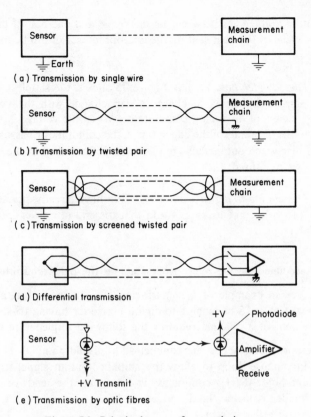

Figure 76. Principal types of transmission

III.7.2.2. The analog multiplexer. The role of the analog multiplexer is to connect one of the sensors onto the data-acquisition chain. Using the chosen form of transmission the multiplexer will possess, for each channel, one, two, or three wires. Slow multiplexers can be realized by means of multi-contact relays. Fast multiplexers are realized using field-effect transistors or MOS. These multiplexers carry an internal decoder for channel selection, using a binary address sent by the microprocessor and memorized in a register internal or external to the multiplexer.

III.7.2.3. The amplifier. The amplifier can have fixed or programmable gain. In the latter case, programming can be manual, remote, or automatic. It can be manual when the output voltages of the sensors have more or less equal and constant amplitudes. The gain can be remotely programmed, that is, by the microprocessor when it is convenient to give each channel a fixed gain but not necessarily the same gain from one channel to another. Programming can be automatic when the magnitudes of the output voltages can vary greatly from one channel to the other as well as along the same channel. In this latter case the microprocessor executes an optimization algorithm which then ensures that the

126

amplifier output voltage lies between the full range and one half of this value. In this case the value of the gain sent by the microprocessor has to be memorized in a register.

III.7.2.4. The sampler/holder. As Figure 75 shows, the simplest way of constructing a sampler/holder is to charge a capacitance with the voltage to be measured by means of an analog commutator. When the voltage is sampled, i.e. transmitted to the terminals of the capacitance, the commutator passes to the open state, which places the output voltage of the amplifier linked to the capacitor at the value to be measured.

III.7.2.5. The analog-to-digital converter. We have already studied this component (pp. 118–120). Let us simply add that the end of conversion signal can trigger an interrupt.

III.7.3. Interconnecting the microprocessor and the data-acquisition chain

Figure 77 gives an example of the interfacing of a 16-channel data-acquisition circuit or board to an 8-bit analog-to-digital converter having tri-state outputs. The measurement of a channel requires the following sequence of operations:

(1) The microprocessor sends the channel address and gain;
(2) 'Momentary pause' loop to allow the amplifier output signal to stabilize;
(3) Sample-and-hold (S/H) command is sent, at the end of which the sampler/holder is in the 'hold' mode;
(4) A conversion order is sent;
(5) The end of conversion signal is tested (if we are operating in programmed mode);
(6) The converted data is read.

III.8. Interfacing a keyboard

An industrial application of a microprocessor can involve several command keys and/or a numerical keyboard for entering certain values into the system; the value

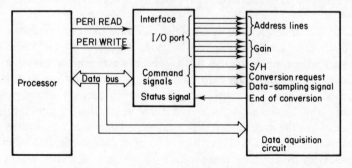

Figure 77. Interfacing a data-acquisition circuit

of some threshold, for example. The microprocessor should be able to recognize which key is pressed and from it deduce the required code. For keyboards with 16 or 20 keys the key push is translated by short-circuiting the row and column at whose intersection the key has been pressed. In Figure 78 pressing the B key causes a short-circuit between row 2 and column 3, and only between this row and column.

Thus if we sent a zero on rows 0, 1, 2, and 3 this zero level would only be found in column 3. Conversely, if we sent a zero on columns 0, 1, 2, and 3 this zero level would only be found on row 2. It is on this principle that decoding of such a keyboard is carried out. Thus, in our example, we have formed the binary word 0111 on the columns and 1011 on the rows. The juxtaposition of these two 4-bit words constitutes an 8-bit word specific to the pressed key.

Sending a logic zero on the rows first and then on the columns is easily effected by using an intermediate parallel interface I/O port. In the first phase, the bits of the I/O port linked to the rows are programmed for output and the bits used for the columns are programmed for input. A zero is then sent on each of the rows; this is the rest, or wait, state of the keyboard. All key touches cause the 'service request' signal to change to level '1', which acts as a status bit in the programmed mode, or an interrupt request in the interrupt mode.

The service request received by the microprocessor is then treated as follows. The 4-bit word formed by the four columns is read and memorized. This completes the first phase.

In the second phase, the bits of the I/O port linked to the columns are programmed for output and the bits linked to the rows are programmed for input. Sending the binary word 0000 on the four columns is followed by reading the

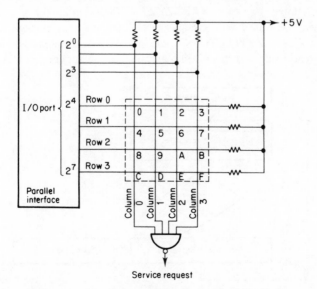

Figure 78. Hexadecimal keyboard and its interfacing

binary word picked up by the four rows. The word just read is then memorized and concatenated with the first word in order to form the 8-bit word specific to the pressed key. A branch-table of 256 8-bit words gives, for each key-specific 8-bit word, the code corresponding to this key – the ASCII code, for example. In order to do this the specific 8-bit word forms the address of the memory location containing the appropriate code. However, this method requires 256 addresses even though only 16 are used. Let us see, therefore, how to reduce the size of the table.

Each 4-bit word encodes only four numbers: the numbers 0, 1, 2, and 3 of the row or column. Each 4-bit word can, therefore, be put into a 2-bit word by a decimal-binary conversion (Figure 79). In juxtaposing two 2-bit words we obtain a 4-bit word, which is the address of the memory location containing the appropriate code for the pressed key. But this requires that the lowest address be 0000 in hexadecimal, and this is often not possible. To overcome this, we need to change the most significant byte of the table addresses by means of the most significant part of the index. Thus if we wish the code for the 4-bit binary word 0000 to be 1000 in hexadecimal, we put 10 in hexadecimal into the most significant part of the index. As for the decimal–binary conversion it suffices to locate, by successive shifts into CARRY, the position of '0' in the 4-bit word formed by the columns or the rows. For this we shall use register B, which will be set in advance to zero, and which will be incremented until the bit of accumulator A shifted into CARRY becomes zero. This decimal–binary conversion forms a subroutine which we call CDB. The subroutine supposes that the 4-bit word to be converted is in A. The converted 2-bit word is now contained in bits 2^0 and 2^1 of register B.

If the converted word corresponding to reading the columns is 000000XX in binary, the converted word corresponding to reading the rows has to be in the form 0000YY00. The addition of these two words gives 0000YYXX. If the low address of the table is given by ZZZZZZZZ00000000 in binary, pressing a keyboard key will have the final consequence of loading the index register with the binary value ZZZZZZZZ0000YYXX, the YYXX part being specific to the key. A memory read using this index will then put into the accumulator, A, the code

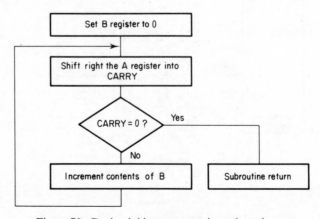

Figure 79. Decimal–binary conversion subroutine

129

appropriate to the key that has been pressed. Figure 80 shows the different operations required to arrive at the desired result, while Table XXII illustrates the working of the table in the following case: the most significant byte of the index is 04 in hexadecimal, and the keyboard code is the ASCII code. In this example, pushing key C gives the successive binary words 1110, 0111, 1100, then the address 040C and finally the ASCII code 43.

The final question to ask is: how does the microprocessor become aware that the operator has pressed a key? The answer to this depends on the mode of I/O transfer that is used: programmed mode with polling, or interrupt mode. Every key touch triggers an interrupt request or sets to '1' a status bit which is tested regularly by the microprocessor.

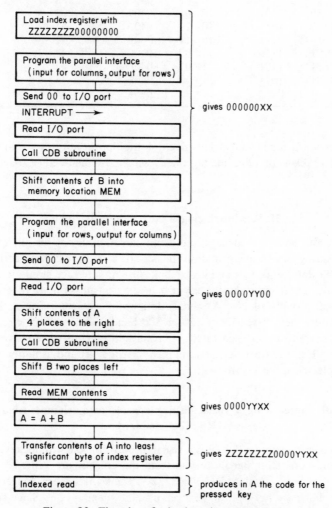

Figure 80. Flowchart for keyboard management

130

Table XXII. Binary words, address, and code for each key of the hexadecimal keyboard of Figure 78

N	Row	Contents	YY	XX	Index contents in hex	Memory address contents
0	1110	1110	00	00	0400	30
1	1110	1101	00	01	0401	31
2	1110	1011	00	10	0402	32
3	1110	0111	00	11	0403	33
4	1101	1110	01	00	0404	34
5	1101	1101	01	01	0405	35
6	1101	1011	01	10	0406	36
7	1101	0111	01	11	0407	37
8	1011	1110	10	00	0408	38
9	1011	1101	10	01	0409	39
A	1011	1011	10	10	040A	41
B	1011	0111	10	11	040B	42
C	0111	1110	11	00	040C	43
D	0111	1101	11	01	040D	44
E	0111	1011	11	10	040E	45
F	0111	0111	11	11	040F	46

This keyboard management has given us the opportunity to see in detail the important problem of table management, which we shall return to in the next chapter.

III.9. Interfacing a current-loop teletype

The teletype is a very frequently used communication device for microprocessor systems during the implementation phase. It is designed for receiving and transmitting data sequences and is also linked by an interface circuit to a UART; that is, to a serial interface for asynchronous transmission. It functions as a current loop, usually of 20 mA, and is designed for transmission at 110 baud. Certain models accept speeds of 150 or 300 bauds. The interface circuit, which allows a current to be generated or received, is constructed from several transistors (Figure 81(a)). The circuit can provide ground isolation by using photocouplers (Figure 81(b)).

III.10. Interfacing a visual display console or a teletype using the RS232C standard

When the communication device is a visual display console with its keyboard, the transfer and command signals to and from the console are generally designed using the American standard EIA – RS232C. The signals are no longer activated by current-intensity but by voltage level, usually + and −12 V. Since such levels are not TTL-compatible and cannot be provided by the microprocessor or its

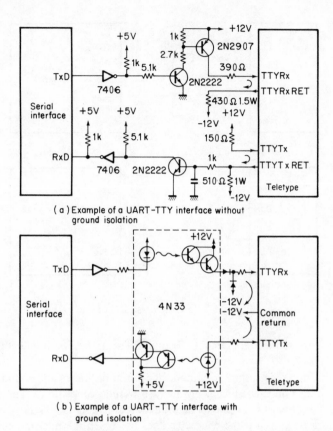

(a) Example of a UART–TTY interface without ground isolation

(b) Example of a UART–TTY interface with ground isolation

Figure 81. UART–TTY interface

associated circuits, a physical interface is interposed. Moreover, such interfacing is easily carried out using two integrated circuits developed by MOTOROLA – the MC1488 and the MC1489. Certain teletypes operate using the RS232C standard, and in this case the interfacing is identical to that of the visual display console. Note that the American RS232C standard has given rise to a CCITT European version which is called the V24 standard.

The transfers to and from the communication device can be made in 'half duplex' or in 'full duplex'. When a keyboard key is pressed the information is sent to the serial interface which transmits it to the microprocessor. In a 'full duplex' link, operation generally takes place in ECHO mode, which is a means of ensuring accurate information transmission. For this, the microprocessor displays on the console, or prints on the teletype, the character which it has just received. This method is also useful for clearing the keyboard which originated the character transfer. Two communication signals are provided, with this in mind, in the RS232C standard; these are the signals $\overline{RTS}$ and $\overline{CTS}$. However, these signals are only necessary for synchronous transmission. With a communication device the transmission is generally asynchronous and it then suffices, for the case of a 'full

132

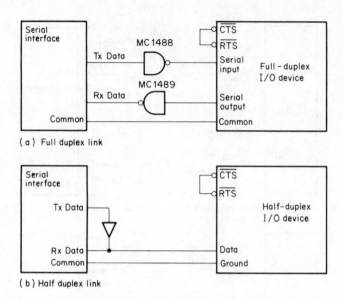

(a) Full duplex link

(b) Half duplex link

Figure 82. Interfacing an I/O device

duplex' link, to connect together $\overline{\text{CTS}}$ and $\overline{\text{RTS}}$ at the communication device (Figure 82(a)).

In a 'half duplex' link the serial input and serial output of the communication device are interconnected, which produces a pseudo-echo mode. The character typed on the keyboard is displayed or printed, and is done so directly, by a communication device, even if the character does not reach the microprocessor. The fact that the serial input and output are connected introduces one constraint on the logic level of the communication device: the latter is *always in a receiving mode except when transmitting*. The serial output is, therefore, always in a high impedance state, except during the transmission of a character. In this latter case, the signal is transmitted on the serial output of the communication device (pseudo-echo mode) and arrives on the Rx Data serial input of the serial interface. A unidirectional buffer prevents this signal from reaching the Tx Data serial output of the serial interface. When the serial interface sends a character to the communication device the signal emitted on Tx Data arrives on Rx Data (provided it is not busy), then passes along the serial input of the communication device without perturbing the serial output of the device, since this output is at high impedance. A 'full duplex' link is used whenever possible.

III.11. Interfacing a stepper motor

A stepper motor allows one to turn through an axis by a precise angle, this angle being *n* times the unit of angular displacement, which we call the STEP. This unit of angular displacement depends on the type of motor: it is either 7.5, 15, 45, or 90 degrees for large-angle motors; 1.8 or 5 degrees for small-angle motors. The

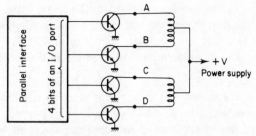

(a) Windings and interfacing circuits for a stepper motor

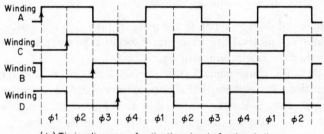

(b) Timing diagrams of activation signals for the windings

	A	B	C	D	←Windings
ϕ1	1	0	0	1	
ϕ2	1	0	1	0	
ϕ3	0	1	1	0	
ϕ4	0	1	0	1	

(c) Truth table for the activation of windings A, B, and C

Figure 83. Interfacing a stepper motor

displacement of the rotor by one step in one direction or the other, is obtained by the appropriate command to the four motor windings.

The signals applied to windings A and B are opposite in phase; the signals applied to windings C and D are also opposite in phase and, in addition, are 90 degrees out of phase with the signals applied to A and B (Figure 83(b)). These phase-shifts lead to four distinct phases ϕ1, ϕ2, ϕ3, and ϕ4 such that

during phase ϕ1 the windings A and D are activated;
during phase ϕ2 the windings A and C are activated;
during phase ϕ3 the windings B and C are activated;
during phase ϕ4 the windings B and D are activated.

The activation of the windings as a function of these four phases is given in the truth table of Figure 83(c). The four 4-bit words forming this table are put into memory and are sent one at a time to four outputs of a parallel interface I/O port.

A level '1' on one of these four outputs drives the power transistor, generally preceded by a Darlington stage, and the corresponding winding is activated, the winding serving as a load for the power transistor or **VMOS**. The order in which the four phases take place determines the direction of displacement of the motor:

(1) The sequence $\phi1$, $\phi2$, $\phi3$, $\phi4$, $\phi1$, $\phi2$, $\phi3$, $\phi4$, $\phi1$, $\phi2$, etc. produces a movement of the motor axis in a given direction (clockwise, for example);
(2) The sequence $\phi4$, $\phi3$, $\phi2$, $\phi1$, $\phi3$, $\phi2$, $\phi1$, $\phi4$, $\phi3$, etc. produces a movement of the motor axis in the opposite direction (anti-clockwise, for example).

Each phase is given a concrete realization in the following way:

(1) The 4-bit word corresponding to the phase is loaded in the parallel interface. Those outputs at level '1' drive the associated power transistors and the corresponding windings are activated;
(2) This 4-bit word is maintained in the interface for a time θ defined by a timer. The duration of the phase is therefore approximately equal to θ.
(3) At the end of the time θ the next 4-bit word is loaded in the parallel interface and the above process is repeated for the next phase.

The displacement speed of the motor is determined by the value of θ and by the supply voltage to the windings. When the displacements to be made are large it is possible to increase the displacement speed of the rotor by using the technique of *overactivation*.

This consists of taking a supply voltage to the windings at a value much higher than the nominal value (24 V, for example, instead of 5 V), this value being used at the beginning of each phase for just a small fraction of the phase duration (100 ms, for example). This technique increases the motor torque considerably.

Overactivation is generally used in conjunction with another technique called *overspeed*. This consists of modulating the speed of displacement of the rotor in cases where the displacement is large enough to justify such a technique. Starting from its nominal value, the speed is increased gradually until it reaches a maximum steady value. This steady value is maintained for a certain time and then the speed decreases gradually back to the nominal value, as shown in the graph of Figure 84(b). This curve is obtained by adjusting the duration, θ, of the phases. To each point on the graph, and therefore to each speed, there corresponds a value of θ. The successive different values of θ required to produce this graph are determined experimentally and then put into memory. They are then read out in turn and programmed into a timer. It is clear that these techniques of overactivation and overspeed justify using a microprocessor to drive a stepper motor (Figure 84).

III.12. Interfacing a cathode ray tube

We know that during the implementation phase of a microprocessor system a communication device is indispensable. The latter could be a visual display unit

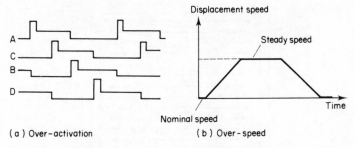

Figure 84. Over-activation and over-speed

(VDU), a teletype (TTY), or something equivalent. A visual display unit which comprises an ASCII keyboard and a cathode ray tube is available commercially and manufactured by a number of firms, but the price is relatively high. Instead, it is possible to obtain a 'cathode ray tube' by using an ordinary television set and an LSI integrated circuit called a *CRT controller*. The cost of a black and white television set is low and do-it-yourself enthusiasts can easily buy a second-hand set cheaply. Certain industrial applications require messages to be shown on the screen and here, too, a CRT controller will be desirable.

III.12.1. Operating principles of a television set

A television transmitter transmits a UHF signal (called the carrier), which is frequency-modulated by the transmitted picture and sound signals. The UHF signal is received by the television aerial. The carrier undergoes a frequency change and yields an intermediate frequency of 4.5 MHz. After amplifcation, the new signal passes into a 'video detector' circuit whose function is to carry out electronic detection so as to reconstitute the combined image and sound signals, which form the *video signal*. The latter is sent successively to different circuits linked to the television cathode ray tube with the aim of

(1) Suppressing the carrier;
(2) Separating out the image signal, sound signal, and synchronization pulses;
(3) Amplifying the image signal so as to modulate efficiently the intensity of the spot on the cathode ray tube. In this way we create, on the screen, a more or less distinct dot;
(4) Amplifying the sound signal and sending it to the loudspeaker;
(5) Sending HORIZONTAL SYNC pulses for the horizontal flyback of the spot and VERTICAL SYNC pulses for the vertical flyback of the spot.

In fact, in a television set, the image is formed by a cluster of electrons forming a point on the screen, called the SPOT. This spot scans the screen from the top left-hand corner and generates several hundred horizontal lines going from left to right and from top to bottom (Figures 85 and 86). During the flyback of the spot from right to left and from bottom to top the luminosity is zero so that the return

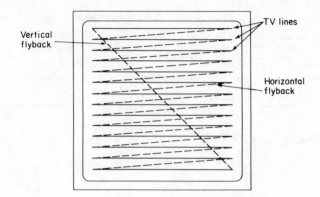

Figure 85. Sweeping a cathode ray tube

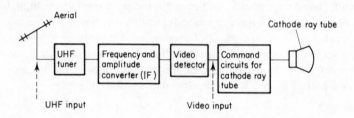

Figure 86. Schematic of television set principles

is invisible. The image signal modulates the luminosity of the screen during all these line scans in such a way as to construct the transmitted image.

The collection of lines on the screen forms a FRAME. Of course, these lines are sufficiently close together for the spaces between them to be invisible to the eye, taking into account the sharpness of human vision.

Note. Another possibility is to produce the complete image on the screen starting with two interlaced frames: this is a technique known as *interlacing*.

III.12.2. The principles of character display on a cathode ray tube

In order to display characters on the screen we form each character by illuminating appropriate points in a collection of points which are disjoint but sufficiently close for the eyes not to perceive the unlit spaces within the character (Figure 88). We can already note two important differences in comparison with television set operation:

(1) On the one hand, in a television set the intensity of the cluster of electrons is variable, but continuous, for each line scan, which we shall call a TV line. By contrast, for displaying characters, the intensity of the cluster of electrons is discontinuous, since it is a matter of displaying not so much a line but a collection of aligned and equidistant points.

(2) On the other hand, in a television set the spot-intensity can take on any value so as to produce all shades between black and white. For displaying characters using two shades (and two only) we require just white (illuminated point) and black (unlit point).

These two differences are fundamental since they take us from an analog modulation of the spot, in the case of the television set, to a logical modulation of the spot, in the case of character display. In fact, in the latter case the signal modulating the intensity of the cluster is a logic signal, since a line is a collection of points which are close but discontinuous.

This fundamental property is illustrated in Figure 87. Figure 87(a) shows the realization of a TV line as a succession of points (squares, to be precise, in our diagram) and they alone have the possibility of being illuminated by the spot. This means that if we want an entire line to appear white on the screen we illuminate all the points in Figure 87(a). This gives the modulation signal of Figure 87(b), which is, of course, a logic signal. Apart from its amplitude, the signal is simply a clock: more precisely, it is obtained by means of a clock with the given frequency and phase, called the DOT CLOCK, whose amplitude conforms to logic level '1' of the technology used (for example, 3.5 V for TTL technology). We note that the analog signal of Figure 87(b) is the VIDEO SIGNAL. We recall that in this example of displaying a complete white line the illuminated points are sufficiently close for the eye to gain the impression of continuity.

The display of alphanumeric characters, made up from dots, requires certain dots of Figure 87 to be lit up and others not to be. Figure 87(c) represents an example of a TV line, while Figure 87(d) shows the corresponding video signal. Since each dot can either be illuminated or not, we can, very simply, represent a dot which has to be lit by a logic '1' (Figure 87(e)). This results in an alphanumeric character which is, we recall, a suitable configuration of lit dots within a rectangular matrix of dots, perhaps represented by several bit-configurations and thus by several binary words, as shown in Figure 88. Figure 88(a) shows the visual image of the letter E using a 5 x 7 dot matrix. This matrix is itself embedded in a 7 x 10 dot matrix. In fact, the characters have to be separated from each other

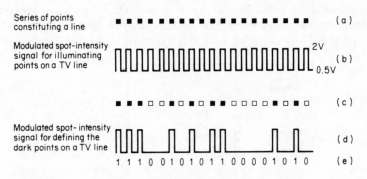

Series of points constituting a line (a)

Modulated spot-intensity signal for illuminating points on a TV line (b)

(c)

Modulated spot-intensity signal for defining the dark points on a TV line (d)

1 1 1 0 0 1 0 1 0 1 1 0 0 0 0 1 0 1 0 (e)

Figure 87. Modulated spot-intensity signal for a TV line in the character display example

138

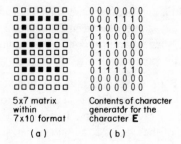

5x7 matrix
within
7x10 format

Contents of character
generator for the
character **E**

(a)   (b)

Figure 88. Representation of the
character **E** in a 5 × 7 matrix

by the same amount horizontally as vertically, in order to be pleasing to the eye. Thus, in 7 x 10 format the first and seventh columns are never lit, neither are the first and tenth rows. The ninth row is used to underline a character if this is required. The character E can be considered as a collection of ten 7-bit words stored in a dedicated memory. The same applies to all other characters. The ten 7-bit words for each alphanumeric character will be arranged in a ROM or PROM called a *character generator*. To represent a character completely on the screen, ten TV lines will be necessary since each row of Figure 88 will have to be displayed as a TV line. In order to display a character, therefore, we need to access the character generator ten times and to supply ten distinct addresses to it, remembering that it is nothing more than dedicated memory. To do this, the address of a 7-bit word in the memory is composed of two parts:

(1) A 7-bit address specific to the character to be displayed. This address is simply the ASCII code of the character. We shall call this the CHARACTER ADDRESS;

(2) A 4-bit address specific to the line of dots (or TV line) to be displayed and therefore indicating the number of the corresponding 7-bit word. We shall call this the TV LINE ADDRESS.

Thus we see that, in the case of 7 x 10 format, ten TV lines are necessary for representing a row of characters. We shall call this row of characters a LINE OF TEXT, or a ROW if we wish to distinguish it from the TV line (Figure 89).

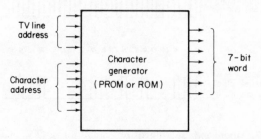

Figure 89. Character generator

III.12.3. The principle of generating addresses and synchronization signals for text display on a screen

A cathode ray tube permits the display of several lines of text, each consisting of several characters. To explain, as clearly as possible, the principle of generating addresses and the HORIZONTAL SYNC and VERTICAL SYNC signals (which we have already met), we are going to describe the case of a screen which allows the display of four lines of text, each of four characters. To be even more specific, let us suppose that the text to be displayed on our screen is (Figure 90(a)):

EPI

ROSE

1980

END

This text for display is stored in RAM memory, by a microprocessor, for example, so that we can access it easily, as often as required. In fact, for all our text to appear on the screen the spot must scan the screen at least twenty-five times a second with the same text, to avoid a visually unstable image. This implies that the RAM memory has to be accessed many times for each character. For this reason, the RAM is sometimes called the REFRESH MEMORY; we shall call it the SCREEN MEMORY. It contains, in our example, the ASCII code for each of the 16 characters to be displayed. The fourth character in the first line of the text is the 'space' or 'blank' character which in ASCII code is equal to 00100000 or 20

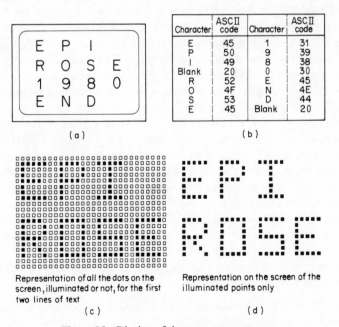

Character	ASCII code	Character	ASCII code
E	45	1	31
P	50	9	39
I	49	8	38
Blank	20	0	30
R	52	E	45
O	4F	N	4E
S	53	D	44
E	45	Blank	20

(a)   (b)

Representation of all the dots on the
screen, illuminated or not, for the first
two lines of text

(c)

Representation on the screen of the
illuminated points only

(d)

Figure 90. Display of the text on our screen

hexadecimal. The sixteen characters to be displayed will be stored in contiguous addresses, the E of the EPI in the lowest address, the P in the following address and the space following the letter D in the highest address. In Figure 90(c) we have represented all the dots in the upper half of our screen, indicating in black the dots which have to be lit. The white squares of the unlit dots do not appear on the screen, so that the latter displays the characters as shown in Figure 90(d). Of course, the illuminated dots will be much closer together on a real screen. The clock, which we shall call the DOT CLOCK, consists of $4 \times 7 = 28$ pulses for each TV line. A complete frame, that is, a scan of the whole screen, requires 28×10 TV lines x 4 lines of text = 1120 clock pulses. Since we must scan at least twenty-five times a second, to ensure a continuous retinal image, our dot clock must have a minimal frequency of $1120 \times 25 = 2800$ Hz. Every seven pulses of this clock we must pass to the following character on the line of text by incrementing the text line address and by sending a read command to the screen memory.

To do this, the dot clock is sent to a divide-by-7 circuit whose output is the CLOCK CHARACTER. This serves as input for a modulo 4 counter called the CHARACTER COUNTER and for a READ signal to the screen memory. The two output bits of this counter form the CHARACTER ADDRESS. The character counter serves also as a divide-by-4; for this purpose, it produces a clock with frequency $f_2 = f/(7 \times 4) = f/28$. Each pulse of this clock corresponds to the end of a TV line and is used, therefore, to control the horizontal flyback of the spot and the incrementing of the TV line. Such a clock is called the HORIZONTAL SYNC clock. Every ten TV lines, and therefore every ten pulses of the HORIZONTAL SYNC signal, it is necessary to increment the text line number. This same signal also functions as a clock input to a modulo 10 counter, which we shall call the TV LINE COUNTER. This counter can also be used as a divide-by-10, which then delivers a signal with frequency $f_3 = f_2/10$ to serve as input to a further modulo 4 counter called the TEXT LINE COUNTER, whose content is the TEXT LINE ADDRESS. This latter counter is now used as a divide-by-4 and the output of this division is the vertical flyback command for the spot; that is, the VERTICAL SYNC signal.

The collection of circuits shown in Figure 91 ensures that for every seven pulses of the dot clock the character generator sends a 7-bit word to a 7-bit shift register. These bits are serialized during the following seven dot-clock pulses and are sent to the video input of the television set, with all-or-nothing modulation of the cathode ray tube, so long as the bit issuing from the shift register is '1' or '0'.

The signals which we have just been discussing are shown in Figures 92 and 93 for our example of a screen having four lines of text each of four characters.

Figure 94 shows that the video signal also contains vertical synchronization pulses. These synchronization pulses and the all-or-nothing intensity modulation pulses are sent to a mixer circuit, whose output is a composite video signal which can have three possible amplitudes:

(1) Amplitude of 0 V (representing INFRABLACK). This level corresponds to the synchronization pulses;

(2) Amplitude of 0.5 V (representing BLACK). This level denotes the absence of illumination.

(3) Amplitude of 1.5 to 5 V, depending on the cathode ray tube (representing WHITE). This level corresponds to the illuminated points on the screen.

The composite video signal output can be sent directly to a television video input (see Figure 86). If the video input of the television set is not easily accessible it is always possible to send the video signal through a UHF modulator whose output can then be sent to the television set's aerial input. This is the solution used in television games packages.

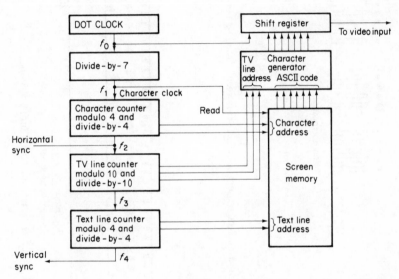

Figure 91. Circuits generating H-SYNC and V-SYNC as well as different addresses

III.12.4. Features and characteristics of a visual display screen

III.12.4.1. Visual display formats

(1) Number of characters and lines of text. At present, the standard format consists of sixteen lines of text each of thirty-two characters, but other formats are, of course, possible.

(2) Dot matrix for character representation. The two main formats for this matrix are 5 x 7 (which we chose in our example) and 7 x 9, which is more useful for representing lower-case letters. To either of these basic formats are added blank rows and columns for separating the characters, at least one row above and one column each on the right and left. Underneath, there are often several rows, one of

142

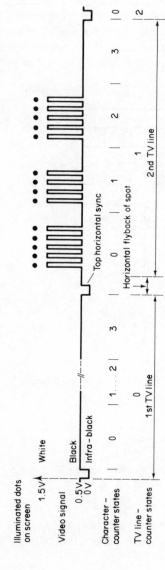

Figure 92. Video signals and character-counter states for a sweep of the first two TV lines

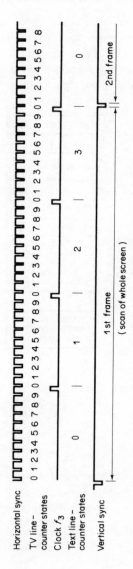

Figure 93. Counter signals and states during a frame scan

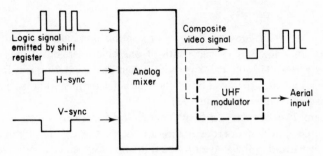

Figure 94. Obtaining the composite video signal

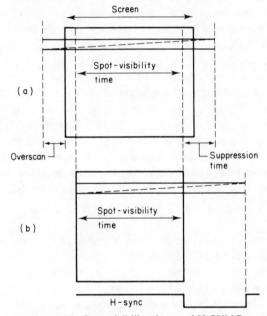

Figure 95. Spot-visibility time and H-SYNC

which is used for underlining a character (UNDERLINE); its thickness can be
one, or many, TV lines.

(3) Time. The actual time taken up by a TV line spot is greater than the time
required simply to scan the visible part of the screen, since one must add on the
duration of the horizontal synchronization pulses. During these pulses, the spot
has to be unlit. Moreover, the spot never illuminates the complete screen. For a
graphic illustration of the different times it is current practice to use the set-up
shown in Figure 95(a), where the useful scan time for a TV line is incremented by
two 'suppression times' during which the spot is unlit. Figure 95(b) is an alterna-
tive way of representing the different times; it consists of taking the spot-visibility
time and adding to it the duration of a horizontal synchronization pulse required
for the horizontal flyback.

144

III.12.4.2. Other features

(1) Cursor. The cursor can be a flashing or non-flashing indicator. This indicator is usually an underline having the width of one character, but it may also be a square or an arrow. This indicator is useful when one is entering text from a keyboard: it then indicates the position of the character pointer (that is, the contents of the character counter of Figure 91).

(2) Light pen. The light pen is a tiny· photoelectric cell to which are attached electronic circuits which operate a flip-flop when the cell is illuminated. The system is constructed in the shape of a pen, the tip of which is a photoelectric cell. When the light pen is brought up to the screen and is activated by operating a push-button, the flip-flop changes to state '1' when the spot illuminates the cell, in other words, when the character the pen is pointing at is displayed by the spot. This transition of the flip-flop to '1' can be used for recording the co-ordinates for the character that the pen is pointing at (these co-ordinates being the text line number and the character number within the line).

(3) SCROLL. This possibility consists of scrolling up the text on the screen. For this one must be able to preset the address of the first line of the text.

(4) Altering a character or a group of characters. It is sometimes necessary to alter one or more characters easily. Let us suppose, therefore, that an operator X transmits text to an operator Y who receives the text on a cathode ray tube. If he detects an incorrect character he signals this fact to operator X. It is then desirable that the latter be able to alter, easily, the incorrect character. In this situation, operator Y requires a technique for pinpointing the character. Several techniques are possible:

(a) Video inversion: the character or group of characters to be altered appear as black-on-white instead of white-on-black;
(b) High intensity: the character or group of characters to be altered is illuminated more brightly than the others;
(c) Flashing: the character or group of characters to be altered flashes at a frequency either fixed in advance or program-selected from several possible frequencies;
(d) Underlining: the character or group of characters to be altered is underlined.

(5) Special graphics. These special graphics enable the formation of geometric figures such as those shown in Figure 96. They are not part of the character generator.

(6) Reducing the load on the DMA controller. We shall see in the next section that a screen memory is not necessary provided we use a DMA controller. In order to disturb the operation of the microprocessor as little as possible we must not use the DMA controller when the processor is involved in searching memory for a row of 'blanks' that terminate a line of text (or even the whole frame when the final text lines are composed solely of blanks).

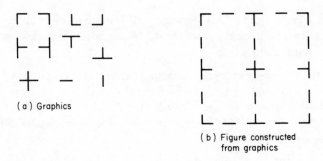

(a) Graphics

(b) Figure constructed
from graphics

Figure 96. Special graphics and their uses

III.12.5. Transfers to and from the microprocessor

III.12.5.1. Using a screen memory. The text to be displayed is first stored in the screen memory. For a screen connected to a microprocessor system this store operation is performed by the microprocessor.

The screen memory, therefore, receives its address

(1) Either from the microprocessor address bus when the latter writes a character into RAM;
(2) Or from the text line counter linked to the character counter during the scan of the screen.

An address-multiplexing circuit is therefore required. The fact that the microprocessor has priority leads to the simplest scheme. The multiplexer is controlled by the CS SCREEN MEMORY ADDRESS signal sent by the microprocessor. The microprocessor data bus has to be capable of being connected to the screen memory inputs for writing into this memory and also to the outputs in order to read the contents of the memory. Additionally, a bi-directional buffer has to be inserted between the data bus and the input/output pins of the screen memory. During the microprocessor operations of reading and writing the screen memory the memory output should not be sent to the character generator. Also, a further buffer, this time uni-directional, should be inserted between the screen memory outputs and the address inputs from the character generator ROM. Only the microprocessor can send a write command to the screen memory. On the other hand, as far as the read command for this memory is concerned, such a command can either be that of the microprocessor MEMORY READ or can be from the character clock. The screen-memory read command is therefore provided by a multiplexer output selected by using CS SCREEN MEMORY ADDRESS as the multiplexer address.

III.12.5.2. Using dual line-buffers. Everything we have so far seen concerning text display on a cathode ray tube has presupposed the use of screen memory containing the text to be displayed. This latter text is written into screen memory by the microprocessor, from its RAM memory. It is quite possible not to use screen memory but, instead, to treat part of the RAM as such. In this case, the following two factors require attention:

(1) Arbitration of memory cycle requests that are addressed to RAM by the microprocessor and by the interface circuits of the cathode ray tube;
(2) The high frequency of transfers between the RAM and the interface circuits of the cathode ray tube, which makes the microprocessor considerably slower in program execution.

These two problems, fortunately, have a common solution: this is to use a DMA controller, linked to two line buffers, where the latter denotes a register having a large capacity (80 ASCII characters, for example). The screen memory is replaced by a line buffer containing all the characters of the line of text. To avoid having to alter the line buffer after the display of each line of text, two line buffers are used. While one is being emptied onto the screen the other is being filled from RAM. This replenishment of one or other of the line buffers, so as to obtain a complete screen display, is a sequence which needs to be repeated indefinitely. The collection of characters in a frame forms a block of data which the DMA controller can easily transfer from RAM into the line buffers in its 'auto-load' mode, since the parameters of the block are constant. Thus the cathode ray tube interface circuits have to address transfer requests regularly to the DMA controller. Each transfer is of one or more characters and is preceded by one or two clock cycles to allow the DMA controller to take control of the bus; in the same way, the transfer is followed by one or two clock cycles to allow the microprocessor to regain bus control. It is therefore desirable to transfer several characters at once so as not to waste too many cycles in removing or returning bus control (Figure 97).

III.12.6. CRT controller

The leading microprocessor manufacturers have designed an LSI circuit which performs the main functions necessary for interfacing a visual display unit: this integrated circuit is called a CRT CONTROLLER. A CRT controller usually generates

(1) The character address;
(2) The TV line address;
(3) The text line address;
(4) The H SYNC signal;
(5) The V SYNC signal.

In addition it provides:

(1) Cursor management;
(2) Light pen management

and various other possibilities which we have mentioned.

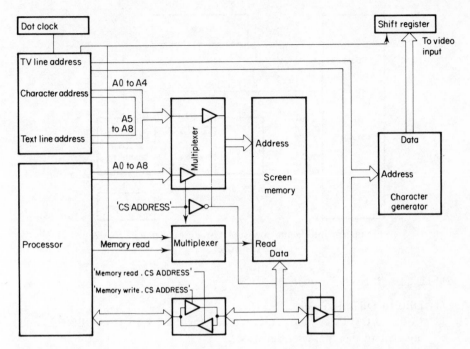

Figure 97. Connection of screen memory and a character generator to a microprocessor

The CRT controller is, of course, a programmable circuit so that it can be adapted for a large number of different screens. In addition, different formats and characteristics can be programmed by the user.

III.12.7. Application to the INTEL 8275 controller

This CRT controller is designed for data transfers to/from RAM by means of an intermediate DMA controller (Figure 98).

III.12.7.1. The registers of the 8275 controller. This controller has three registers:

(1) A COMMAND REGISTER (8 bits), known as CREG, which can only be written;
(2) A PARAMETER REGISTER (8 bits), which can be both read and written. As the name suggests, it allows one to send, to the 8275 controller, the different parameters required for its operation;
(3) A STATUS REGISTER (8 bits), which can only be read, and so can have the same address as the command register.

This means that a single address bit, A0, suffices for selecting the registers.

A0 = 0 PARAMETER REGISTER SELECTED
A0 = 1 STATUS OR COMMAND REGISTER SELECTED

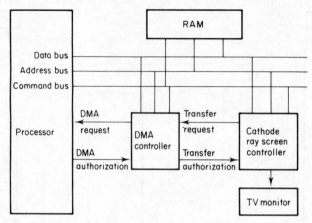

Figure 98. Interfacing a visual display screen to a DMA
controller

III.12.7.2. The 8275 signals

(1) DB0 to DB7: Data bus.
(2) LC0 to LC3: these four output bits are for the TV LINE ADDRESS and are sent to the character generator.
(3) CC0 to CC6: these seven output bits, provided by the line buffer, are the ASCII code of the character to be displayed. They are sent to the character generator.
(4) HRTC (HORIZONTAL RETRACE): this is the HORIZONTAL SYNC output.
(5) VRTC (VERTICAL RETRACE): this is the VERTICAL SYNC output.
(6) VSP (VIDEO SUPPRESSION): this signal sets the video signal to the black level during the horizontal or vertical flyback of the spot and at various other times when the spot is scanning the screen.
(7) CCLK (CHARACTER CLOCK): this input is the CHARACTER CLOCK. We note that the 8275 controller expects the CHARACTER CLOCK rather than the DOT CLOCK, which requires that one or the other be generated by external logic.
(8) $\overline{\text{RD}}$ read signal (input) linked to $\overline{\text{I/OR}}$ of the processor.
(9) $\overline{\text{WR}}$ write signal (input) linked to $\overline{\text{I/OW}}$ of the processor.
(10) DRQ: this is the TRANSFER REQUEST output addressed to the DMA controller.
(11) $\overline{\text{DACK}}$: this is the TRANSFER ACKNOWLEDGE input received by the DMA controller.
(12) $\overline{\text{IRQ}}$: this is the INTERRUPT REQUEST output. The 8275 offers a number of possibilities, but these can lead, in certain cases (i.e. certain uses of the 'attributes' — see later), to poor programming of the 8275. It is then necessary to modify the parameters. This is done at the end of a frame. The 8275 then indicates the end of the frame by an interrupt.
(13) A0: register selection bit linked to the A0 bit of the address bus.

(14) $\overline{CS}$: chip select input.
(15) LPEN (LIGHT PEN): input signal which receives from the CRT the information that the address register of the light pen has been loaded.
(16) HLGT (HIGH LIGHT): output signal sent by the 8275 to the CRT for high intensity.
(17) RVV (REVERSE VIDEO): output signal sent by the 8275 to the CRT for a reverse video command.
(18) LTEN: this output enables the 'underline' display when at level '1', even if VSP is active.
(19) LA0, LA1, GPA0, GPA1: outputs used with the attributes.

These latter 'attributes' offered by the 8275 are:

(1) Reduction of the DMA controller load; and
(2) Altering a character or a group of characters.

We note also that the 8275 has a FIFO option which allows the number of characters per line to be extended without modifying the parameters. In order to do this the 8275 possesses two FIFO queues of sixteen times 7 bits, which allows the capacity of the line buffers to be increased when one wishes to insert blanks.

III.12.7.3.   Programming the 8275.

(A) The 8275 COMMANDS

(1) INITIALIZATION command. This consists of sending the hexadecimal value 00 to the command register and sending four successive parameters to the parameter register. The parameters are chosen as shown in Figure 99. In this diagram, parameters $N1, N2, N3, N4$, and $N6$ are coded in binary (more precisely, it is their values decremented by one, $N1 - 1, N2 - 1$, etc., which have to be coded in binary). This command suppresses the interrupts and transfer requests and activates the VSP (VIDEO SUPPRESSION) signal.
(2) CURSOR POSITIONING command. The position of the cursor is defined by the position of the character at which it has to be placed: this is given by

(1) The number of the text line; and
(2) The number of the character within this text line.

Initially, the cursor is positioned at the first character on the screen; in other words, the top left-hand corner of the screen, having the co-ordinates $X, Y: X = 0$, $Y = 0$.
To control the cursor position requires reading the command word 80H into the command register, followed by two successive parameters into the parameter register. The elements of this command are:

COMMAND WORD   : 80H
PARAMETER 1   : number of the character within the line of text
PARAMETER 2   : text line number.

(3) COUNTER PRELOAD command. Apart from the horizontal and vertical

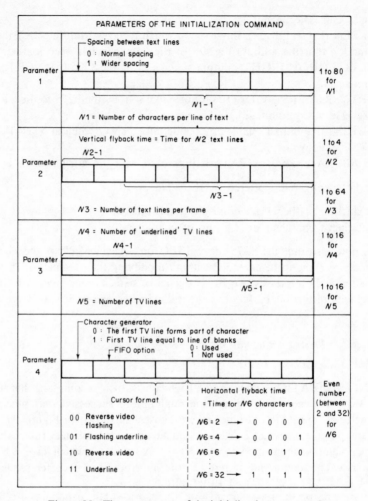

Figure 99. The parameters of the initialization command

flyback times, the spot at any given moment scans one character position within a TV line. This character position is defined by

(1) The text line number;
(2) The character number within this line of text.

These two numbers are provided by the text line counter and the character counter. The aim of the 'counter preload' command is to initialize these counters so that the first character displayed is the first screen character (top left-hand corner). The only element of this command is:

COMMAND WORD   : E0H

After this command, the counters stay in this state until there is some other command.

(4) START DISPLAY command. This command enables the video signal, which was maintained at black level by the initialization command and also activates the interrupt and transfer requests, which place the corresponding status bits in the status register. The command word is defined as shown in Figure 100.

These four commands that we have just considered are sufficient for the 8275 circuit to control the cathode ray tube. However, the circuit also has some further commands.

(5) READ LIGHT PEN REGISTERS command. This command permits one to read the register contents which define the character pinpointed by the light pen. For this, the transmission of the command word is followed by two reads of the parameter register, so that the elements of this command are

COMMAND WORD   : 60H
FIRST PARAMETER READ : character number within the line of text
SECOND PARAMETER READ : text line number.

(6) HALT DISPLAY command. This command disables the video signal as soon as a 'halt display' command arrives:

COMMAND WORD   : 40H

(7) INTERRUPT DISABLE command. This command disables interrupt requests which had initially been enabled by the 'start display' command:

COMMAND WORD : C0H

(8) INTERRUPT ENABLE command. This command re-enables interrupt requests:

COMMAND WORD : A0H

(B) Reading the 8275 status register. The 'interrupt request' status bit is set at '1', if interrupts are enabled, at the start of the display of the final line of text. This

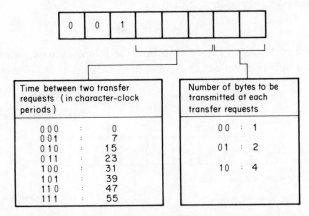

Figure 100. Format of the START DISPLAY command
word

allows the microprocessor to load the DMA controller parameters before a new frame is displayed. This loading of parameters is required when SCROLLING (i.e. shifting the text file up the screen). The status bits IR, LP, IC, DU, and FIFO are reset automatically to zero after the status register is read.

(C) 8275 attributes. INTEL has used the term 'attributes' to refer to certain features of the 8275 such as graphical displays, reduction of the DMA controller's task, and so on. In order to keep our account fairly short and uncomplicated, we shall not go into the details of these 'attributes' in this book.

(D) Example of 8275 programming. Let us assume the following set of conditions:

(1) 80 characters per line of text;
(2) 25 lines of text;
(3) Characters represented by a 5 x 7 matrix within a 7 x 10 matrix, the cursor being on the ninth line in the flashing underlined format;
(4) Frequency of screen refresh: 60 Hz;
(5) Horizontal flyback time: 20 character clock periods;
(6) Vertical flyback time: twice the duration of a TV line scan;
(7) Normal spacing for lines of text;
(8) FIFO option disabled;
(9) 2^7 bit of parameter 4 at zero;
(10) 4 bytes transferred by DMA;
(11) 15 character clock periods between two transfer requests.

The frequency of the H SYNC signal is then

F_{HS} = 60 frames per second x (25 + 2) lines of text per frame x 10 TV lines per line of text;

F_{HS} = 60 x 27 x 10 = 16,200 Hz

The timer period of the signal is then

$$T_{HS} = 1/F_{HS} = 1/16,200 = 61.73 \ \mu s$$

This period corresponds to the scan time for 80 characters, supplemented by the horizontal flyback time, which is equal to the scan time for 10 characters. The

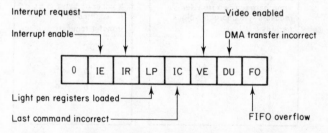

Figure 101. The 8275 status word

character clock period is thus

$$T_C = T_{HS}/(80 + 20) = 61.73/100 = 0.617 \ \mu s$$

so that

$$F_C = 1/T_C = 1/0.617 \times 10^6 = 1.62 \ \text{MHz.}$$

The frequency of the dot clock is

$$F_P = F_C \times 7 \ \text{dots per character} = 11.34 \ \text{MHz}$$

This high frequency necessitates a high operating speed for those logic circuits linked to the 8275 for TV monitor interfacing. These circuits have to provide the dot clock and the character clock of the 8275, as well as the H sync, V sync, and video signals to the TV monitor. If the monitor requires a time period incompatible with that provided by the 8275 for the H sync or V sync signals, then the signal can be provided by a monostable inserted between the 8275 output and the corresponding input of the TV monitor. The monostable needs to be triggered by the rising edge of the signal provided by the 8275.

The video signal to the TV monitor input is the serial output of the line buffer, modulated by two 8275 signals: VSP, whose role is to suppress the illumination of the spot, and LTEN, whose role is to illuminate the 'underline' of a character (even if VSP is activated). Figure 102 illustrates this modulation.

Let us return to programming the 8275.

We have, for the initialization command:

parameter 1 : 01001111 or 4FH
parameter 2 : 01011000 or 58H
parameter 3 : 10001001 or 89H
parameter 4 : 01011001 or 59H

If we enable the 8275 ($\overline{\text{CS}}$) by address bit A5, our addresses will be

11011110 or DE for the parameter register
11011111 or DF for the command and status registers,

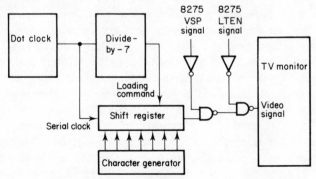

Figure 102. Principle of video-signal modulation by VSP and LTEN

154

which gives the following program for the 8275:

```
MVI   A,00H  ⎫  INITIALIZATION command word
OUT   DF     ⎭
MVI   A,4FH  ⎫
OUT   DE     ⎪
MVI   A,58H  ⎪
OUT   DE     ⎬  transmission of INITIALIZATION command parameters
MVI   A,89H  ⎪
OUT   DE     ⎪
MVI   A,59H  ⎭
OUT   DE
MVI   A,80H  ⎫  CURSOR POSITIONING command word
OUT   DF     ⎭

MVI   A,00H  ⎫
OUT   DE     ⎪  transmission of parameter for positioning the cursor in the
MVI   A,00H  ⎬  top left-hand corner of the screen
OUT   DE     ⎭
MVI   A,E0H  ⎫  COUNTER PRELOAD command word
OUT   DF     ⎭

MVI   A,2AH  ⎫  START DISPLAY command word
OUT   DF     ⎭
```

III.12.7.4. Interfacing scheme for the 8080A. Figure 103 shows the connections between the different circuits necessary for displaying characters on a cathode ray tube. These circuits form a card for interfacing a TV monitor. Thanks to the LSI 8275 controller, the number of integrated circuits is hardly more than a dozen, which means that this card is relatively easy to construct.

III.13. Interfacing a floppy disk or a mini-floppy disk

Floppy disks have appeared only recently, but they have developed rapidly because they are, in effect, direct access auxiliary memories with substantial reliability. An even more recent device is the mini-floppy disk, whose control is practically identical to that of floppy disk; this puts a low-cost and convenient storage medium onto the market. Diskettes and mini-diskettes have already made an impact on data collection, and in microprocessor development systems.

The mechanism of a floppy or mini-floppy disk requires currents which are large enough to drive motors. The currents are provided by electronic power circuits whose power is directly linked to mechanical devices. The mechanical system, together with the power circuits, forms a DRIVE, or a 'floppy-disk unit'. This drive is set up to receive command signals at TTL levels. All these control signals are implemented on the electronic board which constitutes the CONTROLLER board. The number of integrated circuits on this board has been

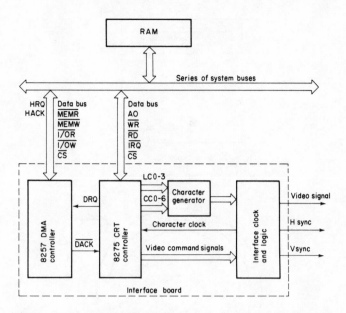

Figure 103. CRT interface board for the 8080A or the 8085A

reduced considerably following the very recent availability of LSI disk controllers, denoted by FDC (FLOPPY-DISK CONTROLLER), such as the well-known WESTERN DIGITAL FDC 1771 circuit.

In this section we shall study diskettes, clarifying, where necessary, the difference between diskettes and mini-diskettes.

III.13.1. Physical description of a floppy disk

The memory part of a diskette is provided by a floppy disk of flexible Mylar, whose surface is coated with magnetic oxide. This disk, with flat surfaces, turns at constant speed in a cardboard jacket, coated inside with a plastic material to reduce friction. In this cover, a radial slot permits the reading head to access all the disk tracks. The envelope contains at least one further aperture, this time circular and much smaller, through which a hole in the floppy disk can be noticed. This hole signals the beginning of each track and is called the INDEX; it is detected by a photo-electric cell placed on one side of the disk, which receives the light from a small lamp placed on the other side (Figure 104).

Like a hard disk, a floppy disk consists of concentric tracks divided into sectors (Figure 105). There are 77 tracks to each disk. Track 00, the furthest out, is the index channel. It is not used for data but for sectoring (in the soft-sectoring case), that is, for marking each sector-beginning. For certain diskettes, sectoring is accomplished by a series of holes in the diskette, one hole for the start of each sector. Tracks 75 and 76 are only used as replacements for one or two tracks which may have been found defective after several fruitless attempts at writing.

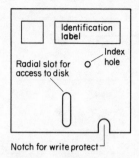

Figure 104. Floppy-disk appearance

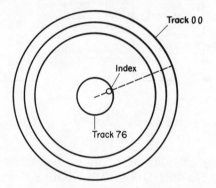

Figure 105. Tracks and index

The recording of data on a disk is carried out at single density (3268 bits per inch) or double density (6536 bits per inch). Moreover, certain floppy-disc drives are provided with two read/write heads which allow the storage of data on both sides of the disk.

In spite of its compact appearance, the floppy-disk unit often contains two 'drives' numbered 0 and 1.

The diskette is an auxiliary memory which is practical and reliable (Table XXIII). A holder placed at the side of the disk drive, containing several dozen floppy disks, allows one to store rather substantial files in a small space. Moreover, inserting and unloading floppy disks is simple and quick.

III.13.2. Formatting a floppy disk

As with a hard disk, identification data has to be placed on the floppy disk in order that data can be altered and recognized. This information is in zones called IDENTIFIERS. The sectors are separated by intervals called GAPS. Before writing data on a floppy disk one must position the identifiers and the gaps; this is called FORMATTING. Figure 106 shows the representation of data, identifiers, and gaps and also of marks, called ADDRESS MARKS, in the IBM 3740

Table XXIII. Diskette and mini-diskette characteristics

Characteristics	Diskettes	Mini-diskettes
Size	8 in. or 20.32 cm	5.25 in. or 13.33 cm
Number of tracks	76 tracks + index track	35 tracks + index track
Number of sectors per track	26	16
Number of bytes per sector	128	128
Density	3268 bits per inch for single density 6538 bits per inch for double density	3268 bits per inch for single density
Rotation speed	360 revolutions per minute	60 to 300 revolutions per minute
Capacity	253K bytes	94K bytes

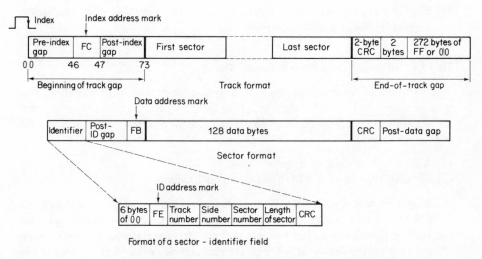

Format of a sector - identifier field

Figure 106. Format of information on a floppy disk

format. The CRC (CYCLIC REDUNDANCY CHECK) is a set of two control characters. This diagram shows that the formatting of data occupies a non-negligible space on the floppy disk. During the formatting operation the value 05 is provisionally given to each byte of data.

Formatting is not often carried out by the LSI diskette controller except for the INTEL 8271. It is thus necessary to write, in RAM, all the bytes for a given track of the floppy disk. Some high-level languages possess a formatting command.

III.13.3. Writing data to a floppy disk

The way in which information is physically recorded on a floppy disk depends on the technique chosen by individual diskette manufacturers; generally speaking,

158

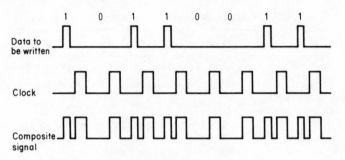

Figure 107. Data format

this involves frequency-modulation. On the other hand, information has to be sent to the floppy-disk unit using some well-defined format. This format involves the interlacing of clock pulses with the data bits at level '1', as shown in Figure 107. Writing and reading data is carried out in the normal way with the sector functioning as the unit of transfer.

III.13.4. Reading data from a floppy disk

The operation of reading data, like that of writing, occurs at the drive output. It is then necessary to extract the data bits from the composite signal and to perform a serial-parallel conversion of these bits. The extraction of the data bits is carried out

(1) Either with the aid of a monostable;
(2) Or with the aid of a PLO (phase-locked oscillator).

The gaps which are sets of FF (and thus of '1' bits) or of 00 (and thus of '0' bits) allow the monostable or the PLO to be synchronized by clock pulses after the read of the 00 bytes. The first bit of the address mark which follows (being always at '1') is then easily detected by the monostable or the PLO. This latter has the advantage of following the slow pulse variations and therefore of adapting itself, automatically, to the very small variations in speed of the floppy disk.

III.13.5. Positioning the head

We have seen that the floppy disk is always rotating. The writing head, situated above the radial slot in the cover, is at rest, situated at a sufficient distance from the disk to avoid any vibration. After every read or write operation we must send a command to position the head. The head positions itself above the correct track, then places itself on the track and is thus ready to read or write data.

III.13.6. Floppy-disk controller signals

To effect the different functions which we have just discussed the floppy-disk controller, in the form of a LSI circuit, must have certain minimum command or status signals, which are:

(1) 2 bits for *drive selection*. These bits allow one to select a floppy-disk drive when the controller controls a single dual-drive system. In fact, the system is equipped with two floppy-disk drives and can therefore control two floppy disks. This is necessary for duplicating files. Some LSI controllers can control several disks (in other words, several dual-drive set-ups) at the price of adding external multiplexer logic. In this case, the unit selected is encoded onto two drive select bits.

(2) DIRECTION. This output provides the floppy-disk drive with the direction in which the head should be displaced in order to position itself on the correct track.

(3) HEAD ADVANCE. This output signal moves the read/write head one step in the direction indicated by the preceding signal. One requires, on this output, as many pulses as are needed to move from one track to the next. Of course, this number of displacements will be programmed into the LSI controller. Some controllers, like the INTEL 8271, offer, as an option, the possibility of generating command pulses by external logic. The displacement time from one track to the next is generally programmable and is called *head-displacement time*. Once the head is positioned on the correct track one must wait for the head to stabilize: this is *head-stabilization time*.

(4) HEAD LOADING. This signal commands the read/write head to lower onto the floppy disk so as to be ready to perform a read or write operation.

These four command signals take care of head-positioning operations.

Note. In the case of a diskette the motor running the floppy disk is always turning. By contrast, for a mini-diskette the motor is generally cut after a read or write operation, provided that, within a few seconds of the end of the operation, no other operation has been called for. Setting the motor in motion has to be followed by a stabilization time of the order of 1 s.

(1) WRITE. This command enables the writing, onto the floppy disk, of the data on the DATA FOR WRITING output. These items of data have been previously serialized by the LSI controller.

(2) DATA FOR WRITING. This signal is the serial output for data.

(3) SAMPLING WINDOW. This signal is sent to the LSI controller by the monostable or the PLO when the floppy-disk unit sends a composite signal to the DATA READ input of the LSI controller.

(4) DATA READ. This signal signifies the serial input of data, in turn, into the monostable, or the PLO, and thence to the LSI controller (Figure 108).

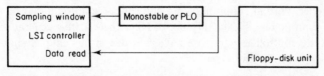

Figure 108. SAMPLING WINDOW and DATA READ signals

(5) PLO/MONO. This input signal tells the LSI controller whether the separa-
tion of data and the clock signals is carried out by a monostable or a PLO.
The sampling window is, in fact, different for these two circuits.

(6) TRANSFER REQUEST
(7) TRANSFER AUTHORIZATION } Signals for transferring data under
(8) INTERRUPT REQUEST direct memory access

(9) READY status bits. These bits indicate the ready status of one or other of
the floppy-disk drives. When the controller has to control several disks the
status of the selected disk is encoded onto two bits.

(10) TRACK 0. When the disk is powered up the program has to position the
read/write head at track 0 before any write or read operation. When this
positioning has been carried out the floppy-disk unit activates the TRACK 0
status bit.

(11) INDEX. On each rotation of the floppy disk the photo-electric cell which
detects the index hole sends a pulse to the LSI controller signalling the beginning of the track: this is called the index.

(12) WRITE PROTECT. Each floppy disk has a notch, detected by an optical
sensor, which stops any writing onto the floppy disk. In order to inhibit
writing one must introduce a special clamp into the notch so as to mask it. If
the clamp is present, the WRITE PROTECT status signal is activated.

These are the principal control signals of the disk controller. Of course, other
options and possibilities are often provided as extras, but they are not essential.

III.13.7. Programming a disk controller

Programming a disk controller is carried out by a set of commands whose aim is
to define the operating mode for the disk controller and to provide the latter with
all its necessary parameters. These are, in general:

(1) Head-displacement time;
(2) Head-stabilization time;
(3) Head-loading time;
(4) The number of defective tracks (two at most);
(5) The operation code to be performed;
(6) The floppy-disk address to which data will be transferred. The unit of transfer
is usually the sector. This address is therefore defined by the track number and
the sector number;
(7) The length of certain gaps.

Having outlined the most important commands to carry out for programming a
disk controller, the full study of such a controller would require a more detailed
treatment than is possible in this book. Nevertheless, the general information
about diskette controllers which we have provided in this chapter should make it
much easier to study any type.

Chapter IV

The software of microprocessor systems

The flowchart of Figure 1 has already shown us the various stages in the design and implementation of an industrial system. In Chapter 3 we studied various devices and the hardware problems associated with microprocessor-based systems. In this chapter we shall attempt to study software requirements for industrial application.

IV.1.   The various stages of writing software

IV.1.1.   Functional analysis

This is the partition of the system into functional blocks, each block corresponding to some large system function. Of course, this partitioning is carried out with the help of a system specification. For each block we must define its function, its inputs and outputs, and its interface to other blocks.

IV.1.2.   Detailed analysis

Each functional block is taken and divided into modules, each module carrying out a well-defined small task. Certain large blocks can be subdivided into sub-blocks which, in turn, can be subdivided into modules until the algorithm for the development of these modules becomes evident: this is called modular structured programming. For each of these blocks, sub-blocks, and modules a flowchart should be designed. Examples of modules are:

(1) Input operations;
(2) Output operations;
(3) Calculation of mathematical functions;
(4) Data look-up in a table;
(5) Transfer of a data block from one memory area to another.

161

This detailed analysis comprises

(1) Examination of the nature of input/output transfers, e.g. programmed mode with or without polling, interrupt mode with or without polling, direct memory access.
(2) Evaluation of interfaces. This means determining the nature of the interface, in the widest sense of the word, which should be used for communication between the microprocessor and its industrial environment. Where transmission is concerned the required type of transmission needs to be chosen; e.g. synchronous transmission, asynchronous transmission, HDLC procedure, SDLC procedure. Whenever there is an interface an exchange of data takes place and at this stage of the design the designer should make a point of highlighting the constraints as clearly as possible; e.g.
  (a) Average rate of data transfer;
  (b) Instantaneous constraints. Certain constraints and demands could, in the course of time, lead to high or very high (rather than average) transmission loads. The problem will become even worse if the demands all occur at once. We must, of course, make a list of these constraints and analyse their effect at the interface level. Timing factors associated with these instantaneous demands are one of the problems which can prevent an industrial system from operating satisfactorily in all the situations where it is expected to serve.
(3) Evaluation of memories. Should static or dynamic memories be chosen?
(4) Evaluation of controllers. What sort of controllers should be used? What tasks should be assigned to them?

The results of this functional analysis should be assembled in a document called a system analysis report.

IV.1.3. The programs

Each flowchart describing a module is translated into a program, which is often a subroutine that can be used to implement several functional blocks: such a subroutine is often called a *utility subroutine* or, simply, *a utility*.

A subroutine will normally take one or more parameters or *arguments*. These should be set up in registers or memory locations by the calling program, rather than in the subroutine itself. If, for example, a timing subroutine is to produce an N ms delay, the quantity N would probably be the argument to the subroutine. If the number N were to be loaded in an index register, this register would constitute the subroutine's input and the subroutine will presume that the number N has been preloaded into that register. All programs calling this utility must preload the argument N into the index register, which will then transmit this argument to the subroutine. Were this value to be set up within the subroutine only a single delay value could be produced.

A subroutine may also pass one or more output parameters back to the calling program. These, and any inputs to the subroutine, should be documented at the start of the routine, as should the registers overwritten by the subroutine and, of course, the purpose of the routine. Together this information constitutes a heading which will be considered as a comment. For example:

```
MODULE       : ADEC
OBJECT       : DECIMAL ADDITION OF 4 BYTES
INPUTS       : FIRST OPERAND ADDRESS = (HL) 4 BYTES
             : SECOND OPERAND ADDRESS = (DE) 4 BYTES
OUTPUTS      : RESULT ADDRESS = (BC) 4 BYTES
REGISTERS
DESTROYED    : ALL
```

Every subroutine should be liberally commented and should be easy to understand. For this reason, any approach which allows the saving of one or two bytes, but which confuses the user, should only be adopted if the reasons for doing so are compelling.

IV.1.4. Translation and implementation

Programs written on paper in assembler or high-level languages are entered into memory by a service utility and translated into binary by another service utility; i.e. by an assembler, compiler, or interpreter. These service programs are a part of the development system.

IV.2. Assembler programming

Assembler programming avoids the longhand translation of programs into hexadecimal and allows the benefit of using various development tools for the implementation of these programs. A program written in *assembler*, also called *assembler language*, is a series of instructions presented in the forms of lines. This series of instructions is a *source program*. In order to be executed this program must be translated into binary. The hexadecimal representation of this binary program is the *object program*. The translation is carried out using a program devised by the manufacturer, which translates each assembler instruction into a binary instruction. This translation program is also called an *assembler*. Because of its length (several K-bytes), it is stored in auxiliary memory, usually a diskette, and when assembly (translation of a source program into binary) takes place, it is loaded into the development system RAM by a special command: ASM, for example.

IV.2.1. The fields of an assembler instruction

Every assembler language instruction consists of several separate parts called FIELDS, which, from left to right, are

The LABEL FIELD
The OP-CODE FIELD
The OPERAND FIELD
The COMMENT FIELD

An instruction always contains one or more of these fields. The fields are separated by at least one blank (space) and when the label field is missing it is replaced by a blank.

IV.2.1.1. The label field

INTEL	MOTOROLA
One to six alphanumeric characters	One to six alphanumeric characters
The first character should either be a letter of the alphabet or @ or ?	The first character should be a letter of the alphabet
A colon should follow the last character	The label should start with the first character of its field (not preceded by a blank)
Operation codes, names of pseudo-instructions and letters designating registers cannot be used as labels	Operation codes, directive names, and the letters A, B, and X, which designate registers, cannot be used as labels
A label should only exist as an instruction address in one place in the program	A label should only exist as an instruction address in one place in the program
When the first non-blank character of a line is the symbol ';', the whole line becomes a comment field. To leave a blank line, therefore, we only need to place a semicolon at the beginning of the line	When the first character of a line is the symbol '*', the whole line becomes a comment field. To leave a blank line, therefore, we only need to place an asterisk as the first character in the line

IV.2.1.2. The op-code field. This field contains either the mnemonic expression for an executable instruction or the mnemonic expression for one of the following pseudo-instructions or directives:

INTEL pseudo-instructions: DB, DS, DW, END, ENDIF, EQU, IF, ORG, SET, TITLE

MOTOROLA directives: END, EQU, FCB, FCC, FDB, MON, NAM, OPT, ORG, PAGE, RMB, SPC

The register, or registers, involved in an executable instruction for the 8080A are not listed in the op-code field, but in the operand field.

IV.2.1.3. The operand field. The operand field contains:

(1) The immediate addressing symbol for an instruction using this mode of addressing (only for the MOTOROLA 6800);
(2) The register, or registers, affected by such an instruction;
(3) The operand (if the instruction includes an operand) expressed as one or two bytes. This operand could be a number, a symbol, or an expression.

INTEL

(1) The operand can be a NUMBER in the form:

DECIMAL: written either without a suffix, or with an optional D suffix;

```
MVI   A,47
MVI   A,47D
LXI   H,2140
```

HEXADECIMAL: written with the suffix H and starting with a numeric character (0 to 9).
A zero should be inserted before every operand which starts with a hexadecimal letter;

```
MVI   A,7EH
MVI   A,0A5H
```

OCTAL: is written either with the suffix O, or Q;

```
MVI   A,47O
MVI   A,47Q
```

BINARY: is written with the suffix B;

```
MVI   A,11101000B
```

ASCII: is written between two primes;

```
MVI   A,'T'   (A = 54)
LXI   H,'BU'
```

(2) The operand can be a SYMBOL. In this case it is

(a) either LABEL or a MNEMONIC of 1 to 6 alphanumeric characters, the first being an alphabetic. This mnemonic cannot be a letter designating a register (A, B, C, D, E, H, L, M);

(b) or the SYMBOL $, designating the contents of the instruction location counter; that is, the address where the first byte of the instruction containing this $ symbol is located.

(3) The operand can be an EXPRESSION. This is a combination of symbols and numbers linked by the following arithmetic or logic operations:

+ addition of 2 operands

MOTOROLA

(1) The operand can be a NUMBER in the form:

DECIMAL: written without a prefix or suffix;

```
LDA A   #47
LDX     #2140
```

HEXADECIMAL: is written either with the prefix $, or with the suffix H;

```
LDA A   #$47
LDA A   #47H
```

OCTAL: written either with the prefix @, or with the suffix O or Q;

```
LDA A   #@47
LDA A   #47O
LDA A   #47Q
```

BINARY: is written either with the prefix % or with the suffix B;

```
LDA A   #%11101000
LDA A   #11101000B
```

ASCII: is written with the prefix ';

```
LDA A   #'T   (A = 54)
LDX     #'BU
```

(2) The operand can be a SYMBOL. In this case it is

(a) either LABEL or MNEMONIC of 1 to 6 alphanumeric characters, the first being a letter of the alphabet. This mnemonic cannot be a letter designating a register (A, B, X);

(b) or the SYMBOL designating the contents of the instruction location counter; that is, the address where the first byte of the instruction containing this symbol is located.

(3) The operand can be an EXPRESSION. This is a combination of symbols and numbers connected by the following arithmetic operations:

+ addition of 2 operands

− subtraction of 2 operands

– subtraction of 2 operands
* multiplication of 2 operands
/ integer division of 2 operands
MOD: this modulo operation gives the integer part after the division of the first operand by the second.
NOT : complement each operand bit.
AND : bitwise logical AND of operands
OR : bitwise logical OR of operands
XOR : bitwise logical EXCLUSIVE OR of operands
SHR : shift the first operand right by the number of positions specified in the second operand. Zeros introduced on the left.
SHL : shift, first operand left by the number of positions specified in the second operand. Zeros introduced on the right.
If : CONV = 14A3H
MVI   A,CONV SHL 8
is equivalent to
MVI   A,A3H
The operators MOD, SHL, SHR, NOT, AND; OR, XOR should be separated from their operand, or operands, by at least one blank.
The expressions are calculated in the following order:
(1) expressions in parentheses. The deepest parenthesized expression is the first to be calculated.
(2) *, /, MOD, SHL, SHR
(3) + , −
(4) NOT
(5) AND
(6) OR, XOR
Examples:
MVI   A,49H + 17/2
The operand is 73 + 08 = 81
LXI   H, $ + 12
if the first byte of this instruction is located at address 1000H
the operand is
1012H.

* multiplication of 2 operands
/ integer division of 2 operands.
The assembler calculates the expression from left to right, without parentheses, and without a priority order for the operators. A fractional result, total or partial, is rounded to the nearest whole number. The calculation of the expression is performed by the assembler at assembly time and not by the microprocessor at run time: for example;
LDA A   #$49 + 17/2
the operand is 73 + 08 = 81
LDX   #* + 12
if the first byte of this instruction is located at address $1000 then the operand is $1012.

NO LOGICAL OPERATORS FOR THE MOTOROLA ASSEMBLER

IV.2.1.4. The comment field. This is optional and is used by the programmer to describe the effect of the operation, but it is ignored by the assembler.

INTEL	MOTOROLA
The comment field should start with the symbol ';'	The comment field is not identified by any particular symbol other than the blank separating the fields
MVI A,12 ; contents of A = 12	LDA A #12 contents of A = 12

IV.2.2. Pseudo-instructions, or directives

Programming in assembler language always involves using assembly commands, which are called PSEUDO-INSTRUCTIONS by INTEL and DIRECTIVES by MOTOROLA. We shall study each of these assembly commands in turn.

IV.2.2.1. Initialization of the instruction location counter. In *The Use of Microprocessors* we saw that hexadecimal programming requires us to calculate the absolute address of the first byte of each instruction. This tedious chore does not occur with assembler programming. All that the programmer has to do is to define an absolute address to act as a starting point for the locating of the program; the first address of each individual instruction is then calculated by the assembler program. To define the absolute address of the first byte of the program we initialize the location counter with the required value. This is done using the assembly command called ORG by both INTEL and MOTOROLA. If this initialization is not carried out the assembler sets the location counter to zero.

INTEL	MOTOROLA
ORG 1000H	ORG $1000
MOV A,B	TBA
The instruction MOV A,B is located at hexadecimal address 1000. The next instruction will be located at 1001H.	The instruction TBA is located at hexadecimal address 1000. The next instruction will be located at $1001.

Several ORG assembly commands may occur in a program and the initialization values do not have to be in numerical order. The ORG command could also be used to place data tables into memory.

IV.2.2.2. Reserving a single address, or an address table. In the course of a program one may need to place some data, or a result, into a memory location which is thereafter designated by a label: MEM1, for example. It is evident that an absolute address should be assigned to this label before the program can be executed. When several bytes of results have to be moved they are moved to contiguous addresses. Together these contiguous addresses constitute a TABLE. This table will be defined:

(1) By its start address;
(2) By the number of locations it occupies.

The location of the first address is obtained either directly from the ORG command or from the address of the preceding instruction (and thus indirectly from the ORG command). This process, in effect, defines the address of each byte of each instruction.

The number of addresses to be reserved is defined by an assembly command called DS (define storage) by INTEL and RMB (reserve memory bytes) by MOTOROLA.

INTEL	MOTOROLA
ORG 2000H	ORG $2000
MEM1: DS 1	MEM1 RMB 1
TAB1: DS 10H	TAB1 RMB $10
address MEM1 = 2000H	address MEM1 = $2000
address TAB1 = 2001H to 2010H	address TAB1 = $2001 to $2010
This pseudo-instruction does not have to contain a label. The address reservation, nevertheless, always takes place starting from the current contents of the location counter.	This directive does not have to contain a label. The address reservation, nevertheless, always takes place starting from the current contents of the location counter.

IV.2.2.3. Attributing values to symbols. It is often useful in an assembler instruction to designate an operand by a symbol rather than by its numeric value. This is especially the case with command words and I/O port addresses on a parallel or serial interface. It is then absolutely necessary to ascribe a unique value to such a symbol. This is done by the assembly command EQU (equate).

The value attributed to the symbol becomes the operand for the command EQU. In addition, this value takes on all the properties of an operand representation.

INTEL	MOTOROLA
VAL1 EQU 18	VAL1 EQU 18
VAL2 EQU 0AE1H	VAL2 EQU $0AE1
VAL3 EQU VAL1 + 2	VAL3 EQU VAL1 + 2
Only one value should be assigned to the symbol by the pseudo-instruction EQU. The INTEL assembler, however, has another pseudo-instruction with essentially the same function as EQU, but which allows us to assign different values to a symbol in the course of writing a program: this is the pseudo-instruction SET	Only one value should be assigned to the symbol by the directive EQU.

```
VAL1    SET     17
        MVI     A,VALI
         •
         •
         •
         •
VAL1    SET     0AH
        MVI     A,VAL1
```

IV.2.2.4. Planting data, or a data table, in RAM. A program usually contains one or more pieces of data, or even data tables. It is important, therefore, to place the data in RAM at specific addresses. This now becomes a question of assigning two attributes, i.e. an address and a value, for each data byte. When addresses are assigned, the first one to be assigned is the one supplied by the contents of the location counter. The value assigned to the data, however, is that indicated in the operand field of an assembly command. This latter command is

(1) DB (define byte) or DW (define word) for INTEL depending on whether 8- or 16-bit data are involved;
(2) FCB (form constant byte) or FDB (form constant double byte) or FCC (form constant characters) for MOTOROLA depending on whether 8-bit data, 16-bit data, or ASCII characters are involved.

The assembly command can, on the same line, define several items of data by separating them with a comma.

INTEL
```
        ORG     1000H
DATA:   DB      23,5,18H,20H
        DB      25,15H,88H +2
TABLE:  DB      'VALUE:'
```

hexadecimal address	hexadecimal contents
1000	17
1001	05
1002	18
1003	20
1004	19
1005	15
1006	8A
1007	56
1008	41
1009	4C

MOTOROLA
```
        ORG     $1000
DATA    FCB     23,5,$18,$20
        FCB     25,$15,$88 + 2
```

hexadecimal address	hexadecimal contents
1000	17
1001	05
1002	18
1003	20
1004	19
1005	15
1006	8A

Two formats exist for the directive FCC:
(1) The number of ASCII characters,

100A	55
100B	45
100C	3A

A table of ASCII characters is defined by the pseudo-instruction DB, the only condition being that we enclose the ASCII data in primes.

```
        ORG   1000H
MEM1 DW    START
TAB1: DW    2010H,1A3CH,5
```

if the value of START is 135H we have

hexadecimal address	hexadecimal contents
1000	50
1001	13
1002	10
1003	20
1004	3C
1005	1A
1006	05
1007	00

The data is stored with the least significant byte first.

comma, text. The text can include trailing blanks.

(2) Text between two identical delimiters, the delimiter being a character chosen at random.

```
        ORG   $1000
TABLE   FCC   6,VALUE: or
TABLE   FCC   /VALUE:/
```

hexadecimal address	hexadecimal contents
1000	56
1001	41
1002	4C
1003	55
1004	45
1005	3A

```
        ORG $1000
MEM1   FDB   START
TAB1   FDB   $2010, $1A3C,5
```

if the value of START is $1350 we have

hexadecimal address	hexadecimal contents
1000	13
1001	50
1002	20
1003	10
1004	1A
1005	3C
1006	00
1007	05

The data is stored with the most significant byte first.

IV.2.2.5. End of program indicator. An assembler program should always be terminated by some command signalling 'end of program' to the assembler; generation of the object program can then commence. The required command is called END. It has neither a label nor an operand.

IV.2.2.6. Other assembly commands (optional). In addition to the fundamental assembler commands which we have just seen, an assembler usually offers one or more assembler options, which are not vital but which facilitate the programmer's work. Let us briefly look at these different commands.

INTEL	MOTOROLA

INTEL

(1) TITLE

A pseudo-instruction gives a source program its title. This title, composed of 1 to 66 ASCII characters, written between two primes, will then be written at the beginning of each page of the assembler-produced program listing. The title is written under the page number; if there is no title, the page number is followed by a line of blanks.

(2) IF and ENDIF

These two assembly commands allow for one part of the program to be considered only if a certain condition is satisfied. This condition is true if the operand of the pseudo-instruction IF has the value 1.

```
ETIQ   IF      VAL1 + 2
  –          this part
  –     }    of the program
  –          is assembled
  –          if VAL1 + 2 = '1'
ENDIF
```

MOTOROLA

(1) NAM

A directive which gives a name to the source program. This name will then feature at the top of the assembler-produced program listing.

(2) PAGE

This directive allows for the pagination of program listings. Each time this directive is encountered it means that the paper is moved on to the beginning of the following page.

(3) SPC n

When the assembler encounters this directive it leaves n blank lines, n being specified in the operand field of the directive.

OTHER MOTOROLA DIRECTIVES

(3) OPT. This directive offers the programmer different possibilities in contents listing.

– OPT M	The assembler loads the binary program FILE.LO into RAM
– OPT NOM	The assembler does not load the binary program FILE.LO into RAM. (This is the default option which is chosen if neither M nor NOM is explicitly stated)
– OPT S	The assembler prints the symbols at the end of the second pass
– OPT NOS	The assembler does not print the symbols (default option)
– OPT NOL	The assembler does not produce a listing of the assembled program
– OPT L	A program listing is produced (default option)
– OPT NOP	Non-pagination of listing
– OPT P	Pagination of listing (default option)

172

– OPT NOG   The assembler prints only one line of any data defined by FCB, FCC, FDB

– OPT G   The assembler prints out all data defined by FCB, FCC, FDB (default option)

The different selected options are separated by commas. For example, OPT, S, NOP.

(4) MON. This directive returns the control to the monitor at the end of assembly. It should be placed at the end of the source program. The assembler then places the following question on the input/output device:

READY

If yes, the program types

EOF (end of file)

Note. At the end of this book (pp. 207–217) we give tables indicating the syntax of instructions and pseudo-instructions when written either with automatic console tabulation (INTEL) or without tabulation (MOTOROLA). With the INTEL system, it is, of course, possible to draft a program without using the tabulation option.

IV.3. Programming techniques and utility subroutines

In this section we shall describe several basic programming techniques, which we shall illustrate by the study of some subroutines of wide applicability called utilities.

IV.3.1. Table management

A table is characterized by a series of memory locations occupying contiguous addresses. The simplest application of this is when we successively read or write the contents of all memory locations from the lowest address to the highest or the other way round. The fact that the addresses are contiguous allows us to use an index register. But it is possible to obtain the same result by using indirect register addressing. We shall study both these techniques.

IV.3.1.1. Index addressed table management. The MOTOROLA 6800 has a true index register. The INTEL 8080A does not have one: only register indirect addressing is possible with the 8080A. We shall illustrate the management of an index addressed table by means of a concrete example; the setting to zero of memory locations $1000 to $1020 inclusive. The index register is initially loaded with the low address of the table, i.e. 1000. The writing of 00 in each memory location is then done by indexed addressing. Each table address is compared with the final address, i.e. 1021 in this example, thereby allowing the program to exit from the loop when it has finished.

Example: 6800

	LDX	#$1000	Load the lowest address into the index register
BCL	CLR	0,X	Clear the memory location pointed to by the index
	INX		Increment the index
	CPX	#$1021	Compare index contents with $1021
	BNE	BCL	Jump to BCL if index contents are not equal to $1021

When the table is located in page 0 of the memory, that is, at addresses whose most significant byte is 00, the index can be used in another way: as a simple down-counter. Let us suppose that we want to zeroize the memory locations at hexadecimal addresses 0040 to 0060 inclusive. The program would be

	LDX	#$21	Load X with the number of memory locations
BCL	CLR	$3F,X	Zeroize the memory location at address (X) + 3F
	DEX		Decrement the index
	BNE	BCL	Jump to BCL provided index contents are not zero

In this program the first memory location re-set to zero is at address $3F + $21 (= $60); that is, the highest table address. The comparison instruction is no longer required, and an instruction can therefore be saved.

IV.3.1.2. Table management by register indirect addressing

Example: 8080A

The 8080A performs well with this type of addressing since three or, more precisely, three pairs of its registers allow this addressing. Nevertheless, one of these pairs, the HL pair, is a special case because it has numerous specific instructions. These instructions carry an M reference in their mnemonic expression: 'MVI M data', for example. The HL double register is, then, the first choice to be used. But the double registers BC and DE can equally well be used. Two instructions are specific to BC and DE: an indirect read instruction LDAX pr (pr = pointer register), and an indirect write, STAX pr.

We shall illustrate table management via register indirect addressing with the concrete example of setting to zero the memory locations at addresses 1000H to 1020H inclusive.

The classic program will use the HL register pair. The number of memory locations to be re-set to zero, 21 in hexadecimal, is loaded into register D, which is used as a down-counter:

```
        MVI      B,21H      ; load into B the number of memory
                            locations
        LXI      H,1000H    ; load the start address into HL
BCL:    MVI      M,00       ; zeroize the memory location pointed to
                            by HL
        INX      H          ; increment HL
        DCR      B          ; jump to address BCL as long as (B) is not
                            ; equal to zero
        JNZ      BCL        ; decrement the number of memory
                            locations
```

This program could, however, also be executed using the register pairs BC or DE. The instruction used is then STAX pr since a write operation has to be performed. This gives two other possible programs:

INDEX = BC   INDEX = DE

```
        MVI      E,21H                       MVI      B,21H
        LXI      B,1000H                     LXI      D,1000H
        MVI      A,00                        MVI      A,00
BCL:    STAX     B                  BCL:     STAX     D
        INX      B                           INX      D
        DCR      E                           DCR      B
        JNZ      BCL                         JNZ      BCL
```

Example: 6800

The MOTOROLA 6800 allows register indirect addressing only with the stack pointer, and this particular use of the stack pointer calls for certain precautions to be taken. First of all, the 6800 microprocessor must inhibit all interrupts while the stack pointer is being used as an indirect address register. Then, the initial contents of the stack pointer should be saved before it is used for indirect addressing and should be restored afterwards. Finally, the read and write instructions for indirect addressing using a stack pointer (which are PUL Y and PSH Y) are automatically accompanied by an incrementing of the stack pointer BEFORE the read, and a decrementing AFTER the write, respectively.

From this last point, the following can be seen:

(1) That the reading of a table, using indirect addressing via the stack pointer, is simplest when the latter is loaded with the lowest table address minus one (to allow for the automatic incrementing before the read);

(2) That writing a table using indirect addressing via the stack pointer is simplest when the latter is loaded with the highest table address.

We denote the saving of the stack pointer in a memory location which we shall call SAVE.

Our program to zeroize the memory locations at hexadecimal addresses 1020 to 1040 inclusive is:

	STS	SAVE	Save the contents of the stack pointer
*	LDA B	#$21	Load into B the number of memory locations to be zeroized
*	LDS	#$1040	Load the stack pointer with the highest address
	CLR A		Zeroize A
BCL *	PSH A		Zeroize memory location pointed at by the stack pointer
	DEC B		Decrement B
*	BNE	BCL	Jump to BCL provided that the contents of B are non-zero
*	LDS	SAVE	Return initial contents to stack pointer

IV.3.2. Simultaneous management of two tables

The address of a piece of data in a data table is completely defined by two pieces of information:

(1) The address of the table: this is either the lowest or the highest table address. We designate it by a general mnemonic TAB1, TAB2 etc. or by a mnemonic signifying a table;
(2) The position of the data in the table: this position is defined by its displacement from the data table address, the word 'data' being taken in a general sense. We designate this data position by POST1 for table 1 and POST2 for table 2.

The two pieces of information about the table, TAB and POST, allow for the calculation of the address at which the read or write in the table should be carried out. We designate this address by a mnemonic obtained by adding X to the mnemonic for the table. Thus, if TAB1 and TAB2 designate the lowest addresses of tables 1 and 2, we have

TAB1X = TAB1 + POST1
TAB2X = TAB2 + POST2

Programs which necessitate the management of two tables can be divided into two categories:

(1) Those for which POST2 = POST1
(2) Those for which POST2 ≠ POST1

In the latter case, POST2 must be calculated. We shall now examine each of these two cases.

176

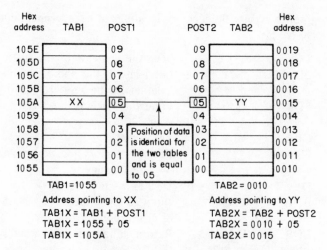

Figure 109. Example of two data tables in which the position of
an item of data is expressed by the same number in each table

IV.3.2.1. Simultaneous management of two tables where POST2 = POST1.
This management is illustrated in Figure 109, which gives an example of
two tables, TAB1 and TAB2, having addresses 1055 and 0010 in hexadecimal,
respectively. The position, POST1, of the data item **XX** read from TAB1 is the
same as the position, POST2, of the data item **YY** written to TAB2. In Figure 109
this common position is the required number of increments of the index register or
the indirect addressing register.

We shall illustrate this type of two-table management by studying the transfer
of one data table from one part of memory to another.

MEMORY AREA TRANSFER PROGRAM

Let us suppose that a data table is to be situated starting at the address TAB1.
This table consists of N addresses: TAB1, TAB1 + 1, TAB1 + 2, ...,
TAB1 + $(N - 1)$. We wish to transfer this table into another part of memory,
starting with the address designated by label TAB2 situated outside the memory
region assigned to the initial data table, TAB1.

Example: 8080A

```
        LXI     H,TAB1      ; load HL with lowest address of TAB1
        LXI     D,TAB2      ; load DE with lowest address of TAB2
        MVI     B,N         ; load N into B
BCL:    MOV     A,M         ; transfer into A the data pointed
                            ; to by HL
        STAX    D           ; move this data to the address pointed
                            ; at by DE
        INX     H           ; increment HL
        INX     D           ; increment DE
```

```
DCR     B               ; decrement B
JNZ     BCL             ; jump to BCL if contents of B are
                        ; non-zero
```

In this program the position of the data is the value added to the indirect address register. It is 0 for the first item of data, 1 for the second item of data, and $N + 1$ for the last item of data. Note that, at the end of program execution, the registers HL and DE do not point to the last address of their tables but to the last address + 1. This, incidentally, does not cause any problem, but we must be aware of it: the supplementary + 1 arises from the fact that the test is carried out after the index register has been incremented.

It is, of course, possible to increment the index after the test. We shall illustrate this possibility with a subroutine which uses the 8080A conditional return instructions RZ, RNZ, RC, RNC, RP, and RM. We shall also make another significant modification. In our example program above the addresses TAB1, TAB2, and the data N constitute the *parameters* or *arguments* of a subroutine. The placing of these arguments into specific registers does not form part of the subroutine. It is the calling program which should load the parameters into their proper registers. This allows subroutines to be called with different parameters and, in addition, allows subroutines to be shared by several programs. We have already met the concept of arguments (also called parameters) in section IV.1.3 (p. 162). Consequently we shall give the heading for a subroutine which we shall call UTRA (transfer utility).

In addition, we show this subroutine accompanied by the pseudo-instructions necessary for assembler programming, so as to explain the use of the pseudo-instructions that we met at the beginning of the chapter.

```
; MODULE          : UTRA
; PURPOSE         : MEMORY COPY FROM TAB1 TO TAB2
; INPUTS          : INITIAL TABLE TAB1 POINTED TO BY HL
;                 : AMOUNT OF DATA TO BE TRANSFERRED
;                 : INDICATED BY B
;                 : FINAL TABLE TAB2 POINTED TO BY DE
; OUTPUT          : TABLE OF DATA SITUATED AT TAB2
; REGISTERS
; DESTROYED       : A, B, D, E, H, L
;
;
;
;
;
                ORG 4000 H
;
UTRA:   MOV     A, M            ; transfer into A the data pointed to by HL
        STAX    D               ; move this data to the address pointed
                                ; to by DE
```

178

DCR	B		; decrement B
RZ			; return from this subroutine if contents of
			; B = 0
INX	H		; increment index HL
INX	D		; increment index DE
JMP	UTRA		; jump to address UTRA
END			

Example: 6800

Index register X is used to point to the final data table, TAB2. The stack pointer is used to point to the initial data table, TAB1. This latter table will then be read by PUL A instructions. Remember that this instruction begins by incrementing the stack pointer prior to transferring into the accumulator the item of data which is being pointed to. The stack pointer, therefore, should be loaded with the lowest address of the table minus one; i.e. TAB1 − 1. If the lowest address is $0000 we need to load the stack pointer with the value $FFFF because $FFFF + 1 = $10000, which becomes $0000, since the 1, being the seventeenth bit, is ignored.

	STS	SAVE	Save contents of stack pointer
	LDS	TAB − 1	Load stack pointer with lowest address
*			of TAB1
	LDX	TAB2	Load index register with lowest address
*			of TAB2
BCL	PUL A		Increment stack pointer and transfer
*			to A the data pointed at by the
*			stack pointer
	STA A	0,X	Store data in TAB2
	INX		Increment index
	CPX	TAB2 + N	Compare index contents with TAB2 + N
	BNE	BCL	Jump to BCL if index contents TAB2 + N
	LDS	SAVE	Restore the stack pointer contents

The use of the stack pointer as an indirect address register is not absolutely essential. By using two pairs of memory locations to serve as extra indexes, loaded, in turn, into register X, it is possible to dispense with the stack pointer. Before any read or write operation is carried out the contents of one of these double memory locations is loaded into the index X (unless it is there already). We designate these two memory location pairs INDEX1 and INDEX2 as a reminder of their role.

In view of its potential usefulness we shall set up the next program as a utility subroutine, leaving to the calling program the tasks of loading the arguments or parameters. In the heading of the subroutine we give the necessary instructions for its use within an assembler program. We call this subroutine UTRA (transfer utility).

```
* MODULE          : UTRA
* PURPOSE         : N-BYTE MEMORY REGION TRANSFER FROM
*                   ADDRESS TAB1 TO ADDRESS TAB2
* INPUTS          : LOWEST ADDRESS OF INITIAL TABLE
*                   TAB1 IN X
*                 : LOWEST ADDRESS OF FINAL TABLE TAB2
*                   IN MEMORY LOCATIONS $2022 AND $2023
*                 : NUMBER OF BYTES, N, IS IN B
*                   (AS HEX-ENCODED BINARY)
* OUTPUT          : TABLE OF DATA SITUATED STARTING
*                   AT TAB2
* REGISTERS
* DESTROYED       : A, B, X
*
*            NAM      UTRA
             ORG      $2000
UTRA         STX      INDEX1     Store contents of X in INDEX1
             LDA A    X          Indexed read of data from TAB1
             LDX      INDEX2     Load X with the contents of INDEX2
             STA A    X          Indexed write of data into TAB2
             INX                 Increment X and then contents of INDEX2
             STX      INDEX2     Store new value of X in INDEX2
             LDX      INDEX1     Load X with the contents of INDEX1
             INX                 Increment X and then contents of INDEX1
             DEC B               Decrement B
             BNE      UTRA       Jump to UTRA if contents of B non-zero
             RTS                 Subroutine return
INDEX1       RMB      2
INDEX2       EQU      $2022
             END
```

Note. If the two tables TAB1 and TAB2 are both contained in a memory region of less than 256 bytes, and if, in addition, their low addresses are separated by 128 bytes or less, one single index is sufficient. Index X is initialized to the lowest address of TAB1. The lowest address of TAB2 is defined by its displacement, positive or negative, relative to TAB1; we shall call this value DIS2 (displacement of table 2). The memory location address of TAB2 is then

TAB2 = (X) + DIS2

which gives the following program:

```
             ORG      $2000
*
             LDX      #TAB1      Load address of TAB1 into X
BCL          LDA A    X          Indexed read from TAB1
             STA A    DIS2,X     Indexed write from TAB2
```

```
        INX                     Increment index
        CPX     #TAB1 + N       Compare index contents to TAB1 + N
        BNE     BCL             Jump to BCL if index < TAB1 + N
TAB1    EQU     $C000
DIS2    EQU     $70
N       EQU     $40
```

IV.3.2.2. Simultaneous management of two tables where POST2 ≠ POST1.
This is a more complex case than when POST2 = POST1. We still have two
tables of data, but the position of data in table 2 is not expressed by the same
displacement as the position of data in table 1; or, in other words, POST2 (position of data within table 2) is different from POST1 (position of data within table
1). Figure 110 shows two tables of data, one of 10 bytes and one of 6 bytes. The
reading of data XX, for which we have POST1 = 05, eventually causes the data
YY to be written to the position POST2 = 03 of table 2. The value of POST2,
which is different from the value of POST1, has to be calculated. We shall
illustrate this situation by looking at a specific program.

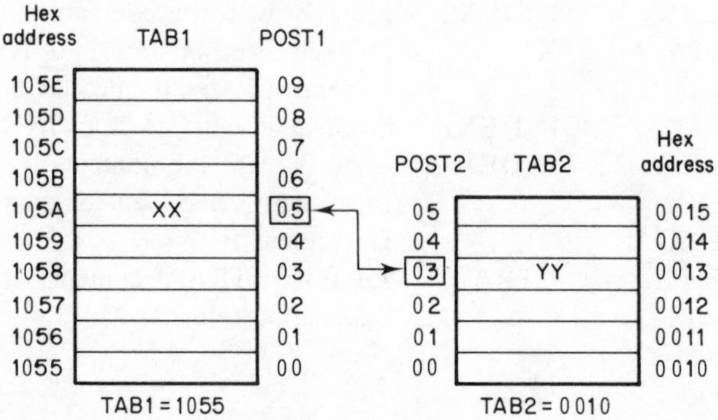

Figure 110. Example of two data tables where POST1 ≠
POST2

PROGRAM FOR CALCULATING A HISTOGRAM FROM AN ASCII DATA AREA

Let us consider a table of data, which we shall call DATA. The names TAB1 and
TAB2, used previously, are too general for our present purpose; it is advisable
that mnemonics be as informative as possible. This table, of undefined length, contains decimal numbers represented in ASCII. The end of the table is indicated by
04. We shall calculate

(1) The number $N0$ of 0's contained in the DATA table;
(2) The number $N1$ of 1's contained in the DATA table;
(3) The number $N2$ of 2's contained in the DATA table;
....
(4) The number $N9$ of 9's contained in the DATA table.

The numbers $N0$, $N1$, $N2$, ... $N9$ will be arranged in a histogram which we shall call HISTO (TAB2 = HISTO), the number $N0$ being placed at the start address of the table, the number $N1$ at start address + 1, etc. For each indexed read of the DATA table, it is necessary to calculate POST2 and then HISTOX. The ten memory locations of the HISTO table should first be set to zero, as in the program shown in section IV.3.1 (p. 173).

The calculation of POST2, that is, the position of data in the HISTO table, is easily carried out by zeroing the 4 most significant bits of the items read from the DATA table. For example, if the data read from the DATA table is 37, we shall obtain 07 when the four most significant bits have been set to zero. Now this value is exactly POST2; that is, the position to be incremented in the HISTO table. It only remains to increment by one unit the contents of the memory location at address HISTOX = HISTO + 07. This entails adding 07 to the address of the table; that is, to HISTO. Using our two assembly language syntaxes we shall indicate the required assembly commands for this program. The DATA table must end with a character differing from those contained in the table; we designate this character by EOT (end of table). We shall give EOT the value 04.

Since this program is not of general interest we shall not program it as a utility subroutine. Consequently this program, which we call HISTO, loads its own parameters.

Example: 8080A
The HISTO table is pointed to by the HL register while the DATA table is pointed to by the DE register. Nonetheless, the HISTO table must be set to zero, in advance, with the aid of the HL register.

```
; MODULE          : HISTO
; PURPOSE         : HISTOGRAM OF A TABLE OF ASCII-
                    ENCODED DECIMAL NUMBERS
; INPUT           : DATA TABLE ENDING WITH EOT
; OUTPUT          : HISTO TABLE: 10 BINARY VALUES
EOT      EQU       04 H
         ORG       4000 H
; SET TO ZERO THE TEN MEMORY LOCATIONS OF TABLE
; 'HISTO'
         MVI       B,10
         LXI       H,HISTO
RAZ:     MVI       M,00
         INX       H
         DCR       B
         JNZ       RAZ
; SET UP HISTO TABLE POINTED TO BY HL
; AND DATA TABLE POINTED TO BY DE
         LXI       D,DATA    ; Load DE with the start address of
                             ; DATA
```

182

```
        MVI      B,0        ; Zero the B register
BCL:    LDAX     D          ; Indexed read of DATA table
        CPI      EOT        ; Compare data just read to EOT
                            ; character
        JZ       FINI       ; Jump to finish if data = EOT
        SUI      30         ; POST2 = ASCII data - 30
        MOV      C,A        ; Transfer POST2 into C
        LXI      H,HISTO    ; Load HL with the value of HISTO
        DAD      B          ; HISTOX = (HL) + POST2 =
                            ; (HL) + (BC)
        INR      M          ; Increment memory contents at address
                            ; HISTOX
        INX      D          ; Increment DE
        JMP      BCL        ; Unconditional jump to BCL
FINI:   NOP
; PROGRAM DATA
; DATA TABLE AT ADDRESS 5000H
        ORG      5000H
DATA:   DB       '34509711'
        DB       '22359068'
        DB       '785'
        DB       EOT
; HISTO TABLE AT ADDRESS 5100H
        ORG      5100H
HISTO:  DS       10
        END
```

In this program let us designate by 'HISTOX' the address whose content is incremented via the indexed instruction INR M; this address is calculated as follows. The value POST2 is obtained by simply zeroing the 4 most significant bits of the data which has just been read. The value POST2 is then placed in register C. The DAD instruction adds the contents of HL to that of BC and transfers the result to HL. The contents of HL then become HISTO + POST2 (i.e. HISTOX). The DATA table is placed in memory and initialized using the DB pseudo-instruction. The data is written in the form of decimal digits but is stored in the DATA table as ASCII characters because all the decimal figures are enclosed between two apostrophes.

Ten memory locations, starting at address 5100H, are reserved for the HISTO table by a combination of the two instructions ORG 5100 H and DS 10.

We also notice in this program several lines starting with a semi-colon; such lines are reserved for comments.

Example: 6800

The 6800 has only one index register, which is insufficient for performing the addition HISTOX = HISTO + POST2 directly. Thus we use a pair of memory locations to serve as a kind of index for the HISTO table. We call this pair of memory locations INDEX2. Similarly, we use a pair of memory locations, INDEX1, for the DATA table. The addition HISTOX = HISTO + POST2 is now carried out by storing HISTO (start address of the table) in INDEX2 and then adding POST2 to the least significant byte of INDEX2; i.e. to the contents of address INDEX2 + 1. Thus, if POST2 is in A and HISTO in X we perform the following:

```
ADD A INDEX2 + 1      (A) = (A) + (INDEX + 1)
STA A  INDEX2 + 1      (INDEX2 + 1) = (A) + (INDEX2 + 1)
```

This addition could, however, involve a carry into the most significant byte of INDEX2. Therefore, the CARRY flag must be tested and, if it is '1', INDEX2 must be incremented, which yields the following instructions:

```
BCC FOLLOW        jump to FOLLOW if carry = 0
INC  INDEX2        increment INDEX2 if carry = 1.
```

We give below the assembler instructions for this program.

```
* MODULE            : HISTO
* PURPOSE           : HISTOGRAM OF A TABLE OF ASCII-
*                     ENCODED DECIMAL NUMBERS
* INPUT             : DATA TABLE ENDING WITH EOT
* OUTPUT            : HISTO TABLE: 10 BINARY VALUES
            NAM       HISTO
EOT         EQU       4
            ORG       $2000
* SET TO ZERO THE TEN MEMORY LOCATIONS OF TABLE
* HISTO
            LDA B     #10
            LDX       #HISTO
RAZ         CLR       0,X
            INX
            DEC B
            BNE       RAZ
* SET UP HISTO TABLE POINTED TO BY INDEX2
* AND DATA TABLE POINTED TO BY INDEX1
            LDX       #DATA      Load X with address of DATA
            STX       INDEX1     Store DATA address in INDEX1
BCL         LDX       #HISTO     Load X with address of HISTO
            STX       INDEX2     Store HISTO address in INDEX2
            LDX       INDEX1     Load X with DATA address
            LDA A     0,X        Indexed read of the DATA table
            CMP A     #EOT       Comparison of data with EOT
            BEQ       FINI       Jump to finish if data = EOT
            AND A     #$0F       Obtain POST2 by masking bottom
*                                four bits
```

ADD A *	INDEX2 + 1	(A) = POST2 + least signficant byte of HISTO
STA A *	INDEX2 + 1	Least signficant byte of HISTO is incremented by POST2
BCC	FOLLOW	Jump to FOLLOW if carry = 0
INC	INDEX2	increment INDEX2 if carry = 1

FOLLOW	INX		Increment index
	STX	INDEX1	Shift contents of X into INDEX1
	LDX	INDEX2	Load contents of INDEX2
	INC	0,X	Increment contents of HISTOX
	JMP	BCL	Jump to BCL
FINI *	NOP		
	ORG	$2300	
DATA	FCC	/3450971122359068/	
	FCB	EOT	
HISTO	RMB	10	
INDEX1	RMB	2	
INDEX2	RMB	2	
	END		

IV.3.2.3. The use of a jump table

Let us assume that, in the framework of an industrial application, we have to execute one out of N subroutines depending on the value, V, of a number encoded in n bits. If the value of this number is $V1$ we must execute subroutine No. 1, which we designate SR1; if the value of the number is $V2$, we execute SR2, etc., ... This is illustrated in the flowchart of Figure 111.

This problem can be solved using a more elegant method wherein a jump table is used which contains the address of every subroutine. The value V of the

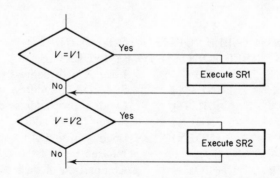

Figure 111. Flowchart illustrating jumping to a subroutine

encoded number is tested and, as a result of the test, we jump to the address of the subroutine to be executed. It is important to understand this operation well in order to carry it out, and we shall describe it carefully. We shall employ our previous notation for tables and use TAB to designate a table which contains addresses rather than data. We can think of our table as being composed of pairs of memory locations. The address of a given pair we shall call TABX. The first operation to be performed is the calculation of TABX. The second operation is then to transfer the contents of TABX into the index, X (the indirect addressing register).

This second operation depends on the instruction set. We shall therefore explain things for each of our two microprocessors, using a polling subroutine called POLL.

POLLING PROGRAM

The encoded number is the contents of an 8-bit I/O port like the one shown in Figure 11. Several I/O devices can simultaneously ask for service, in which case the encoded number contains several '1's. In order not to drown the explanation of branching techniques by the peculiarities of this polling program, we shall only deal with one part of the program, and we shall suppose that the encoded number contains only one '1'. The problem is, therefore, as follows:

to branch to SUB1 if the contents of the I/O port are 00000001
to branch to SUB2 if the contents of the I/O port are 00000010
to branch to SUB3 if the contents of the I/O port are 00000100
to branch to SUB4 if the contents of the I/O port are 00001000
to branch to SUB5 if the contents of the I/O port are 00010000
to branch to SUB6 if the contents of the I/O port are 00100000
to branch to SUB7 if the contents of the I/O port are 01000000
to branch to SUB8 if the contents of the I/O port are 10000000

The jump table, which we call TAPOL, will contain one address. or two bytes, per subroutine. For subroutine addresses we shall take the hexadecimal addresses 5100 for SUB1, 5200 for SUB2, 5300 for SUB3, etc., ending with 5800 for SUB8.

Example: 8080A
The essence of the program is to transfer the contents of TAPOLX into the program counter, PC. This operation is carried out in three stages after TAPOLX has been calculated.

(1) The contents of TAPOLX, that is, the address of the subroutine to be executed, is transferred into the register pair DE.
(2) The contents of DE are transferred to HL. Thus, the subroutine address is in HL.
(3) The contents of HL are transferred to the program counter PC. Now that the address of the subroutine is in the program counter the subroutine will be executed.

186

```
; MODULE        : POLL
; PURPOSE       : JUMP TO APPROPRIATE POLLING SUBROUTINE
; INPUT         : START ADDRESS OF TAPOL TABLE IN HL,
;                 CONTENTS OF I/O PORT IN ACCUMULATOR
; OUTPUT        : AUTOMATIC JUMP TO APPROPRIATE
;                 SUBROUTINE
; REGISTERS
; DESTROYED     : A, D, E, H, L
          ORG   4000H
TEST:     RAR              ; rotate right accumulator contents
                           ; into carry
          JC    CHARGT     ; jump to CHARGT address if carry = 1
          INX   H          ; double incrementing of index to point to
          INX   H          ; start address of the next subroutine
          JMP   TEST       ; jump to TEST for testing the next
                           ; accumulator bit
CHARGT:   MOV   E,M        ; load into E the least significant byte
                           ; of subroutine address
          INX   H          ; increment HL
          MOV   D,M        ; load into D the most significant byte
                           ; of subroutine address
          XCHG             ; exchange (DE) and (HL) where (HL) =
                           ; appropriate
                           ; subroutine address
          PCHL             ; (HL) → PC which causes a jump to
                           ; appropriate subroutine

;
; TAPOL JUMP TABLE
TAPOL:    DW    5100H, 5200H, 5300H, 5400H
          DW    5500H, 5600H, 5700H, 5800H
          END
```

Note that the return from the subroutine has to be provided by the subroutine itself.

Example: 6800

The index register of the 6800 permits an easy transfer of the contents of TAPOLX into X: this is effected by an indexed load into the index itself and is achieved by the instruction LDX 0,X. If (X) = TAPOLX, the instruction LDX 0,X transfers into the index X the contents of the memory location at address (X), i.e. TAPOLX. Thus the contents of TAPOLX, which constitute the address of the appropriate subroutine, are transferred into X. In order to jump to this subroutine we only need to execute the instruction: JMP 0,X (jump to the address contained in X- and thus to the address of the subroutine to be executed).

```
* MODULE          : POLL
* PURPOSE         : JUMP TO APPROPRIATE POLLING
*                   SUBROUTINE
* INPUTS          : START ADDRESS OF TAPOL TABLE IN X
*                 : I/O PORT CONTENTS IN ACCUMULATOR
* OUTPUT          : AUTOMATIC JUMP TO APPROPRIATE
*                   SUBROUTINE
* REGISTERS
* DESTROYED       : A,X
          NAM       POLL
          ORG       $2000
TEST      LSR A               Shift right contents of A into carry
          BCS       CHARGT    Jump to CHARGT if carry = 1
          INX                 Double incrementing of X to point the
          INX                 next subroutine address
          JMP       TEST      Jump to TEST
* LOAD SUBROUTINE ADDRESS IN X THEN IN PC
CHARGT LDX       0,X
          JMP       0,X
* TAPOL JUMP TABLE
TAPOL     FDB       $5100, $5200, $5300, $5400
          FDB       $5500, $5600, $5700, $5800
          END
```

IV.3.2.4. Transmission of data to a subroutine

We have already pointed out that, for subroutines, it is desirable to have the parameters (arguments) loaded by the calling program. However, to carry out its function a subroutine frequently requires data – in the form of a data table, for example. The subroutines we have studied so far have had their data defined once and for all. We shall now study the possibility of the calling program imposing not only the subroutine parameters but also the data of its choice. Let us suppose that in the 'polling' program example, which we have just discussed, there were several I/O ports containing status bits for I/O devices requesting service from the microprocessor. The eight subroutines corresponding to I/O device No. 1 are then different from the eight subroutines corresponding to I/O device No. 2, and so on.

In this event, the calling program itself defines:

(1) The subroutine parameters;
(2) The location and contents of the data table.

Furthermore, suppose that the addresses of the subroutine corresponding to I/O device No. 1 are those which we chose for the preceding program, POLL, and that the addresses corresponding to I/O device No. 2 are contained in another table designated by TAPOL2.

188

The addresses of TAPOL2 subroutines will be: 6100, 6200, 6300, 6400, 6500, 6600, 6700, 6800.

Example 8080A
The main, or calling, program is represented as follows:

```
        –
        –
        –
        LXI    H, TAPOL1     ; load TAPOL1 start address into HL
        CALL   POLL          ; call POLL subroutine which uses
                             ; TAPOL1 data
TAPOL1  DW     5100H, 5200H, 5300H, 5400H
        DW     5500H, 5600H, 5700H, 5800H
        –
        –
        LXI    H,TAPOL2      ; load TAPOL2 start address into HL
        CALL   POLL          ; call POLL subroutine which now uses
                             ; TAPOL2 data
TAPOL2  DW     6100H, 6200H, 6300H, 6400H
        DW     6500H, 6600H, 6700H, 6800H
        –
        –
        –
```

Example: 6800
The main, or calling, program is represented as follows:

```
        –
        –
        –
        LDX    #TAPOL1       load TAPOL1 start address into X
        JSR    POLL          call POLL subroutine which uses
*                           TAPOL1 data
TAPOL1  FDB    $5100, $5200, $5300, $5400
        FDB    $5500, $5600, $5700, $5800
        –
        –
        LDX    #TAPOL2       load TAPOL2 start address into X
        JSR    POLL          call POLL subroutine which now uses
*                           TAPOL2 data
TAPOL2  FDB    $6100, $6200, $6300, $6400
        FDB    $6500, $6600, $6700, $6800
        –
        –
```

IV.3.2.5. Multibyte operations

When arithmetical or logical operations are carried out with an 8-bit microprocessor on multibyte numbers these operations have to be carried out byte by byte. Such operations are called 'multiple precision': for example, a double precision multiplication. Multibyte operations are necessarily characterized by a connection between each byte operation, this connection being the propagation of some form of carry. The aim of this section is to show this carry in the context of the more frequent logical or arithmetical operations. The multibyte numbers are located in memory at contiguous addresses, the least significant byte being placed at the highest address.

(A) Incrementing an N-byte binary number. The first byte will be the least significant byte, the second will be the next byte as we move towards the most significant byte, and so on. The incrementing of a multibyte number is achieved by incrementing the first byte. If, before incrementing, it is set to FF, it takes on the value 00 after incrementation and the second byte must then be incremented. If the second byte is also at FF before being incremented it takes the value 00 after incrementing and the third byte must then be incremented. The incrementing criterion is the setting to 1 of the Z flag.

The multibyte number is an N-byte binary number arranged in contiguous memory addresses, the least significant byte being at the highest address. We suppose this address to be stored in HL for the 8080A and in X for the 6800, while the number N, in binary, we presume will be in register B.

Example: 8080A

```
INCMO:   INR   M         ; increment byte pointed to by HL
         RNZ             ; return from subroutine if byte ≠ 0
         DCR   B         ; decrement B register
         RZ              ; return from subroutine if (B) = 0
         DCX   H         ; decrement HL
         JMP   INCMO     ; unconditional jump to INCMO
```

Example: 6800

```
INCMO    INC   X              increment byte pointed to by X
         BNE   RETURN         jump to RETURN address if byte ≠ 0
         DEX                  decrement index X
         DEC B                decrement B register
         BNE   INCMO          jump to address INCMO if (B) ≠ 0
RETURN   RTS                  subroutine return
```

(B) Decrementing an N-byte binary number. When the byte is set to 00 it takes on the value FF after decrementing which, in turn, generates a carry. However, the decrement instruction does not affect CARRY, and so we have to replace the decrement by a subtraction of one which does set the CARRY. If CARRY assumes the value 1 the following byte must be decremented, or, to be more precise, one must be subtracted from it. Here again, the n bytes are placed at contiguous memory addresses, with the least significant byte at the highest address, which in the case of the 8080A we assume to be stored in HL, and in the case of the 6800 in X. The value N is stored in register B.

Example: 8080A

```
DECMO:    MOV   A,M        ; indexed read of byte pointed to by HL
          SUI   01         ; subtract one from this byte
          MOV   M,A        ; transfer decremented byte to the address
                           ; pointed to by HL
          RNC              ; subroutine return if CARRY = 0
          DCR   B          ; decrement contents of B
          RZ               ; subroutine return if (B) = 0
          DCX   H          ; decrement HL
          JMP   DECMO      ; unconditional jump to DECMO
```

Example: 6800

```
DECMO     LDA A X          indexed read of the byte pointed to by
*                          index X
          SUB A #01        subtract one from this byte
          STA A X          transfer the decremented byte to address
*                          pointed to by X
          BCC   RETURN     jump to RETURN if CARRY = 0
          DEX              decrement index X
          DEC B            decrement contents of B
          BNE   DECMO      jump to DECMO if (B) ≠ 0
RETURN    RTS              subroutine return
```

(C) Shifting an N-byte binary number by one place left. The transfer of the MSB of a byte into the LSB of the next byte is performed with the help of CARRY. A zero is placed into the LSB of the lowest byte. The highest bit of the first byte, or MSB1, becomes the lowest bit of the second byte, after two rotate left instructions (Figure 112).

The N bytes of the binary number are once again at contiguous addresses. The least significant byte is at the highest address and this address is pointed to by HL for the 8080A and by X for the 6800. The register B contains N.

Example: 8080A

```
DECG:     XRA   A          ; reset CARRY to zero
BCL:      MOV   A,M        ; indexed read of byte pointed to by HL
          RAL              ; rotate left contents of A, and thus the
                           ; byte
          MOV   M,A        ; transfer of shifted byte to address pointed
                           ; to by HL
```

```
DCR   B        ; decrement contents of B
RZ             ; subroutine return if (B) = 0
DCX   H        ; decrement HL
JMP   BCL      ; jump to BCL
```

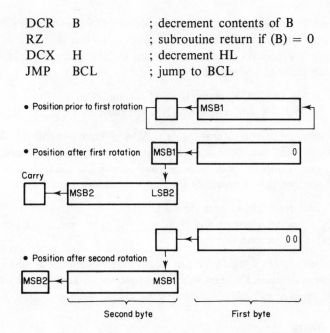

Figure 112. Shifting a 2-byte number one place to the left

It is important to note that the first RAL rotation transfers the MSB of a byte into the CARRY. This MSB is only transmitted into the LSB of the adjacent byte on the next occasion that the RAL instruction is met, which is after the execution of all the instructions in the loop. We require that these instructions do not themselves modify the CARRY. Note that this is true in the present example.

Example: 6800

```
DECG   CLC            reset CARRY to zero
BCL    ROL   X        rotate left the byte pointed to by X
       DEC B          decrement the contents of B
       BNE   JUMP     jump to JUMP if (B) ≠ 0
       RTS            subroutine return if (B) = 0
JUMP   DEX            decrement index X
       BRA   BCL      branch to BCL
```

It is important to note that the rotation ROL X transfers the MSB of the byte pointed by X into CARRY. This MSB is only transmitted into the LSB of the following byte when the instruction ROL X is next encountered, which is after the execution of all the instructions in the loop. We require that these instructions do not modify the CARRY. Happily, this is the case here.

(D) Shifting an *N*-byte binary number by one place right. When a right shift is being performed it is important to begin by shifting the most significant byte,

192

which should, in consequence, be initially pointed to by the index. It follows also that the index will be incremented rather than decremented.

The program is therefore identical to the one we have just seen, except that the following substitutions are made:

RAL by RAR and DCX H by INX H for the 8080A
ROL X by ROR X and DEX by INX for the 6800.

(E) Twos-complement (negation) of an *N*-byte binary number. When the microprocessor does not have a negate instruction this task is carried out by forming the ones-complement of each byte and adding 1 to the first complemented byte. It follows that the treatment of the first byte differs from that of the others:

First byte: ones-complement and then add 01;
Other bytes: ones-complement and then add the carry resulting from the treatment of the preceding byte.

The number is, once again, arranged in memory at contiguous addresses. The highest address contains the least significant byte and is pointed to by the index, while the B register indicates the number of bytes.

Example: 8080A
The complementing of bytes is carried out in the accumulator

COMP2:	MOV	A,M	; indexed read of first byte
	CMA		; ones-complement of first byte
	ADI	01	; addition of 01 to first ones-
			; completed byte
BCL:	MOV	M,A	; transfer of complemented byte to the
			; address pointed to by HL
BCL:	DCR	B	; decrement contents of B
	RZ		; subroutine return if (B) = 0
	DCX	H	; decrement HL
	MOV	A,M	; indexed read of byte pointed to by HL
	CMA		; ones-complement of this byte
	ACI	00	; addition of carry from the preceding
			; byte
	JMP	BCL	; jump to BCL

We notice in this program that the first byte is treated by the first three instructions. The other bytes are treated in a loop.

When the number of bytes is reduced to 2, it is possible to use a register pair. The two bytes are, first of all, ones-complemented. An increment instruction for the register pair then immediately effects the negation (twos-complement).

COMP2:	MOV	C,M	; transfer first byte into C
	CMA		; ones-complement of the first byte
	DCX	H	; decrement HL

```
        MOV   B,M           ; transfer second byte into B
        CMA                  ; ones-complement of the second byte
        INX   B             ; increment contents of BC, which
                             ; effects a negation (twos-complement)
        MOV   M,B           ; return second byte to its memory location
        INX   H             ; increment HL
        MOV   M,C           ; return first byte to its memory location
```

Example: 6800

This microprocessor has an instruction for negation (twos-complement) and also for ones-complement. However, if the first byte is 00, the negation gives FF + 1, or 00, with 1 to be carried. This carry must be added to the next byte which, if it is set to 00 before being complemented, produces, in turn, another carry.

```
COMP2   NEG   X             twos-complement of first byte
BCL     DEC B               decrement contents of B
        BNE   JUMP          jump to JUMP if (B) = 0
        RTS                 subroutine return
JUMP    DEX                 decrement index
        BCS   COMP2         if CARRY = 1 form twos-complement of
                            the next byte
        COM   X             if CARRY = 0 form ones-complement of
                            the next byte
        JMP   BCL           jump to BCL
```

In this program the twos-complement of the first byte, if it is already 00, sets CARRY to 1. In this case the treatment of the next byte amounts to a twos-complement, which is performed by the instructions BCS COMP2 and NEG X.

The instructions DEC B, BNE JUMP, RTS, and DEX should not, themselves, modify the CARRY. If the first byte is not 00, the following bytes are ones-complemented.

(F) Comparison of 2 N-byte positive numbers situated in RAM. The comparison is performed starting with the most significant byte. The result of comparing the two numbers $N1$ and $N2$ is shown by the value of the CARRY and ZERO flags. If the two most significant bytes are equal, the comparison must be continued with the next bytes.

Example: 8080A

The MSB of number $N1$ will be pointed by DE and the MSB of number $N2$ by HL, while register B contains the byte count. The least significant byte of $N1$ or $N2$ is at the highest address.

```
; MODULE        : COMPAR
; PURPOSE       : COMPARE TWO N-BYTE POSITIVE NUMBERS
; INPUTS        : NUMBER N1 POINTED TO BY DE (MSB)
;               : NUMBER N2 POINTED TO BY HL (MSB)
```

194

```
:                      : BYTE COUNT IN B
; OUTPUT               : RESULT OF COMPARISON INDICATED BY CY
:                        AND Z
:                      : N1 > N2 if CY = 0 AND Z = 0
:                      : N1 = N2 if CY = 0 AND Z = 1
:                      : N1 < N2 if CY = 1 AND Z = 1
; REGISTERS
; DESTROYED            : A, B, D, E, H, L
COMPAR:  LDAX  D              ; indexed read of byte pointed to by DE
         CMP   M              ; compare byte pointed to by HL
         RC                   ; subroutine return if CY = 1. N1 < N2
         RNZ                  ; subroutine return if CY = 0 and Z = 0.
                              : N1 > N2
         DCR   B              ; decrement byte count
         RZ                   ; if byte count = 0 return from subroutine
                              ; with CY = 0 and Z = 1. N1 = N2
         INX   D              ; if not, increment DE, then
         INX   H              ; increment HL, then
         JMP   COMPAR         ; jump to COMPAR for comparison of
                              : the next byte
```

Example: 6800

If the value $2N$, where N is the number of bytes in $N1$ or $N2$ and is always less than 256 in decimal, then we need only the X index register.

Let us suppose $N = 3$, and that $N1$ is located at hexadecimal addresses 2430, 2431, and 2432, with $N2$ located at hexadecimal addresses 2435, 2436, and 2437. To read the most significant $N1$ byte, which is at address 2430, we can load 2430 into X and perform an indexed read:

```
LDX   #$2430
LDA A  X
```

The read of the most significant $N2$ byte is then

```
LDA A  $05,X
```

The number of bytes being 3, we could also place $N2$ at addresses following those of $N1$ and read the most significant $N2$ byte by

```
LDA A  3,X
```

We shall adopt the first solution by letting DEPN2 be the least significant byte of the highest $N2$ address. Thus, in our example DEPN2 = 05.

The byte count will be in B:

```
* MODULE               : COMPAR
* PURPOSE              : COMPARE TWO N-BYTE POSITIVE NUMBERS
```

```
* INPUTS           : ADDRESS OF MSB OF N1 IN X
*                  : ADDRESS OF MSB OF N2 = (X) + DEPN2
* OUTPUT           : RESULT OF COMPARISON INDICATED BY
*                      C AND Z
*                  : N1 > N2 IF C = 0 AND Z = 0
*                  : N1 = N2 IF C = 0 AND Z = 1
*                  : N1 < N2 IF C = 1 AND Z = 0
* REGISTERS DESTROYED : A, B, X
*
COMPAR    LDA A 0,X          read byte N1
          CMP ADEPN2,X       compare with byte N2
          BCS    RETURN      jump to RETURN if C = 1 (N1 < N2)
          BNE    RETURN      jump to RETURN if C = 0 and Z = 0
*                            (N1 > N2)
*         DEC B              decrement byte count
          BEQ    RETURN      if byte count = 0 jump to RETURN
*                            with C = 0 and Z = 1 (N1 = N2)
          INX                increment X
          BRA    COMPAR      jump to COMPAR for comparison of next
*                            byte
RETURN    RTS                return from subroutine
```

(G) Binary addition of two N-byte numbers N1 and N2. We always suppose that these numbers are placed in memory with the least significant byte at the highest address. The result of the addition will be transferred to the memory locations of N1 (i.e. $N1 = N1 + N2$).

Example: 8080A
The least significant byte of N1 will be pointed to by HL and the least significant byte of N2 will be pointed to by DE. The byte count will be presumed to be in B.

```
ADBIN:    XRA   A      ; reset CARRY to 0
BCL:      LDAX  D      ; indexed read of byte pointed to by DE
          ADC   M      ; add contents of A to byte pointed to by HL
          MOV   M,A    ; transfer result to address pointed to by HL
          DCX   D      ; decrement DE
          DCX   H      ; decrement HL
          DCR   B      ; decrement byte count
          JNZ   BCL    ; if byte count ≠ 0 jump to BCL
          RET          ; subroutine return
```

Example: 6800
We shall suppose that all the bytes of N1 and N2 are located in a memory region of less than 256 bytes. The least significant byte of N1 will be pointed to by index X. The byte count will be presumed to be in B.

```
ADBIN       CLC                reset CARRY to zero
BCL         LDA A X            read byte N1
            ADC ADEPN2,X       add byte N1 + byte N2 + CARRY
            STA A X            transfer result to byte N1
            DEX                decrement index X
            DEC B              decrement B
            BNE    BCL         jump, to BCL if (B) ≠ 0
            RTS                subroutine return
```

(H) Decimal (BCD) addition of two N-byte numbers $N1$ and $N2$. The programs are the same as those just given, except that the indexed addition instruction must be followed by the DAA instruction (decimal adjust accumulator).

(I) Binary subtraction of two N-byte numbers $N1$ and $N2$. The operation is $N1 = N1 - N2$. The result will then be transferred to the locations of $N1$. The least significant byte of $N1$ and $N2$ will be situated at the highest address.

Example: 8080A
The highest addresses of $N1$ and $N2$ will be pointed to by DE and HL respectively. The byte count will be in B.

```
BINSUB:     XRA    A           ; reset CARRY to zero
BCL         LDAX   D           ; indexed read of byte pointed to by DE
            SBB    M           ; subtraction: (A) – byte pointed to by HL
            STAX   D           ; shift result to address pointed to by DE
            DCX    D           ; decrement DE
            DCX    H           ; decrement HL
            DCR    B           ; decrement byte count
            JNZ    BCL         ; jump to BCL if (B) ≠ 0
            RET                ; subroutine return
```

Example: 6800
We shall assume, once again, that all the bytes of $N1$ and $N2$ are located in memory at addresses within a 256-byte memory region and can thus be accessed via the index register X. The least significant byte of $N1$ or $N2$ will be at the highest address. The byte count will be in B.

```
BINSUB      CLC                reset CARRY to zero
            LDA A X            read byte N1
            SBC A DEPN2,X      subtract byte N1 – byte N2 – CARRY
            STA A X            transfer of result to byte N1
            DEX                decrement index X
            DEC B              decrement B
            BNE    BCL         jump to BCL if (B) ≠ 0
            RTS                subroutine return
```

(J) Decimal (BCD) subtraction of two N-byte numbers $N1$ and $N2$. The operation is $N1 = N1 - N2$. The least significant byte of $N1$ or $N2$ is located at the highest address. The byte count is in B.

The decimal subtraction $N1 - N2$ is carried out by adding to $N1$ the 10^n complement of $N2$, obtained as follows:

(1) The lowest byte of $N1$ is represented by its 100s complement;
(2) The other bytes are replaced by their 99s complement.

The 100s complement can result in a carry which is then propagated to the next byte.

Thus the subtraction $N1 - N2$

$$N1 = 483945$$
$$-N2 = 319116$$

will be replaced by the addition $N1 + N2'$

$$
\begin{array}{ll}
N1 = & 483945 \quad 84 = \text{100s complement of 16} \\
+N2' = & 680884 \quad 08 = \text{99s complement of 91} \\
& \quad 68 = \text{99s complement of 31} \\
\hline
& 1\ 164829
\end{array}
$$

The last carry which generates the value 1000000 is not counted; it can be thought of as a last subtraction in the following operations:

$$
\begin{aligned}
483945 - 319116 &= 483945 + (1000000 - 319116) - 1000000 \\
&= 483945 + 680884 - 1000000 \\
&= 164829
\end{aligned}
$$

The decimal value 99 is loaded into accumulator A. The simple subtraction 99 – byte gives immediately the 99s complement of the byte. As for the 100s complement of the first byte, this is obtained in the same way, except that the carry is first set to 1. The value 99 becomes 9A: thus the 100s complement of the first byte (16) is calculated as follows:

$$
\begin{array}{l}
9A = 1001\ 1010 \\
-16 = 0001\ 0110 \\
\hline
 1000\ 0100
\end{array}
$$

The result, 84, is the 100s complement of 16.

Example: 8080A
DE points to the LSB (highest address) of $N1$
HL points to the LSB (highest address) of $N2$
Register B contains the byte count

```
DECSUB: STC                 ; CARRY set to 1
BCL:    MVI    A,99         ; load 99 into A
        ACI    0            ; add CARRY to the accumulator
        SUB    M            ; 100s- or 99s-complement of the byte
                            ; pointed to by HL
        XCHG                ; exchange contents of HL and DE
```

```
          ADD    M              ; add the N1 byte to A
          DAA                   ; decimal correction
          MOV    M,A            ; transfer result to N1 byte
          XCHG                  ; exchange contents of HL and DE
          DCX    D              ; decrement DE
          DCX    H              ; decrement HL
          DCX    B              ; decrement B
          JNZ    BCL            ; jump to BCL if (B) ≠ 0
          RET                   ; subroutine return
```

Example: 6800
LSB of N1 is pointed to by X and the byte count is in B.

```
DECSUB    SEC               set CARRY to 1
BCL       LDA A  #99        load 99 into A
          ADC A  #0         add CARRY to accumulator
          SUB A DEPN2,X     100s- or 99s-complement of the N2 byte
          ADD A  X          add N1 byte to A
          DAA               decimal correction
          STA A X           transfer result to N1 byte
          DEX               decrement index X
          DEC B             decrement B
          BNE    BCL        jump to BCL if (B) ≠ 0
          RTS               subroutine return
```

IV.3.2.6. Programmed implementation of combinations of logic functions

(A) The 'OR' function. If an industrial application requires us to perform the OR operation on several logic variables, eight, for example, this operation can be carried out in the following way. The logic variables are connected to the microprocessor system via a tri-state buffer which constitutes an I/O device. Reading the contents of this buffer automatically executes the OR function of the eight logic variables because, in effect, this OR function is none other than the complement of the ZERO flag.

If there are only six logic variables placed in the LS bits of the I/O port, it will be necessary, after reading the I/O device, to set the unused bits to zero (i.e. the two MS bits) by the masking technique. The complement of the Z flag will then immediately give the OR function of the six variables.

Note. The instruction IN of the 8080A does not affect the Z flag. We must, therefore, mask the contents of the accumulator with 11111111 (FF) if there are eight logic variables or with 00111111 (3F) if there are six logic variables.

(B) The 'AND' function. The contents of the I/O port receiving the eight logic variables are read and then ones-complemented. The ZERO flag is then the AND function of the eight logic variables. If, for example, there are only six logic variables, the unused bits must be reset to zero, by masking, after the ones-complement.

(C) The AND–OR function. The combined function of Figure 113, frequently encountered in hard-wired logic, is easily realized using a microprocessor. It suffices to connect to the microprocessor system the sixteen logic variables of two I/O ports (two tri-state buffers, for example), as shown in Figure 113. By creating the logical AND of the contents of the two I/O ports, the Z flag immediately provides the complement of the desired AND–OR function.

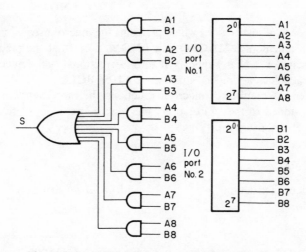

Figure 113. AND–OR function of sixteen variables

IV.3.2.7. Use of macro-instructions. A macro-instruction is, in a sense, a special instruction created by the programmer and permits a frequently used instruction sequence to be designated by a single mnemonic.

(1) Use of a macro-instruction without parameters. We take as an example a 2-ms timer which will be declared as a macro-instruction. We shall call it TEMP02 and we assume that it is used several times in the program. It is used as follows:

Example: 8080A

without macro-instruction			with macro-instruction
	–		–
	–		–
	–		–
	MVI	B,00	TEMP02
BCL1:	DCR	B	–
	JNZ	BCL1	–
	–		–

```
                    –                                    –
                    –                                    –
                    –                        TEMP02
                    –                                    –
          MVI       B,00                                 –
BCL2:     DCR       B            TEMP02:  MACRO
          JNZ       BCL2                  MVI       B,00
                    –            BCLX:    DCR       B
                    –                     JNZ       BCLX
                                          ENDM
```

The sequence of instructions which performs the macro-instruction is contained between the mnemonics MACRO and ENDM. Note that the macro assembler (i.e. an assembler which supports macro-instructions) will replace BCLX by acceptable absolute addresses; that is, BCL1 or BCL2.

The larger the number of macro-instructions the more numerous will be the instructions added to the source program. Macro-instructions are often located at the end of the program.

Example: 6800

without macro-instruction   with macro-instruction

```
                    –                                    –
                    –                                    –
                    –                                    –
          LDA B     #$FA                   TEMP02
BCL1      DEC B                                          –
          BNE       BCL1                                 –
                    –                                    –
                    –                                    –
                    –                                    –
                    –                      TEMP02   MACRO
                    –                                LDA B     #$FA
          LDA B     #$FA                   BCLX     DEC B
BCL2      DEC B                                      BNE       BCLX
          BNE       BCL2                             ENDM
```

The instruction sequence which implements the macro-instruction is between the mnemonics MACRO and ENDM. Note that the macro-assembler (i.e. assembler which supports macro-instructions), will replace BCLX by correct absolute addresses, i.e. those of BCL1 or BCL2.

The greater the number of macro instructions, the more numerous the instructions added to the source program. Macro-instructions are often located at the end of a program.

(2) Use of a macro-instruction with parameters. A macro-instruction may have one or many variables (parameters) which will be named in the program just after

the macro-instruction call. When three parameters are involved, this is written in the following form:

NAME   MACRO   PARAMETER 1, PARAMETER 2, PARAMETER 3

We take as an example a program which allows the writing of some data, which we represent by 'DATA', into all the memory locations of an N-byte memory region, the start address of which is designated by TAB. This macro-instruction is called INIT (initialization) and is written in the following form:

INIT N, TAB, DATA

Example: 8080A

```
–
–
–
–
–
INIT     30H, 1200H, 00
–
–
–
–
–
INIT     100, 2000H, 20H
–
–
–
–
–
INIT     MACRO N, TAB, DATA
         MVI     B,N
         LXI     H,TAB
BCLX     MVI     M,DATA
         INX     H
         DCR     B
         JNZ     BCLX
         ENDM
```

The macro-assembler will replace INIT 30H, 1200H, 00 by the following instruction sequence:

```
         MVI     B, 30H
         LXI     H,1200H
BCL1:    MVI     M,00
         INX     H
```

Example: 6800

```
–
–
–
–
–
INIT     $30, $1200, 00
–
–
–
–
–
INIT     100, $2000, $20
–
–
–
–
–
INIT     MACRO N, TAB, DATA
         LDA B   #N
         LDX     #TAB
         LDA A   #DATA
BCLX     STA A   0,X
         INX
         DEC B
         BNE     BCLX
         ENDM
```

The macro-assembler will replace INIT $30, $1200, 00 by the following instruction sequence:

```
         LDA B   #$30
         LDX     #$1200
         LDA A   #00
BCL1     STA A   0,X
```

```
        DCR     B                          INX
        JNZ     BCL1                       DEC B
                                           BNE     BCL1
```

In the same way, it will replace INIT 100, 2000H, 20H by the following instruction sequence:

```
        MVI     B, 100
        LXI     H, 2000H
BCL2:   MVI     M, 20H
        INX     H
        DCR     B
        JNZ     B
                BCL2
```

Strictly speaking, labels BCL1 and BCL2 will not be created, but the macro-assembler will give BCLX an appropriate absolute value, taking into account the location of the macro-instruction in the program. The object program is the same, regardless of whether or not macro-instructions are used.

In the same way, it will replace INIT 100, $2000, $20 by the following instruction sequence:

```
        LDA B   #100
        LDX     #$2000
        LDA A   #$20
BCL2:   STA A   0,X
        INX
        DEC B
        BNE     BCL2
```

Strictly speaking, labels BCL1 and BCL2 will not be created, but the macro-assembler will give BCLX an appropriate absolute value, taking into account the location of the macro-instruction in the program. The object program is the same, regardless of whether or not macro-instructions are used.

(3) Benefits of macro-instructions. *A priori*, macro-instructions are of less importance than subroutines because, unlike subroutines, the object program is in no way shortened by their use. The use of subroutines, however, necessitates the use of a stack, and thus of dynamic memory allocation. Macro-instructions lead to a more rapid execution of the object program since the return address has neither to be saved nor stored. But macro-instructions are primarily of interest when they include a subroutine call. Then their role is to transmit parameters to the subroutine and have the advantage of being a simple and efficient tool for the programmer.

IV.4. The use of development tools

Once a program has been written in assembler language, it is necessary

(1) To place it in RAM via an I/O device: this function is carried out with the help of a service program called a *text editor*.

(2) To assemble it, that is, to translate it into binary, which creates a new file: the object program. This translation, including a listing of the source program, the object program, and the syntax errors, is carried out by a service program called the assembler.

(3) Load it into the development system RAM. This assembly has created a new file, the object program, which has now been placed in the backing store of the development system (probably a diskette). Before executing the object

program one must first place it in RAM. This transfer is carried out by another service program, called DEBUG by INTEL and LOAD by MOTOROLA.

(4) To execute and implement it. This is carried out by another service program, generally called the *monitor*.

Together these service programs add up to a substantial size which causes them to be stored on backing store (e.g. a diskette). The reading or writing of a file (a general term which, in our case, is either a service program or a utility program) necessitates a complex sequence of operations. All of these diskette-management operations are also provided by a service program. This latter program, together with other service programs stored on a diskette, constitute the DISK OPERATING SYSTEM or DOS; it is called ISIS by INTEL and MDOS by MOTOROLA. The management of the conversational device, and of the development system in general, is handled by a mini-computer, called MDS by INTEL and EXORCISER by MOTOROLA.

Thus a development system comprises:

(1) A specialized mini-computer: this contains the RAM;
(2) A conversational device: a VDU console, Teletype, Texas Silent, etc.;
(3) A diskette;
(4) A fast printer if the conversational device is a VDU console.

IV.4.1. Text editing

Text editing can only be carried out if the text editor is transferred into the RAM of the specialized mini-computer. This transfer is made using the EDIT command. The user program, which is entered using a keyboard, leads to the creation of a file called the source program. A name will be given to this file. Normally, a suffix is added to the name which defines one of the many different files created for a program before it is executed. We have already met a diskette system having two drives numbered 0 and 1. This number is also given to the file name. So if we wish to create and edit the program ADDI we type the following on the I/O device keyboard:

```
■ EDIT        ∧   :  F0  : ADDI     S80       for the INTEL system
      ↓            ↓    ↓      ↓          ↓
ISIS symbol   Blank  drive 0  name of   source
             (space)          program   program


═ EDIT        ∧   ADDI . SA  :  0       for the MOTOROLA
      ↓            ↓            ↓     ↓                 system
MDOS symbol   Blank          source  drive 0
             (space)         program
```

This command causes the text editor to be transferred into RAM and passes control to this program, which is indicated by the symbols

* for the INTEL text editor
@ for the MOTOROLA text editor.

We have gathered together all the text-editor commands at the end of this book (p. 207).

We can therefore use the various text-editor commands to enter our program instructions, one at a time, to make modifications, add instructions, delete others, etc. Each command is terminated by $$ ($ = ESCAPE key). Instructions, comments, and assembly commands, which are typed on the keyboard, are entered in a region of RAM called the text-editor buffer.

The INSERT command, designated by I, permits us then to insert our program. To make modifications, we have at our disposal a pointer whose position is defined by the line number and by the character number within the line. The text-editor commands allow us to position on any character of the text which we want to insert, erase, or modify, by simply altering the pointer position.

We illustrate the use of a text editor with an example (see also the table of EDIT commands on p. 208):

INTEL		MOTOROLA	
▬ EDIT ∧ : F0 : ADDI.S80		▬ EDIT ∧ ADDI.SA:0	
* B$$	position pointer at the start of the buffer	@B$$	position pointer at the start of the buffer
($ = escape key)		($ = escape key)	

We enter the program as follows:

INTEL			MOTOROLA		
* I	TITLE	'ADDITION'	@ I	NAM	ADDITION
	ORG	4000H		ORG	$4000
OPER1:	EQU	18	OPER1	EQU	18
OPER2:	EQU	12	OPER2	EQU	12
	MVI	A,OPER1		LDA	A #OPER1
	MVI	B,OPER2		LDA	A #OPER2
	ADD	B		ABA	
	DAA			DAA	
	END$$			END$$	

INTEL:

If, by mistake, we type OPERI instead of OPER1 we position the pointer on the letter I as follows:

* B$$

* FOPER$$ the pointer is now positioned on I, the first character after OPER.

We replace I by 1 as follows:

* SI$1$$

MOTOROLA:

If, by mistake, we type OPERI instead of OPER1 we position the pointer on the letter I as follows:

@ B$$

@ SOPER$$ the pointer is now positioned on I, the first character after OPER.

We replace I by 1 as follows:

@ CI$1$$

We can verify the accuracy of the correction by displaying the modified line:

* 0L↑T$$

We end the edit by

* E$$ which writes our program on the the disk and passes control to ISIS.

How do we insert one or more instructions? Suppose that we have forgotten the DAA instruction. We must position ourselves at the beginning of the line corresponding to the END pseudo-instruction. For this, we do the following:

* B$FEND$0L$I ∧ DAA CR
$$ (CR = return key)

The B$FEND$ positions the pointer on the next character after END. The 0L$ command positions the pointer at the beginning of the line, which then allows us to use the Insert command. This letter should contain the gap corresponding to the label field, followed by DAA and then carriage return. If we forget this we would have:

DAA   END$$ instead of
DAA
END$$

We can verify the accuracy of the correction by displaying the modified line:

@ 0L↑T$$

We end the edit by

@ E$$ which writes our program on the disk and passes control to MDOS.

How do we insert one or more instructions? Suppose that we have forgotten the DAA instruction. We must position ourselves at the beginning of the line corresponding to the END pseudo-instruction. For this, we do the following:

B$SEND$0L$I ∧ DAA CR
$$ (CR = return key)

The B$SEND$ positions the pointer on the next character after END. The 0L$ command positions the pointer at the beginning of the line, which then allows us to use the Insert command. This letter should contain the gap corresponding to the label field, followed by DAA and then carriage return. If we forget this we would have:

DAA   END$$ instead of
DAA
END$$

IV.4.2. Assembly

Here, too, a command is needed to transfer the assembler program into RAM. This command is:

− ASM80 ∧ : F0 : ADDI.S80 for the INTEL assembler
= ASM ∧ ADDI.SA:0 for the MOTOROLA assembler

for the case of our ADDI program.

If the assembler indicates errors, these must be modified with EDIT; that is, the EDIT program must be loaded into RAM. In this case, the A$$ command enters into RAM memory region the first fifty lines of our source program ADDI stored on a diskette.

The assembly sequence is indicated in the table on p. 209. This table also contains the command, or commands, to be carried out prior to program execution; for instance:

DEBUG for the INTEL system
EXBIN then
LOAD for the MOTOROLA system

The listing given by the assembler indicates, for each instruction, its line number, address, hexadecimal code, mnemonic, and finally, any comment:

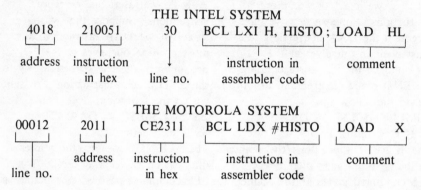

IV.4.3. Program execution

This latter is carried out with commands similar to those we have seen in *The Use of Microprocessors* for the INTEL kit monitor. These commands are assembled in tables at the end of this book.

The main innovation with regard to kit commands is the important possibility of using GO commands with a breakpoint.

IV.4.4. Other DOS commands available for the INTEL and MOTOROLA systems

* DIR. This command gives the contents of a disk.
* COPY. This command allows for a program listing, or a copy of a program from another part of the same disk, or from another disk.
* DELETE. This command erases a program from the disk.

IV.4.5. Command tables for INTEL and MOTOROLA systems

We have assembled below the principal commands of the INTEL and MOTOROLA development systems in the form of tables. These tables will spare the reader from having to go through large quantities of documentation in order to use INTEL and MOTOROLA development systems.

TO START THE INTEL SYSTEM

Using monitor only	*Using monitor and ISIS (DOS)*

– PRESS BOOT
– RESET
– PRESS THE 'SPACE' BAR OF
  THE I/O DEVICE (CRT or TTY)
– RELEASE BOOT
– The monitor prints out:
∗ MDS MONITOR, VX.X
  (version VX.X)
	– POWER UP THE MICROPROCESSOR
	  DEVELOPMENT SYSTEM (MDS) AND ITS
	  I/O DEVICE
	– POWER UP THE DISK DRIVE
	– INSERT THE DISK, LABEL TO THE LEFT,
	  SLOT TO THE FRONT
	– CLOSE FLAP OF DRIVE
	– PRESS BOOT
	– RESET
	– PRESS 'SPACE' BAR OF
	  I/O DEVICE
	– RELEASE BOOT
	ISIS prints out:
	– ISIS, VX.X (version VX.X)

TO HALT THE INTEL SYSTEM

- WHEN THE 'DRIVE BUSY' LIGHT GOES OUT, OPEN THE FLAP
- TAKE OUT THE DISK
- SWITCH OFF POWER SUPPLY TO FLOPPY DISK
- SWITCH OFF POWER SUPPLY TO MDS AND THE I/O DEVICE

PRINCIPAL COMMANDS OF THE INTEL SYSTEM

Isis	*Monitor*	*Ice*	*Isis*	*Monitor*

▬	•	∗	– ASM
			– ATTRIBUTE
			– COPY
			– DEBUG
			– DELETE
			– DIRECTORY
			– EDIT
			– ICE 80
			– RENAME
				● ASSIGNMENT
				● DISPLAY
				● FILL
				● GO
				● MOVE
				● SUBSTITUTE
				● X (EXAMINE
				  AND MODIFY
				  REGISTERS)

INT0 OR ICE 80	DEBUG	INT0		
	G8			
	INT 4		*PROGRAM NAMES:*	
		INT1	Programs are designated by a combination of three pieces of information:	

INT1	INT0	INT4	– Drive number (this can be omitted for drive 0)
			– Name of program (one to six characters)
			– Program extension: S80, LST, OBJ
			  (S80, can be replaced by S, which is what we do in
			  these tables)
			Example: F1:ADDI.S80 or F1:ADDI.S	

EDIT symbol: *	MAIN ISIS COMMANDS	throughout this page $ = hit ESCAPE
Command and format	*Functions performed*	*Notes*

MAIN ISIS COMMANDS

	Command and format	Functions performed
EDIT	= EDIT ∧ : FX : FILE . S X = drive number: ∅ : right drive 1 : left drive	This command copies to RAM the floppy disk-based text-editor program and then transfers control to this program to allow the source program FILE.S8∅ to be entered
Buffer Replenish	*A$$	places the next 50 lines of the disk-based user program into the text buffer
	*A....A$$	as for A$$ but reads in the next 50 × n lines
Pointer Positioning	*B$$	positions the pointer at the first text character
	*Z$$	positions the pointer just after the last text character
	*F..$$	positions pointer at first character after the text string '..'
	*nL$$	moves pointer forward by n lines (L) or characters (C)
	*nC$$	(backwards if n is preceded by a – sign)
Write Text	*Itext$$	insert the text string delimited by I and $$ starting at pointer position
Read Text	*nT$$	transcribe n lines without alteration starting at pointer position
Delete Text	*nK$$	delete n lines starting from position of pointer
	*nD$$	delete n characters starting from position of pointer
Modify Text	*S..$–$$	replace text string '..' by text string '_'
Flush Buffer	*nW$$	empty first n lines of buffer and write them on the disk
Halt Edit	*E$$	halt command for EDIT, copy buffer contents onto the disk and return control to ISIS

Notes

(1) When the program is on drive ∅, the EDIT command can be reduced to:
= EDIT ∧ FILE.S
(∧ = blank (space))

(2) For the F .. $$ command, when there are several possible matching text strings the pointer selects the first one that it finds starting from the previous pointer position

(3) For long programs, editing must be carried out on pieces of the program by using the REPLENISH BUFFER and FLUSH BUFFER commands

(4) For every command having an n (except nW) n can be negative; we merely precede n by a – sign

(5) When the EDIT command is used it is not necessary to specify file extension (which will be presumed to be S) e.g.
–EDIT ∧ : FX : INDEX

Chaining of commands
Several commands can be put on a single line provided they are separated by $
*AB12L$10T$$
When there is no possible ambiguity, the separating symbol may be omitted:
*AB12L10T$$

ISIS symbol: ▬

MAIN ISIS COMMANDS (cont.)

Command and format	Function performed	Notes
ASM		(1) X = drive number
┌─ CREATION OF FILE USING EDIT ─┐		∅ = right drive
–ASM8∅ ∧ :FX:FILE.S	Transfers the assembler program into RAM, assembles the program FILE and creates two further programs:	1 = left drive
	– FILE.OBJ (object program)	(2) When the program is on drive ∅ one can suppress the :F∅: (e.g. ASM80 ∧ INDEX.S)
ERRORS ? — NO	– FILE.LST (source program + object program)	(3) After re-assembly the corrected file will be FILE.LST. The old version is renamed FILE.BAK
YES		
–COPY ∧ :FX:FILE.LST	listing of FILE.LST to assist error detection	
–EDIT ∧ :FX:FILE.LST	call EDIT again to correct errors	
CORRECTION OF ERRORS UNDER EDIT (terminated by E$$)		
DEBUG		
–DEBUG ∧ :FX:FILE.OBJ	Load the binary program FILE.OBJ into RAM and return control to the monitor	
•AL = C	Assign the listing function to the console; not recommended if the I/O device = TTY	
┌─ TEST AND RUN THE PROGRAM UNDER CONTROL OF MONITOR ─┐		

MONITOR COMMANDS

MONITOR symbol: •

	Commands and format	Functions performed	Notes
A	• A function = peripheral by default the monitor assigns all functions to TTY. To see the assignations, hit Q	assigning a function to a peripheral function { C: console dialogue / P: tape punch / L: listing } peripheral { R: tape reader / C: console / T: teletype / L: lineprinter / P: punch }	(1) Each command is terminated by pressing the RETURN key (2) Commands S, D, and X are identical to those found in the SDK-80 kit
S	• SAAAA △ XX-YY type the underlined symbols only	Displays the contents, XX, of the memory location AAAA and, if required, replaces these contents by YY. Each time 'space' is pressed the address is incremented	
D	• DAAAA,BBBB	Displays the memory contents of addresses AAAA to BBBB inclusive	
G	• GAAAA, – BBBB type the underlined symbols	Executes the program starting at address AAAA up to, but not including, address BBBB	
X	• XrYY-ZZ /\ YY-ZZ • X	Displays contents of r (r = A, B, C, D, E, H, or L) and permits these contents to be modified by simply typing in the new contents, ZZ. The command is halted by hitting RETURN. Pressing 'space' takes us on to the next register. Displays the contents of all registers	
M	• MAAAA,BBBB,CCCC	Transfers the memory region between addresses AAAA and BBBB inclusive to another memory region starting at address CCCC	
F	• FAAAA,BBBB,XX	Writes the constant, XX, into all the memory locations between addresses AAAA and BBBB inclusive	

ISIS symbol: ■	OTHER ISIS COMMANDS	on this page: $ = DOLLAR

	Command and format	Function performed	Notes
DIR	– DIR ∧ TO ∧ : peri : ∧ X – DIR ∧ TO ∧ : peri : ∧ X ∧ I – DIR ∧ TO ∧ : peri : ∧ X ∧ F peri = { CO for CRT or TTY / LP for lineprinter / TP for teletype X = drive number (∅ or 1)	lists to peripheral 'peri' the names of disk-based user programs lists to peri the names of disk-based user and system programs lists to peri the names of disk-based user programs but without the number of blocks and bytes • when the attribute ∧F is not appended to the DIR command the listing shows for each program: – the number of blocks (BLKS column) – the number of bytes (LENGTH column)	(1) The ∅ used to indicate drive ∅ is optional. Examples: DIR ∧ TO ∧ : peri: DIR ∧ TO ∧ : peri: ∧ I (2) When peri = CO the TO : peri : part is optional. Examples: DIR (drive ∅ is used by default) DIR ∧ I ∧ I DIR ∧ F (drive ∅ is used) (3) With ISIS it is possible, by pressing the RUB OUT key n times, to delete the last n characters (4) Each comment is terminated by pressing the RETURN key (5) To delete the line which is currently being input the two keys CTRL and X should be pressed simultaneously
ATTRIB	– ATTRIB ∧ : FX : FILE.EXT ∧ attribute attribute { $I0 prog. visible to DIR / $I1 prog. invisible to DIR / $W∅ prog. not protected / $W1 prog. write-protected } EXT = extension = S or LST or OBJ	modifies the attributes of the program called FILE • $I0 = dollar I zero • a write-protected program can only be deleted if its attribute is first changed	
COPY	– COPY ∧ : FX : FILE.EXT ∧ TO ∧ : peri : – COPY ∧ : FX : FILE.EXT TO ∧ : FX : FILE1 EXT = extension = S or LST or OBJ	produces on peri a listing of the program FILE (peri = CO, LP, or TP as for DIR) copies the program in FILE back onto the disk under a new name (e.g. FILE1) without deleting the first file. This copying process can be performed on the same drive or from one drive to another	
RENAME	– RENAME ∧ : FX : FILE.EXT ∧ TO ∧ : FX : FILE1.EXT EXT = extension = S or LST or OBJ	renames unprotected programs; the program called FILE disappears from the disk, and reappears under the name FILE1	
DELETE	– DELETE : FX : FILE.EXT – DELETE : FX : FILE1.EXT, : FX : FILE2.EXT EXT = extension = S or LST or OBJ	deletes the unprotected program called FILE from the disk deletes from the disk the unprotected programs FILE1.EXT and FILE2.EXT	

212

LAYOUT OF INTEL INSTRUCTIONS AND PSEUDO-INSTRUCTIONS WITH TABULATION

```
               ORG           4000H
;
START:         MVI           A,VAL
               LXI           H,2050H
               DCR           A
               JMP           START        ;JUMP TO START
               STA           MEM1
               SHLD          MEM2
               LXI           TAB1
;
;DATA TABLE AND MEMORY RESERVATION
;
VAL            EQU           04
MEM1:          DS            1
MEM2:          DS            2
TAB1:          DB            23,12,45,18,91,39,57,77
               DB            51,02,66,90,49
               END
```

LAYOUT OF MOTOROLA INSTRUCTIONS AND DIRECTIVES WITHOUT TABULATION

```
NAM  EXAMPLE
SPC  2
ORG  $2000
SPC  2
START LDA A #VAL
LDX  #$2050
DEC  A
JMP  START JUMP TO START
STA  A MEM1
STX  MEM2
LDX  TAB1
*
*DATA TABLE AND MEMORY RESERVATION
*
VAL  EQU  04
MEM1 RMB  1
MEM2 RMB  2
TAB1 FCB  23,12,45,18,91,39,57,77,51,02,66
FCB  90,49
END
```

For both INTEL and MOTOROLA one can optionally intersperse comments, whole lines of comment, and blank lines among the text

TO START THE MOTOROLA SYSTEM

Using the monitor only	*Using the monitor and MDOS*
– PRESS RESTART	– SWITCH ON THE EXORCISER AND THE
– The monitor prints	I/O DEVICE
– EXBUG X, X	– POWER UP THE FLOPPY DISK
– NEXT TYPE OUT THE DESIRED	– LOAD THE DISK, WITH LABEL ON TOP
COMMAND:	AND SLOT TO THE FRONT
– MAID OR PRINT FOR EXAMPLE	– CLOSE THE FLAP
	– PRESS RESTART
	– The monitor prints:
	EXBUG X, X
	– TYPE MAID
	– NEXT TYPE E800 ; G
	– MDOS prints
	= MDOS XX . XX

TO HALT THE MOTOROLA SYSTEM

- IF THE DISK IS NOT IN USE OPEN THE FLAP
- TAKE OUT THE DISK
- SWITCH OFF POWER SUPPLY TO THE FLOPPY DISK
- SWITCH OFF POWER SUPPLY TO THE EXORCISER AND TO THE I/O DEVICE

MAIN COMMANDS OF THE MOTOROLA SYSTEM

Name of program	*MDOS*	*Monitor*
PROGRAMS ARE DESIGNATED BY COMBINING	= ASM	*address/
THREE ITEMS OF INFORMATION:	= BLOCKEDIT	*address;G
– DRIVE NUMBER (THIS MAY BE	= COPY	*address;V
OMITTED FOR DRIVE ∅)	= DEL	*address;U
– PROGRAM NAME (1 to 6 characters)	= DIR	* ;P
	= DUMP	* ;U
	= EDIT	* $R
	= EXBIN	* $V
– THE SUFFIX: SA, LX, LO	= LIST	* $T
(THIS INFORMATION MAY BE	= LOAD	* n;N
OMITTED)	= NAME	* n;P
EXAMPLE: ADDI.SA:1		

MAIN MDOS COMMANDS

EDIT symbol: @   on this page $ = ESCAPE key

	Command and format	Functions performed	Notes
	= EDIT FILE.SA : K drive number: 0: right drive 1: left drive	This command loads into RAM the floppy disk-based text-editor and then transfers control to this program to allow the source program FILE.SA to be entered	(1) When the program is on drive 0, the EDIT command can be reduced to: EDIT ∧ FILE.SA
Buffer replenish	@ A$$ @ A...A$$ } n	places the next 50 lines of the disk-based user program into the text buffer as for A$$ but reads in the next 50 × n lines	(2) For the F...$$ command, when there are several possible matching text strings, the pointer selects the first one that it finds starting from the previous pointer position
Pointer positioning	@ B$$	positions the pointer at the first text character	(3) For long programs, editing must be carried out on pieces of the program using the REPLENISH BUFFER and FLUSH BUFFER commands
	@ Z$$	positions the pointer just after the last text character	
	@ S..$$	positions pointer at first character after the text string '...'	(4) To delete n characters, press CONTROL and H keys simultaneously n times
	@ nL$$ @ nM$$	moves pointer forward by n lines (L) or characters (C) (backwards if n is preceded by a – sign)	(5) To delete the line which is being input, press CONTROL and X keys simultaneously
Write text	@ Itext$$	insert the text string delimited by I and $$ starting at pointer position	
Read text	@ nT$$	transcribe n lines, without alteration, starting at pointer position	
Delete text	@ nK$$ @ nD$$	delete n lines starting from pointer position delete n characters starting from pointer position	
Modify text	@ C..$-$$	replace text string '..' by text string '--'	
Flush buffer	@ nP$$	empty first n lines of buffer and write them on the disk	
Halt edit	@ E$$	halt command for EDIT, copy buffer contents onto the disk, and return control to MDOS. Definitely a command to be remembered	

(EDIT)

Chaining commands
Several commands can be put on a single line provided they are separated by $
@ ASB$12L$10T$$
When there is no possible ambiguity, the separating symbol may be omitted
@ AB12L10T$$

MDOS symbol: =

MAIN MDOS COMMANDS (cont.)

Command and format	Functions performed	Notes
		(1) K = drive number $\emptyset$ = left drive 1 = right drive (2) When the program is on drive $\emptyset$, one may suppress the $\emptyset$ (3) The program suffix is not necessary. By default it is taken equal to SA for ASM to LX for EXBIN to LO for LOAD (4) Only one FILE.LX program and one FILE.LO program can exist (5) If a listing has not been requested before assembly it can be asked for afterwards by the command: ASM $\wedge$ INDEX : K; L = #CN, $-\emptyset$

ASM

```
┌─ ─ ─ ─ ─ ─ ─ ─ ─ ─ ┐
│  Creation of FILE.SA  │
│      using EDIT       │
└─ ─ ─ ─ ─↓─ ─ ─ ─ ─ ─┘
    ┌──────────────────┐
┌──▶│ = ASM ∧ FILE.SA : │
│   │    K option       │
│   └─────────↓────────┘
│          ╱ERRORS ?╲──── NO
│          ╲        ╱
│            YES
│   ┌──────────────────┐
│   │ = DEL ∧ FILE.LX : K │
│   └─────────↓────────┘
│   ┌──────────────────┐
│   │ = EDIT ∧ FILE.SA : K │
│   └─────────↓────────┘
│   ┌──────────────────┐
└───│  Error correction using │
    │  EDIT (terminated by E§§) │
    └──────────────────┘
```

EXBIN
```
┌──────────────────────┐
│ = EXBIN ∧ FILE.LX : K │
└──────────────────────┘
```

LOAD
```
┌──────────────────────┐
│ = LOAD ∧ FILE.LO :    │
│        K option       │
└──────────↓───────────┘
┌─ ─ ─ ─ ─ ─ ─ ─ ─ ─ ┐
│   Test and run the    │
│  program under MAID   │
└─ ─ ─ ─ ─ ─ ─ ─ ─ ─ ┘
```

ASM functions performed:

In order to carry out the assembly it is necessary:
that text editing end with E§§
that FILE.LX should not exist on the disk or for the $-\emptyset$ option to be used

assembly of program FILE.SA and creation of FILE.LX

option {
:L list FILE.SA on lineprinter
:L = #CN list FILE.SA on console
:G list constants generated by FCB, FCC, and FDB
:S list labels
:, $-\emptyset$ the program FILE.LX is not created
}

possible chaining of several options separated by commas; however, there must only be one L option

EXBIN functions performed:

FILE.LX erased if it exists (option $-\emptyset$ not used)

This command not to be used if $-\emptyset$ option is employed

call EDIT in order to correct FILE.SA

conversion of FILE.LX into binary, which can be loaded from the disk; this binary program is FILE.LO. This command requires that FILE.LO does not already exist on the disk prior to the command

LOAD functions performed:

load FILE.LO into RAM

option {
;M returns control to MAID after loading FILE.LO into RAM
;V allows the use of SWI under MAID
}

possible chaining of several options without a separating symbol, e.g. MV

MDOS symbol: =		∧ = space (blank)
	OTHER MDOS COMMANDS	
Command format	*Function performed*	*Notes*
DIR = DIR : K option = DIR ∧ FILE.*:K option = DIR ∧ L*.*option = DIR ∧ *.SS option = DIR ∧ FILE.SS:K option SS = SA, LX or LO { ;S → option { ;E → ; L →	• lists the names of disk-based user programs • lists the names of all programs called FILE whatever their suffix • lists the names of all user programs whose name begins with the letter L (the suffix is immaterial) • lists the names of all user programs having the suffix SS • for this command the option determines the effect system programs are given as well as user programs lists the attributes: no. of first sector, size, entry no. for each program as for option E but listed to the lineprinter	(1) When the program is on drive ∅, one can suppress the ∅ (2) LIST command nnnn: decimal number of one to five digits which must be less than 65536 mmm: decimal number of one to three digits If START is not indicated it is taken to be L1 and S∅ If the listing starts at the beginning of the program and stops before the end the required command is = LIST ∧ FILE.SS:K, END followed by some choice of option
LIST = LIST ∧ FILE.SS: K option = LIST ∧ FILE.SS: K,START, END, opt. START { Lnnnn (line no.) or END { Smmm (sector no.) option { ; L → ; N →	• gives a complete listing of FILE.SS • lists FILE.SS from the line or sector no. indicated by START to the line or sector no. indicated by END listing on lineprinter rather than on I/O device decimal numbering of listed lines	
DEL = DEL ∧ FILE.SS:K = DEL ∧ FILE.*:K = DEL ∧ FILE1.SS, FILE2.SS, FILE3.*	• deletes the unprotected program FILE.SS from the disk • for each of the programs FILE.SS MDOS asks the question: DELETE FILE.SS? Type Y (CR) or N (CR) for yes or no respectively • deletes the unprotected programs FILE1.SS and FILE2.SS from the disk and asks the question DELETE FILE3.SS? for each FILE3 program	
COPY = COPY ∧ FILE.SS:K, #peri peri { CN for console LP for printer CP for teletype = COPY ∧ FILE.SS:K, FILE1.SS:K	• lists the program FILE.SS:K to the selected peripheral copies onto the disk the program FILE.SS:K under a new name (FILE1.SS:K, for example) without deleting the first file. This copy can be performed on the same drive or from one drive to another	

MAIN MONITOR COMMANDS

MAID symbol: *

	Command and format	Function performed	Notes
Display and modification of memory	* AAAA/XX YY ○ type the underlined symbols ○ = (LF) or (↑) or (CR)	• displays the contents, XX, of the memory address AAAA and, if necessary, replaces these contents by YY. Each time (LF) (line feed) is hit, the address is incremented. Each time (↑) (shift N) is hit, the address is decremented. Hitting the (CR) key halts the command. (CR) = RETURN key	**(1)** Registers displayed by the $R command: P = program counter X = index A = accumulator A B = accumulator B C = condition code register S = stack pointer
Breakpoints	* AAAA;V * AAAA;U * $V * ;U	• introduces a breakpoint at address AAAA • removes the breakpoint at address AAAA • displays the address of breakpoint • removes all the breakpoints	**(2)** All the commands shown in this table, except the last one, relate to functions of MAID; the last one, however, is the PRINT function. These two functions are obtained by performing a RESTART. The monitor prints EXBUG X.X and then the function must be typed in. But the MAID functions can be obtained equally well by using the ;MV option with the LOAD command
Program execution	* AAAA;G * ;P * n;P	• executes the program starting at address AAAA • restores program execution starting at address in the program counter and restores register contents • restarts program execution from the breakpoint until this breakpoint has been encountered n times	
Displaying registers	* $R P-YYYY ZZZZ (LF) X-YYYY (LF) A-YY ZZ (CR)	• displays the contents of all the registers P-YYYY X-YYYY A-YY B-YY S-YYYY P-YYYY then displays once again the contents of the first register to modify the contents type in the new contents to go on to the new register type (LF) to stop this command press (CR)	
Program execution with register display	* n;N * $T END ADDRESS.BBBB * AAAA;G	• trace n instructions i.e. execute these n instructions and display the register contents after each instruction • trace all the instructions between start address AAAA and finish address BBBB	
Printing memory contents	EXBUG X.X PRNT BEG ADDR YYYY ZZZZ (CR) END ADDR YYYY ZZZZ (CR) EXEC Y	• print the contents of memory between the start and finish addresses (END ADDR) inclusive, which addresses are typed in on the keyboard. After printing, the monitor prints EXBUG X.X and then the MAID function must be typed in. At this stage type in X.	

Index